D0787935

Bartók and the Piano

A Performer's View

Barbara Nissman

The Scarecrow Press, Inc.
Lanham, Maryland, and Oxford
2002

SCARECROW PRESS, INC.

Published in the United States of America
by Scarecrow Press, Inc.
A Member of the Rowman & Littlefield Publishing Group
4720 Boston Way, Lanham, Maryland 20706
www.scarecrowpress.com

PO Box 317
Oxford
OX2 9RU, UK

British Library Cataloguing in Publication Information Available

Library of Congress Cataloging-in-Publication Data

Nissman, Barbara.
    Bartók and the piano : a performer's view / Barbara Nissman.
        p. cm.
    Includes bibliographical references (p.) and index.
    ISBN 0-8108-4301-3 (alk. paper)
    1. Bartók, Béla, 1881–1945—Criticism and interpretation. 2. Piano—Performance. I.
Title

ML410.B26 N65 2002
786.2'092—dc21   2002017049

For Daniel

Contents

Acknowledgments

Special thanks to Magyar Nemzeti Galèria (Hungarian National Gallery) for their permission to use Béni Ferenczy's drawing of Bartók for the cover of the book; to Faber & Faber for their permission to reprint quotes from *Bartók Essays,* from *Bartók's Letters,* and from *The Bartók Companion*; to Boosey & Hawkes for permission to reprint Bartók's musical examples; to Rigbie Turner, curator at the Morgan Library in New York for his help with Bartók's 1898 *Sonata*; to Dover Publications and Editio Musica Budapest for permission to reprint musical examples from their publications; and to the *Hungarian Quarterly* for their permission to quote from articles originally published in the *New Hungarian Quarterly* and later reprinted in *Bartók Studies.*

I wish to thank my friend Jeffrey Bishop of Oxford University Press for his initial encouragement with this project and Susan Brailove for her time, patience, perseverance, and excellent advice in helping to see this book to its publication. I am grateful to several people who generously advised me in the book's beginning stages: Malcolm Gillies, Elliot Antokoletz, Benjamin Suchoff, Lázsló Somfai, and David Dubal. And to Bruce Phillips, music editor at Scarecrow Press, my special appreciation for his help and advice.

To the wonderful team who produced the compact disc recording included with the book: Dennis Rooney, producer; David Barr, Steinway concert technician; Joe Patrych, music editor; and the staff at Carnegie Hall, Lewisburg, West Virginia—thank you.

And finally, my deepest appreciation to Daniel, without whose inspiration this book could never have been written.

Introduction

I must state that all my music is determined by instinct and sensibility; no one need ask me why I wrote this or that or did something in this rather than in that way. I could not give any explanation other than I felt this way, or I wrote it down this way. I never created new theories in advance. This attitude does not mean that I composed without set plans and without sufficient control. The plans were concerned with the spirit of the new work and with technical problems (for instance formal structure involved by the spirit of the work) all more or less instinctively felt.

—Béla Bartók[1]

Bartók never believed in theories or trusted theorists, and he had good reason, for his music defies pigeonholing. The more deeply one explores his piano music, the more it resists categorization. In other words, there are no easy solutions to tackling Bartók's piano music. There are no sets of prescribed rules or formulas to follow when studying each work. The performer must find and follow the path the composer walked, discarding all preconceptions. Bartók forces the pianist to approach his music with an open mind, a flexible soul, and very good ears.

I am neither a music theorist, nor a historian, nor a musicologist. I am a pianist and a performer. I did not set out to write a book about Bartók's piano music. It would be more accurate for me to say that the book found me. While preparing Bartók's piano music for recording, I started exploring a wide range of literature written about this difficult repertoire in hopes of clarifying my task at the keyboard. (See the annotated bibliography at the conclusion of the book.) I was looking for material from the

Bartók scholars, expert advice I could use to benefit my interpretations at the piano. From some Bartók specialists, I gained an increased understanding of his harmonic language; from others, a heightened awareness of his ethnomusicological frame of reference. But it was the performer's viewpoint I craved. I wanted to know how Bartók, the pianist/performer, approached his music.

I was stunned to discover that Bartók's piano output—a total of more than 300 works, including the 153 pieces from *Mikrokosmos*—had never been thoroughly discussed in print from the perspective in which the music had been conceived: at the piano and from the point of view of the performer. Himself a student of a Liszt pupil, Bartók was primarily a pianist; he played, performed, and edited most of the standard and early keyboard literature.[2] Although he became well known as an ethnomusicologist, Bartók never labeled himself a theorist or musicologist. A formidable pianist, he was probably at his most adventurous and most natural self when composing for the keyboard.

What I gained from my exploration strengthened my determination to return to the piano, to the printed score and the words of the composer. In retrospect, I am delighted to have approached Bartók's piano music without preconceptions, even without those of my teacher, pianist György Sándor, who was a pupil of Bartók. The discipline I imposed on myself was to start with the music, a fresh score without any pencil markings. As I studied this repertoire, I became more comfortable with its new language. I began to discover, and then I began to hear. Fortunately, Bartók has left a vast pianistic legacy with detailed indications and keen observations entered in the scores. The real authority on Bartók's piano music remains Bartók, and the principal source materials are his music and his words.

In trying to extract the composer's intent, a performer must find the way through vast amounts of instruction. Without musical compromise, the performer must then reinterpret, using his or her own voice at the piano and communicating as convincingly as possible a personal interpretation of the composer's wishes. Any one page of Bartók's piano writing is filled with meticulous dynamic, articulation, and metronome markings and with timings calculated to the exact second. This complex music requires intelligence and effort. The brain must first decipher it and organize it; only then can the task of learning begin. Bartók makes pianists learn another language—*his* language—and demands that they speak it as if it were their mother tongue.

I have waded through the mass of details in each of Bartók's scores and wrestled with each work's technical problems and musical difficulties. Perhaps my observations will be helpful in guiding the eye and ear during the initial learning process. At the very least, my conclusions will provide a catalyst for discussion and exchange of ideas. Isn't that why we want to hear different interpretations of the same musical work and also want to hear the same work performed by interesting artists more than once? A phrase in the hands of one pianist sparks an idea, which is then absorbed and digested in a different manner by another. I have written this book not to instruct but to give enabling guidelines to further an understanding of Bartók's piano music.

My concentration is on the major piano works in the repertoire, with separate chapters devoted to the most difficult and challenging masterworks: the *Out of Doors* suite, the *Sonata* (1926), and the three piano concertos. Each chapter also includes an overview and more general discussion of Bartók's related minor works. The decision to focus on the standard repertory of the advanced pianist precluded my writing in depth about more than a selection of pieces from *Mikrokosmos*.

I originally conceived this book chronologically, but I found that the exploration of roots and influences necessary to an understanding of Bartók's pianism did not always follow a chronological order. Chapter 1 progresses from the youthful unpublished 1898 *Sonata* to the transitional *Elegies*, works difficult to pigeonhole because of their combination of romantic pianism and new minimalism. This minimalism was further developed in the *Bagatelles*, a revolutionary work that reflects Bartók's succinct new style, discussed in chapter 2. The *Ten Easy Pieces*, written as a complement to the *Bagatelles*, contain some early folk transcriptions; the Csík songs were also part of this new approach to the piano. The *Seven Sketches*, according to the composer, are more or less written in the same style as the *Bagatelles* [except for no. 4, which could have been included in a discussion of the romantic pianism of chapter 1].

Because this is a book written by a pianist for other performing pianists or lovers of the piano, a chapter on Bartók's pianism and virtuosic music became a necessity, prompted by my learning the difficult *Etudes*. The *Rumanian Dances* and *Allegro Barbaro* also qualified as bravura compositions to be included in chapter 3. In the chapter on folk music (chapter 4), I tried to show the composer's progression from a simple transcription of a folk tune to paraphrases using folk music, culminating with the *Improvisations*, inspired by the folk song tradition but written in a completely original language.

For me as a pianist, form and structure are the most important ingredients in interpretation; the discussion of form in chapter 5 focuses on two major works: the 1926 *Sonata* and the *Sonata* for two pianos and percussion. In chapter 6, Bartók's piano masterwork, the *Out of Doors* suite, is analyzed pianistically and musically. Here I have tried to share with the reader what I discovered as I prepared this work for performance.

Chapter 7 features the suite and explores Bartók's relationship with the past. The oddly titled chapter 8, Ten Plus Nine Plus Two Plus . . . includes

Introduction

many other Bartók works pianists love to play. The rest of the book is devoted to a discussion of Bartók's pedagogical works, including *Mikrokosmos*, an analysis of his three piano concertos, and a survey of the piano/chamber repertoire. Finally, going full circle, the book concludes where it began, with the composer at the piano playing his own music. I believe that this progression presents a logical picture for the pianist's enhanced understanding of a unique composer.

A brief note about Bartók's relationship to detail: Bartók was meticulous in all of his markings; even metronomic markings and timings have been accurately noted. As an editor of other composers' keyboard music, Bartók was very aware of the problem of authenticity within editions and the inclusion in many editions of "arbitrary performing indications by unscrupulous editors."[3] As in Beethoven's works, the authority for Bartók's music rests with his own manuscript. Whatever is indicated in the score reveals "precisely his intentions,"[4] unless there might have been copyist errors in the publication process. While preparing this book, in addition to studying Bartók's published scores, I have gone back whenever possible to autograph sources to further confirm what appeared to be errors. (Note: Currently in preparation by László Somfai at the Budapest Bartók Archives is the forty-eight volume *Béla Bartók Complete Critical Edition*. Several new editions whose revisions benefit from the manuscripts in Bartók's son Peter's possession have recently been issued by Boosey & Hawkes and Universal and are discussed in the appropriate chapters.)

Bartók's piano music defies categorization. Like Picasso, he developed his own language while retaining traditional formal structures. Bartók built upon the foundations of romantic pianism, allowing each piece to dictate its own form and style. What remains constant, however, is the way any performer should approach each composition. All elements—tempos, rhythm, melodic line, dynamics, mood, touch, color, technical demands, compositional technique, harmonic language—must be analyzed, evaluated, and then viewed within the larger structure. Yet ultimately it is the individual pianist/performer who must bring to all of Bartók's indications his or her own intelligence and imagination. I wish you an interesting and challenging voyage.

NOTES

1. Béla Bartók, "Harvard Lectures" (1943), in *Béla Bartók Essays*, ed. Benjamin Suchoff (Lincoln: University of Nebraska Press, 1976), 376.
2. Bartók was responsible for editions of Scarlatti sonatas; works of Couperin; *The Well-Tempered Clavier* and other works of J. S. Bach; nineteen Haydn sonatas; twenty-seven Beethoven sonatas and other miscellaneous works; twenty Mozart

sonatas; and various pieces by Schubert, Schumann, and Chopin, among others, in addition to his piano transcriptions from early Baroque keyboard music. (See chapter 8.)

3. Béla Bartók, "Motion in the Committee of Intellectual Co-Operation of the League of Nations" (1932), in *Béla Bartók Essays*, 499.

4. Bartók, "Motion in the Committee of Intellectual Co-Operation of the League of Nations," 499.

1

✦

The Traditionalist

Nothing absolutely new in the world can be invented: The most unusual looking ideas have or must have had their predecessors.

—Béla Bartók[1]

Bartók's roots were formed at the piano. He received his first piano lessons from his mother at the age of six, and by the age of nine was writing down his original piano compositions. As he states in his *Autobiography*:

> Before I was eighteen, I had acquired a fairly thorough knowledge of music
> from Bach to Brahms (though in Wagner's work I did not get further than
> *Tannhäuser*). All this time, I was busy composing and was under the strong
> influence of Brahms and Dohnányi, who was four years my senior.[2]

It was the pianist and composer Ernö Dohnányi who encouraged the
young Bartók to come to Budapest to study at the Budapest Academy of
Music with Dohnányi's own piano professor, István Thomán, who had
studied with the great Franz Liszt.

Bartók and Dohnányi experienced similar influences in their musical
development, but as composers they grew in opposite directions.
Dohnányi continued to expand his piano writing within the nineteenth-
century romantic tradition, and his music never ventured far from that
realm. Bartók also went through the prerequisite imitative period, heard
in his early works through 1906, but finally found his own path. From
1906 onward, he seemed to know instinctively the direction in which he
had to travel, never allowing any radical departures or detours. This new

and personal style, coinciding with the beginning of his intensive folk music research, represented a strong reaction against any form of expansion, discarding all that was excessive in favor of sparseness. Throughout his life, economy would remain Bartók's most important criterion for judgment of craftsmanship— ". . . how best to employ terseness of expression, the utmost excision of all that is nonessential—after the excessive grandiloquence of the Romantic period."[3]

A study of Bartók's very early works provides a glimpse of what was initially packed in his suitcase as a young man just venturing out in the world, what he discarded when it was no longer useful, and what he retained. These compositions—which include the unpublished Brahmsian four-movement piano *Sonata* of 1898 (part of the Robert Owen Lehman Collection on deposit at the Pierpont Morgan Library in New York); the *Four Early Pieces* of 1903; the Op. 1 *Rhapsody* (the solo version of 1904 as well as the piano and orchestra version of 1905); and two relatively unknown but interesting early works recently made available through publication, the *Piano Quintet* of 1904 and the *Scherzo*, Op. 2 for piano and orchestra of 1905—crystallize the direction he intuitively sought. It was Bartók who said regretfully just before his death in 1945, "I am only sad that I have to leave with a full trunk."[4]

Along with these mostly derivative works, a discussion of the 1908 *Two Elegies*, Op. 8b, is also included in this chapter. These pivotal works embrace Bartók's newly found economy, but pianistically they remain anchored in the previous century. Perhaps because of their emotional significance, Bartók did not allow them to catch up with his new modernism—and therein lies their charm.

SONATA (1898, UNPUBLISHED)

An early unpublished four-movement *Sonata* from 1898, written when Bartók was only seventeen, sounds as if it could have been composed by a young Brahms, with a few bravura passages from Liszt, some full-scale Wagner heroics, and shifting major-minor melodies of Schubert. It is a long, repetitious work that suffers from a lack of editing and some youthful pretension, but it is interesting as a well-crafted example of nineteenth-century potpourri. Occasionally some of the writing feels awkward under the fingers; certainly it is not as pianistic as Liszt's passagework or Bartók's own later pianism, and it qualifies as an early experiment. Within this rather serious and overblown composition, the use of key signatures is taken *ad absurdum*, with the finale notated in seven flats. What a difference ten years can make in a composer's attitude: In the Op. 6 *Bagatelles* written in 1908 (see chapter 2), Bartók pokes fun at the serious music theorists; he indicates, tongue-in-cheek, two different key signatures in his first bagatelle, one for each hand, while at the same time loudly proclaiming its key to be a "Phrygian-coloured C major."[5] Certainly, he has traveled a long way from that seven-flat key signature.

Some excerpts from the unpublished 1898 *Sonata* underscore Bartók's early influences. The opening movement has the heaviness of Brahms, the octaves of Liszt, and the pomposity of Wagner. This passage could have come from a Wagner opera or possibly been extracted from one of Liszt's *Transcendental Studies*.

Example 1.1: *Sonata*, first movement, development section, m. 108–15

Playing through this sonata, it is obvious that Bartók must have been well acquainted with the complete chamber music of Brahms. Hemiola abounds (example 1.2), and the opening themes of the second movement Adagio and the third movement Presto sound like material from one of Brahms's own violin sonatas.

Example 1.2: *Sonata,* first movement, part of second theme, m. 67–70

Example 1.3: Opening from the second movement Adagio, m. 1–5

[Track 1]

Example 1.4: Opening measures of third movement Presto, m. 1–4

[Track 2]

The opening seven measures of the finale's Adagio introduction recall the Liszt *Sonata*, while the wandering, ambiguous tonality in the passage following might have come from Liszt's later works.

Example 1.5: *Sonata*, fourth movement (Adagio introduction), m. 1–18

Bartók's familiarity with the late piano sonatas of Schubert is evident in the principal thematic material from the fourth movement Allegro.

Example 1.6: *Sonata*, fourth movement, m. 25–34

This early work is full of bravura writing, but lacks the pianistic virtuosity of Liszt. (Liszt rarely used three staves!) Passages are awkwardly written but are meant to exploit the full orchestral sonorities of the keyboard.

Example 1.7: *Sonata,* second movement Adagio, m. 43–51 [Track 1]

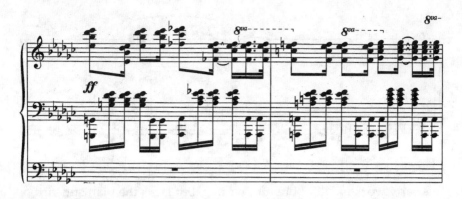

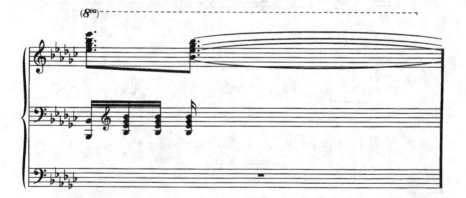

This sonata suffers from having too much material; even a leitmotif from *Tristan* is paraphrased in the return section of the final movement.

Example 1.8: *Sonata*, fourth movement, m. 229–34

After this overblown youthful effort, it was obvious to Bartók that this direction could take him no further.

A chance encounter with the Hungarian peasant woman Lidi Dósa, singing a popular folk song, helped reverse his course, stirring his passion to explore this rich national heritage. As early as 1904, Bartók made his first actual notation of a Hungarian folk song. Even then he understood what an enormous task it would be to document these folk tunes before a peasant generation died, and their culture along with them.

His respect for simplicity and understatement had nurtured an initial attraction to the naïve melodic folk elements heard in some of the music of Brahms, Schubert, and Liszt and in his own early *Four Pieces* and the Op. 1 *Rhapsody*. However, Bartók soon realized that the nineteenth-century melodies used in Brahms's *Hungarian Dances* or the *Hungarian Rhapsodies* of Liszt were not derived from real folk material but were taken from popular tunes, usually of Gypsy rather than Magyar origin, probably composed by amateurs or dilettantes. Armed with very basic recording equipment, Bartók, along with his good friend and colleague Zoltán Kodály, set out for the countryside to trace folk music back to its original source and to discover the "absolute purity of style of the peasant's folk music."[6]

His secure salary as a piano professor gave him the means to pursue his folk music research. For thirty years Bartók taught only piano at the Budapest Academy of Music; he never taught composition. In a letter to Randall Thompson, director of the Curtis Institute, he claimed that "to teach composition was to imperil my own composing."[7] However, he confessed in a letter to the English composer Frederick Delius that "teaching the piano to untalented youngsters who look upon music as a means of earning their living is truly not a thing I can feel enthusiasm for."[8] Collecting folk music was his real passion and became the food for his compositions. He also edited a substantial amount of the piano repertory, including many of the early keyboard masters, for a Hungarian music publishing firm, and was intimately familiar with the entire piano literature.

Occasionally Bartók's wonderful sense of humor and his penchant for musical jokes and "insider" musical quotes is discovered hidden away in some measures of his piano compositions. Musical allusions in his *Elegies* and the *Three Burlesques*, Op. 8c (discussed in Chapter 8), among others, reveal a droll and subtle wit. In the first Burlesque, entitled "Quarrel," Bartók paraphrases Marguerite's theme from Liszt's *Mephisto Waltz*, and thus makes a subtle statement about the feminine charms of one of the quarrel's combatants (his future wife, Marta).

Always present in Bartók's evolving compositional style were his pianistic roots in the nineteenth-century grand bravura tradition. No matter how lean his style became, as in the *14 Bagatelles*, Op. 6, that tradition could not be hidden. The early *Four Pieces* (1903) and the *Rhapsody* Op. 1 are direct descendants of Lisztian virtuosic writing. The *Two Elegies*, Op. 8b, and the fourth Sketch from his *Seven Sketches*, Op. 9b, provide excellent examples of a new compositional style coexisting within the foundations of romantic pianism. Bartók's compositional development never negates his natural pianism. Moreover, it is this solid keyboard foundation that allows him the freedom to transcend the instrument and go beyond the piano's musical limitations. In the *Three Etudes*, Op. 18; the *Two Rumanian Dances* of Op. 8a; and the *Allegro Barbaro* (discussed in chapter 3), extroverted pianistic virtuosity is in the foreground but never dominates musical or formal considerations. Only a master pianist with a superb knowledge and love of the instrument could have written such difficult, but always *pianistic* keyboard music. Virtuosic pianism, evident in the difficult later works such as the 1926 *Sonata*, *Out of Doors*, and the *Suite* Op. 14, becomes totally integrated within the work's formal design and functions only to serve its musical needs.

FOUR EARLY PIECES (1903)

These four pieces show the early influence of Brahms, Liszt, and Strauss on Bartók's work. As Bartók wrote in his *Autobiography*:

> The first Budapest performance of *Thus Spake Zarathustra*, in 1902, came like a flash of lightning which whirled me out of my stagnation. This work, which most of our musicians here at home received with indignation, for me meant a great experience: finally I could see a new direction and a new road. I threw myself into Strauss's scores and began to compose once more.[9]

The first piece, "Study for the Left Hand," was dedicated to Bartók's teacher, István Thomán (a former Liszt pupil), and is a very Lisztian composition. Bartók frequently extracted this piece from the entire set because of its effectiveness, and he performed it often in concert. It is very pianistic, and its harmonic language remains grounded in the nineteenth century.

The contrasting second theme sounds as if it could have been written by Mahler.

Example 1.9: No. 1, *Four Early Pieces,* Dover (1981), p. 5, m. 6–12

(Erratum: On p. 11, m. 116 of the Dover edition, the top E-flat of the first chord should be an E-natural.)

The second piece, "Fantasy I," dedicated to Emma Gruber, a dear friend and confidante who later became the wife of Zoltán Kodály, recalls the opening bars of Brahms's Op. 118, No. 1. Bits and pieces of Strauss's symphonic poems are also easily recognizable.

Example 1.10: No. 2, *Four Early Pieces* p. 17, m. 18–24

(Errata in the Dover edition: In m. 4, a natural sign is missing in front of the B. At m. 31, there should be no accent written over the tied note in the right hand; an accent should appear only in the bass. On p. 20 at m. 68, the B notated in the left hand before the thirty-second note rest should be a sixteenth note; it functions as part of the group of five.)

By 1905, Bartók's love affair with Strauss was waning:

> . . . the magic of Richard Strauss had evaporated. A really thorough study of Liszt's oeuvre, especially some of his less well known works like *Années de Pèlerinage, Harmonies Poétiques and Réligieuses,* the *Faust Symphony, Totentanz* and others had, after being stripped of their mere external brilliance, which I did not like, revealed to me the true essence of composing. For the future development of music, his oeuvre seemed to me of far greater importance than that of Strauss or even Wagner.[10]

The third piece, "Fantasy II," cast in a simple three-part form, is conventional in its rather overblown and predictable nineteenth-century approach. (Erratum: In m. 28–29 of the Dover edition, the time signature should be changed to 2/8; the original time signature of 3/8 returns at m. 30.)

The fourth and largest piece of the set, "Scherzo," a repetitious and overly extended work dedicated to Dohnányi, sounds as if Liszt and Dohnányi together might have written it. (The last six measures also give a nod to Chopin with a paraphrase of his famous A-flat major polonaise.) Bartók explores a national folk character, a style that he himself later criticized in the work of some nineteenth-century composers as being folk-like but not based on the true folk music of the peasants.

Example 1.11: No. 4, *Four Early Pieces* p. 25, m. 41–48

Bartók also exploited the sentimental chromaticism of Strauss:

Example 1.12: No. 4, *Four Early Pieces* p. 28, m. 144–56

This recalls the pianism of the *Hungarian Rhapsodies* of Liszt:

Example 1.13: No. 4, *Four Early Pieces* p. 29, m. 208–15

Bartók also experiments with rhythmic notation in this composition. In the transition to the return, each hand is notated in a different time signature that avoids sharing a downbeat.

These four early pieces show the composer searching for his own voice.

RHAPSODY OP. 1 FOR SOLO PIANO (1904); FOR PIANO AND ORCHESTRA (1905)

Bartók allowed the *Rhapsody* to be published as his Opus 1. (The original manuscript of the *Sonata* of 1898 also indicates Op. 1; however, Bartók withdrew the use of this first opus number many times before the *Rhapsody*, published in 1908, was so labeled.)

In 1905, Bartók entered the first and last competition in which he would
be a piano participant: the Rubinstein competition held in Paris for both
pianists and composers. Bartók did not regret losing in the piano category
to the German pianist Wilhelm Backhaus (he was a good pianist!), but he
resented being excluded in composition because of a very mediocre composer by the name of Attilio Brugnoli. He wrote to his mother:

> I have to inform you with regret that I was not successful in the competition.
> It is not extraordinary and does not hurt me that I did not win the prize for
> piano playing, but the way the prize for composing was handled was just re-
> volting. . . . So Brugnoli was mentioned in the first place. And I shall return
> my (un)honorary diploma to Auer (St. Petersburg) as soon as I receive it. I do
> not want to accept such stupid "honors." I should like to remark that Brug-
> noli's works are just compilations of no value at all. That the adjudicators
> could not see how much better my works were, is perfectly scandalous.[11]

Certainly, time has proven Bartók right in his judgment of the composer
Brugnoli, but Bartok didn't seem to have much luck with competitions.
Several years later, in 1911, Bartók submitted the score of *Bluebeard's Castle* to an opera competition in Hungary. The work was branded "unplayable" and eliminated from the competition.

In comparison to the *Four Early Pieces* of 1903, Bartók seems to have
found his footing. No longer imitating Strauss, Brahms, and Dohnányi, he
is now strongly influenced by the formal design of Liszt's music. However, the voice heard in the *Rhapsody* goes beyond Liszt; Bartók reveals
himself to be an individual and an interesting young Hungarian pianistic
personality. Both composers make use of a contrasting binary dance form
for their rhapsodies: a slow (lassu) introduction, followed by the quick
(friss) dance movement. The inspiration for the *Rhapsody*'s fast second
movement was a folk dance, performed by smiling couples in brightly
embroidered peasant costumes.

The *Rhapsody* Op. 1 is a genuine piece of bravura and must be performed with unabashed virtuosity: no apologies needed for having fun
and showing off at the piano! However, this is not music for everyone; it
is for the pianist with a large enough technique to respond to its youthful
heart-on-the-sleeve emotion without embarassment. The *Rhapsody* Op. 1
then becomes a joy to play. Certainly, its difficulties must be approached
seriously; however, too earnest a performance will diminish and trivialize
its content and also risk losing the fresh, improvisatory quality that this
rhapsodic music requires. (A similar problem exists for the performer of
Liszt's piano music; he must be able to experience the passion and the joy
of discovery embodied within Liszt's virtuosity. Yet the pianist walks a
dangerously narrow line between what will sound tasteful and what
could deteriorate into grotesqueness and mannerism.)

Another difficulty prominent within the solo version is the fragmented quality of the composition. The *Rhapsody* must give an impression of improvisation, but it must also hold together, its many seams not too much in evidence. It suffers from being an overly sectional work, and each sprawling movement needs to be contained within the boundaries of a three-part design.

Its two contrasting movements, played without interruption, share similar thematic material and are unified further by returning to the opening section's closing material at the conclusion of the *Rhapsody*. Like Liszt, Bartók proves himself a master of thematic transformation. The motto theme, introduced in the opening measures, is transformed rhythmically in the dance movement.

Example 1.14: *Rhapsody* Op. 1, Dover (1981), p. 39, m. 1–3

Example 1.15: *Rhapsody* p. 58, m. 378–91

Example 1.16: *Rhapsody* p. 61, m. 486–500

The *Rhapsody* comes full circle with its final five measures reaffirming (in augmentation) the opening four-note motto.

A second motto theme (ritenuto molto), introduced in the first section, reappears to herald the dance movement and is gradually transformed to a folk dance melody.

Example 1.17: *Rhapsody* p. 48, m. 80–81

Example 1.18: *Rhapsody* p. 51, m. 113–22 (transition to dance movement)

Example 1.19: *Rhapsody* p. 52, m. 130–43

It is fun to discover the thematic connections between these two contrasting movements. The interval of the fourth figures prominently in Bartók's vocabulary, and a left-hand motif from the opening recitative section is transformed into the fiddling of a wild Gypsy violinist.

Example 1.20: *Rhapsody* p. 42, m. 29

Example 1.21: *Rhapsody* p. 59, m. 428–38

In much of the first movement's recitative section, Bartók imitates the sounds of the *cimbalom*, the hammered Hungarian stringed instrument, by writing difficult ascending and descending chordal passagework. Keep in mind that these harmonically static passages are written with the intention of prolonging the sound. Over this wash of thick texture, the right hand freely improvises and declaims the melody. These recitatives resemble Spanish and Moorish folk-chant, which Manuel de Falla imitated in his *Nights in the Gardens of Spain* (itself a part of Bartók's performing repertoire). It is essential to follow where Bartók takes the melodic line and to never lose its feeling of forward direction. The underlying harmonies provide the key to understanding the phrase structure of the first movement. The line moves forward and then pulls back, and the pianist needs to capture these rhapsodic, push/pull elements with every performance.

Example 1.22: *Rhapsody* p. 41, m. 20–25

Liszt's pianistic ghost is still lurking in the shadows! Decisions about how much rubato to use must be made by listening and trusting the ear and one's innate good taste. Bartók attempts to write out the rubato desired, aiding the pianist's own discovery of the line's natural declamation. His indications include a wealth of accelerandos, ritardandos, and stringendos, and provide excellent signposts and checkpoints for the performer.

The solo version of the *Rhapsody* is recommended only for the advanced pianist who possesses a good technique and an inclination toward romantic, Lisztian bravura. This piece is not only demanding from the technical and physical perspective, but also extremely difficult musically. I believe that it is always easier to perform a musical masterpiece than to make truly convincing a work of lesser musical stature such as the *Rhapsody*.

Because of the 1905 Rubinstein competition, Bartók revised the solo version of his Op. 1 *Rhapsody* into a work for solo piano with orchestral accompaniment. In its concerto form, the *Rhapsody* becomes a much more effective and virtuosic work, especially the fast second movement. (The only significant difference in the material of these two versions of Op. 1 is the extended introductory cadenza that was added for the concerto version.) With Bartók's revised piano writing of the solo piano part, and the added color resources of the orchestra, the piano writing becomes technically less difficult but still succeeds in sounding extremely virtuosic. However, in its concerto form, the *Rhapsody* now suffers from sounding much more dated than the original solo version.

In evaluating the two versions of this composition, each work must be judged on separate terms, accepting the inherent limitations of the solo medium and the concerto form. (Actually, three different versions exist: A shortened solo version of the slow movement alone was also originally published.[12]) The solo version presents more obvious problems for the pianist; the wide color resources of the orchestra, so helpful in delineating the formal design, are not available. The pianist is now responsible for all contrasts, and technically speaking, the piano writing becomes much more difficult. The solo performer must transcend the weaknesses of the total composition, highlighted in the solo version. What might sound effective as a colorful orchestral interlude, scored for a variety of contrasting instruments, requires a varied and imaginative coloristic palette from the pianist. The solo version also demands more stamina and physical energy; the pianist no longer has the rest breaks of the orchestral tuttis during this seventeen-minute composition. However, I believe that an imaginative pianist, aware of the music's limitations but possessing a bit of charm, spontaneity, and delight in virtuosity, could make the solo piece convincing.

Suggestions for Performance (Applicable to Both Versions)

Mesto: The opening of this movement should sound as sorrowful and soulful as possible. I think of this first page introduction as a conversation between two people with the first two measures being answered by the next three measures, and then followed by another exchange of dialogue before the recitative section begins. (Erratum: At m. 7 of the Dover edition, the B-natural in the third beat of the left hand should be B-flat.) Be flexible with tempo. It should be stretched like a rubber band when necessary, without losing its basic shape. First interpret Bartók's rhythmic directions strictly, and *then* see how much rubato is possible. Only after the rhythm has been confined will it then be able to be freed. Rubato is an essential ingredient of this rhapsodic music, and the pacing of dynamics must be thought out in advance.

Exploit sudden contrasts with dynamics and color effects. Bartók frequently goes immediately from *ppp* to fortissimo. Remember that the ultimate function of the difficult 32nd-note scale passagework is to prolong sound and color; therefore, liberal use of pedal is recommended. It will be more effective to begin slowly and gradually build momentum during the crescendo.

Within such a thickly textured composition, be sure to clarify and identify what is foreground and what is background/filler. In the imitative passages after the recitative, follow the voice lines separately and be aware of their independence. Then, decide how each should be voiced; they must not sound as if they are all of equal importance, nor should they possess a sameness of color. Exploit to the maximum color and virtuosic effects; the cadenzas Bartók writes out should be bathed in pedal and played as freely as possible. Experiment, and imagine all those Gypsy violinists! Five measures from the end of the composition, try rolling the four chords; this will make it easier to bring out the notes of the theme.

A good performance of the *Rhapsody* depends on the strength of personality and the commitment of the performer. All of its technical problems must appear to be easy, to be merely tossed off by the pianist. To call attention to the music's difficulties is to undermine the entire work and cause it to fall flat. If the solo version is studied, it will be helpful to consult Bartók's orchestral score for coloristic suggestions. The concerto version should be learned only after the pianist is already familiar with the more substantial three *Piano Concertos* (discussed in chapter 10). The Op. 1 is a novelty piece, revealing Bartók's youthful passion and Lisztian pianistic roots; an orchestral performance is certainly a rarity but would make for interesting programming combined with one of Bartók's more mature concertos such as the third.

In 1961, sixteen years after Bartók's death, two very early compositions, the *Piano Quintet* and the *Scherzo* Op. 2 for piano and orchestra, were uncovered among Bartók's personal papers by Denijs Dille, the original head of the Budapest Bartók Archives, and are now available in publication by Boosey & Hawkes. Both strongly reflect Bartók's early influences—Brahms, Liszt, Strauss, Wagner, and Franck—and both works are good indicators of what will follow.

PIANO QUINTET (1904)

This very early work, which represents the beginning of Bartók's farewell to romanticism, was composed after his symphonic poem *Kossuth* and just before his Op. 1 *Rhapsody*. Bartók had not yet seriously begun his collecting of folk music.

The Brahms chamber repertory, especially the F minor piano quintet, and the music of Liszt serve as Bartók's models here. From Brahms, he learns how to balance the piano with the string quartet, and Liszt's structural designs become Bartók's formal blueprints. Working within an extended and rather verbose four-movement structure, Bartók links all the movements together by utilizing similar thematic material related to a popular folk song. The movements are successive sets of variations.

Bartók's first wife Marta related a story, which might explain why Bartók never allowed the *Quintet* to be published during his lifetime. When first premiered in 1910 on a program that also included his *Bagatelles* Op. 6 and his *String Quartet* No. 1, the work was a huge success and was very well received by the critics—perhaps too well received. They spoke about the effect of hearing the *Quintet* after listening to the first *String Quartet*, admitting that the *Quintet*, now "sounded like Haydn or Mozart, lovely and melodic." They then went on to say, "What a pity that Bartók abandoned his artistic trends to pay homage to false gods." When the program was repeated in 1921, people once again said that the *Quintet* definitely surpassed Bartók's later works. He flew into a rage and hurled the score into a corner; it was not discovered until 1961.

The *Quintet* is a rather inflated, overblown romantic work, but it is a definite crowd-pleaser. Its exciting finale looks ahead to the final movement of the Op. 1 *Rhapsody* and predicts the finale of the 1926 *Sonata*. It is apparent that Bartók had honed his skills by studying and performing the quartets and quintets of Brahms and Franck.

SCHERZO, OP. 2 FOR PIANO AND ORCHESTRA (1904–1905)

Not only was the *Scherzo* not published in Bartók's lifetime; it was also never played. The premiere was supposed to take place in 1905 in Budapest with the Philharmonic, and with Bartók as piano soloist. At the first rehearsal, the orchestra's obvious lack of preparation and rather hostile attitude angered Bartók, and he left and never returned. He took back the performing rights from the Philharmonic, and the *Scherzo* for piano and orchestra did not receive its first performance until 1961.

Sometimes referred to as *Burlesque* for piano and orchestra, this piece strongly resembles the Strauss *Burlesque*, recalling the *Totentanz* of Liszt as well. (Several passages also remind me of the first movement cadenza from the Grieg *Piano Concerto*.)

Despite the seriousness of the initial piano writing, the *Scherzo* was written as a musical joke, with the woodwinds and brass sounding like Sancho Panza and Til Eulenspiegel sharing some merry pranks. Bartók's orchestration and motivic imitation are responsible for humorous effects. The one-movement form has been influenced by Liszt. Beginning with an adagio introduction, a motto theme in the form of a recitative introduces the opening scherzo (allegro) section, which is followed by the trio (andante) section, representing the slow movement of the piece. The motto theme reappears to introduce the scherzo's return, which is played this time only by the orchestra, except for a six-bar interjection from the pianist. The piano returns only in the coda, with an eighteen-measure expressive and very Straussian adagio interlude.

In this composition, the pianist functions more as an equal partner with the orchestra than as a soloist. In general, the piano writing is a continuation of the romantic, virtuosic pianism of Bartók's Op. 1, but with much more allegiance to Strauss. The youthful *Scherzo* highlights Bartók's wonderful sense of humor, and the orchestral writing in the final return should produce a smile, or at least a chuckle!

TWO ELEGIES, OP. 8B (1908–1909)

The *Two Elegies* evoke an image of Bartók bestriding two centuries; one foot is firmly placed in the modernist world with his new compositional style, and the other foot refuses to move from its nineteenth-century pianistic roots. However, both feet are in balance and the figure remains upright. Bartók described the *Elegies* as "a certain return to the old-style piano technique," and identified No. 1 as D minor and No. 2 as C-sharp minor, to which was added the following comment: "This information is addressed especially to those who like to pigeonhole music they do not understand into the category of atonal music."[13]

Within these two elegies, Bartók makes use of all the trappings gleaned from nineteenth-century pianism: tremolos, cadenzas, arpeggios, trills, octaves, orchestral sonorities. However, Bartók's approach to development of thematic material is the antithesis of romanticism; material is now developed with leanness and sparseness, much more characteristic of Beethoven's early-period classical motivic development than the thematic expansiveness at the end of the century, and more closely associated with the ideals of the twentieth-century minimalists. Here minimalism is merged with maximum pianism, used only to underline and heighten the dramatic intensity and emotional expressivity within these mournful *Elegies.*

Elegy No. 1 in D Minor (1908) [Track 3]

The inspiration for the first *Elegy* was Bartók's painful loss of the young Hungarian violinist Stefi Geyer, whose muse is also present in the first *Violin Concerto*, the thirteenth and fourteenth *Bagatelles*, the *Two Portraits* Op. 5, the *Ten Easy Pieces*, and the first *String Quartet* Op. 7. Shortly after Bartók completed the first *Violin Concerto*, Geyer sent Bartók a letter ending their relationship; the first *Elegy* was written shortly thereafter, and exactly one year later Bartók married Marta Ziegler, his sixteen-year-old piano student. (The dedication score of the first *Violin Concerto*, Op. posth., written for Geyer during 1907–1908, was discovered in Geyer's possession and performed only after her death in 1958.)

It is rare to see Bartók so emotionally revealed at the piano and writing a work so governed by his heart. Perhaps as consolation for the loss of his "ideal companion" or as a lamentation for his pain, Bartók returned to the familiar romantic pianism of his youth, his comfort food at the piano. A fragment from an early letter written to his mother in 1905 sets the tone for these two elegies; this seems to be Bartók's *Heiligenstadt Testament.*

> . . . And I can see in advance, this loneliness of my soul will be my fate. I am looking and searching for an ideal companion, but I feel it is all in vain. Should I find one, disappointment would not be far away. Quiet resignation may sound contrary to my searching for a companion, but I have almost become used to the thought that it cannot be otherwise, I must always be lonely. And I can say this to bring comfort to others: We must attain to a height from where we can view things with sober calmness, with complete indifference. It is difficult to acquire this ability. But to reach this height is the greatest triumph we can have over ourselves, over others, over all that is. Sometimes for awhile I feel I have reached the height. Then comes a terrible fall, then the struggle, the move upward starts again. And so it goes on incessantly. Still, there will be a time when I shall succeed in remaining on the top.[14]

On first hearing, it is difficult to detect Bartók's economy of motivic material and to analyze its many transformations. This elegy sounds as if it is through-composed: a stream-of-consciousness anguished out-pouring of soul. Actually the elegy can be reduced to a simple three-part form, but even this is disguised to fit into a binary structure, similar in its form to the earlier sonatas of Scarlatti. After the grave introduction, based on a variant of Stefi's lost love motif (D/F-sharp/A/C-sharp) the first section uses only material from the leitmotif, inverted, sequenced, rhythmically augmented (example 1.24) and embroidered, and completely dissected.

Example 1.23: *Elegy* No. 1, Dover (1981), p. 119, m. 1–8

Example 1.24: *Elegy* No. 1, p. 120, m. 17–20

It surges with passionate pianism and full-blown seething emotions, but exhibits minimal thematic content and closes with a tritone motif extracted from the theme. The middle section begins with a *ppp* fugato whose subject is based on the opening bars of the composition and then developed; dynamics and emotional intensity reach their climax in this middle section. The Stefi Geyer motif heralds the return section.

Example 1.25: *Elegy* No. 1, p. 123, m. 69–71

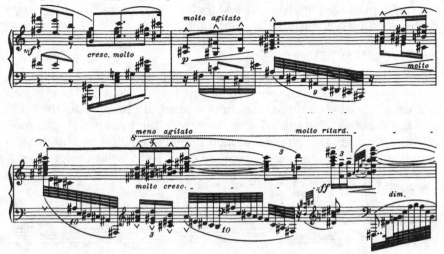

Bartók disguises the return by altering the passagework accompanying Stefi's theme, and by interchanging hands. The piano writing here is reminiscent of Liszt's *La Leggierezza* and also hints at the elaborate arpeggio writing he will use in his second *Etude* (discussed in chapter 3).

Example 1.26: *Elegy* No. 1, p. 125, m. 78–79

Example 1.27: Liszt *Concert Etude* No. 2, Dover (1988), p. 155, m. 49–50

The coda allows Bartók one last emotional outburst using the tritone closing motif, presented in an anguished *ff* chordal eruption. The *Elegy* ends with resolution of the tritone to D minor.

Suggestions for Performance

Grave introduction: Within the larger form of this elegy, this introductory section cries out for molto espressivo playing that should sound improvised and uncalculated even though carefully studied. Try to maintain the back-and-forth rhythm of the left hand along with the improvised, parlando melodic structure. The left-hand motion should resemble a pendulum, also supplying harmony and color; liberal use of the pedal will be helpful.

Example 1.28: *Elegy* No. 1, p. 119, m. 9–12

Long, extended pedals are also recommended for all the extensive arpeggiated left-hand passagework. Change of pedals should coincide with harmonic changes but should not be noticeable. Depending on acoustics, one long pedal from m. 38 until m. 42 might have to be supplemented by a pedal flutter vibrato.

Example 1.29: *Elegy* No. 1, p. 121, m. 38–43

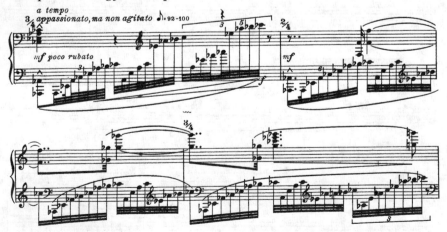

Accents: As does Liszt, Bartók differentiates his accents with varied markings. (The marking ^ is a stronger accent than the marking >. The sforzato marking is the strongest accent of the three.)

Example 1.30: *Elegy* No. 1, p. 121, m. 30–33

Compare this example with the accents Bartók indicates in examples 1.23 and 1.24. The accents in examples 1.30 and 1.24 should stand out more in bold relief than the accents of example 1.23. With his notation, Bartók differentiates between emphatic and expressive accents.

With the first *Elegy*, Bartók challenges the performer on many levels: emotionally, pianistically, and musically. Even though the key is D minor, as confirmed by its last chord, Bartók's tonality is sometimes ambivalent, as in its opening measures, and certainly freed from traditional nineteenth-century harmonic language.

Elegy No. 2 in C-Sharp Minor (1909)

This is the more difficult and elusive of the *Elegies*. Bartók has written a work based on the minimal thematic material of four notes, a variation of the Stefi Geyer chord. His extremely economical compositional techniques are a reaction against the excesses of romanticism, but his four-note theme looks back to a nineteenth-century masterwork, Chopin's B minor *Sonata*.

Example 1.31: *Elegy* No. 2, Dover (1981), p. 127, m. 1–7

Example 1.32: Chopin *Sonata* No. 3, Op. 58, Dover (1981), p. 147, m. 1–5

Bartók proves himself to be a superb minimalist, but this is minimalism within a dramatic three-part structure that exploits repetition and variation for maximum effect. Bartók's compositional craftsmanship is aided by his extraordinary romantic pianism; repetition fosters orchestral colors and sonorities as well as establishing a consistency of mood and dramatic tension. Frequently the ear will be fooled by Bartók's devices of inversion and augmentation of this four-note motif; how well he is able to disguise his limited material! The symbols 0- and -0 are introduced in the score to indicate that the motif should be repeated and the number of repetitions not fixed, but varied according to the amount of rubato required for each individual performance; the symbols mark where this improvisatory practice begins and ends. Bartók has great faith in the *ad libitum* skills of the performer and also trusts his freedom of rubato. (Bartók was years ahead of all the aleatory composers, including John Cage!)

Example 1.33: *Elegy* No. 2, p. 129, m. 17

In the Andante section, Bartók encloses the entire section (m. 28–43) by these symbols (0- and –0), thus indicating that the section should be played with as much rubato as possible. Some of this piano writing suggests the pianism of Rachmaninoff, Franck, or Ravel. (I always am reminded when I play these measures of the beautiful cello solo with piano accompaniment in the middle section of Franck's *Variations Symphoniques*.)

Example 1.34: *Elegy* No. 2, p. 130, m. 29–32

Example 1.35: Rachmaninoff *Prelude* Op. 32, No. 12, Dover (1988), p. 102, m. 1–4

Bartók demonstrates how repetition can create consonance if the repetition occurs often enough. The seventh interval between the first and last note of the motive (see example 1.31) becomes a constant that requires no resolution; Bartók pulls the ear toward it, providing a sense of arrival at the return and conclusion of the composition.

The second *Elegy* is cast in a simple three-part form, with all material germinating from one four-note motif presented in the opening measure. Structural analysis is essential to arriving at any interpretation involving so much repetitive material. The motif will vary in its compositional treatment and performance because of its place in the total design: the same motif functions as melody, accompaniment; is used vertically, horizontally, imitatively; is inverted, augmented. The technique of inversion also enters the vocabulary of Bartók's pianistic notation with special indications given for reverse arpeggios.

Example 1.36: *Elegy* No. 2, p. 137, m. 91–94

Reverse arpeggios will also be used by Bartók in the second *Piano Concerto* as well as in several solo works including the *Sonata* of 1926, the *Improvisations* Op. 20, two *Burlesques*, and the Op. 6 *Bagatelles*. (In the earlier second *Elegy* and seventh *Bagatelle*, Bartók indicates a reverse arpeggio, beginning on the top note of the chord, with an arpeggio marking appearing to the right of the chord instead of its usual placement on the left. In later works Bartók writes all arpeggios to the left of the chord and adds a descending arrow preceding the chord to indicate that the pianist should play the arpeggio in reverse.)

Suggestions for Performance

In the opening measures, Bartók indicates sempre rubato (quasi improvisando). Within these first five introductory measures, the same motif is repeated at least ten times. Each must be varied. I do an echo effect beginning on the last beat of the third measure and gradually introduce the melody that is an augmentation of the motif. Never, ever, lose the melodic line. (See example 1.31.)

Concentrate on the building of sonorities. Bartók uses repetition to create a constant sound filler; this background enhances emotional and dramatic intensity. (Beware of any unnecessary forcing of sound, which will produce only tired muscles and an ugly, strident tone.) A big, full orchestral forte is what is wanted here, and all the varied declamatory accents should be observed. Notice that the 4/8 measure varies the same four-note chord by augmentation and extension.

Example 1.37: *Elegy* No. 2, p. 130, m. 21–28

A special mood and atmosphere must be evoked; long pedals help to color the melody and create the unique wash of sound needed for the accompaniment figures. Experimentation with sonority is necessary with so much repetition of this four-note cluster. The return section at Tempo

I (m. 47) consists basically of repetition of the principal motif and goes from *ff* to *p* with some minor digressions along the way. Make sure the rhythmic variants of these passages are noted and their dynamic design well paced.

Concentrate on the many coloristic possibilities of the final page, which serves as the epigram for the entire work (see example 1.36). The melody must never be lost, and pedals should be kept as long as possible. This page will require strict counting before Bartók's irregular rhythms can be learned and become second nature.

(Errata: On the final page of volume I of the Dover Collection (p. 137), the indication should read "an eighth note = 69–76," not "a quarter note" as written. Also, in the middle stave of m. 59, the change from bass to treble clef where both hands are playing in unison is missing.)

Some confusion surrounds Bartók's use of the indication "Tempo I." Frequently in his writing he will indicate a return to an original tempo with altered metronome markings. In the second elegy there are three different metronome markings given for Tempo I. On page 129, at Tempo I, I would suggest a marking of 88 instead of 69. This makes better musical sense in the shaping of the entire work and relates to the metronome marking of the return section at m. 47. The Tempo I marking at m. 24 before the middle section should also be altered to read 88.

The second *Elegy* demands big bravura piano playing in the grand tradition: exploitation of contrasts, orchestral sonorities, and the freedom needed to improvise while maintaining the larger structural outlines. Formal boundaries must be clearly outlined, and the minimal material used in this composition thoroughly analyzed, preferably away from the piano, to gain further appreciation of the composer's craft. With such thematic economy, experimentation at the keyboard with pedaling and coloristic effects becomes essential. The elegy sounds like a contradiction of extremes; minimum material is exploited for maximum effect, but the result is a poignant, emotional statement in C-sharp minor.

These two mournful elegies are part of a series of lamentations written by Bartók. The thirteenth *Bagatelle* from his Op. 6 set of 1908 was a lament for his lost love, Stefi Geyer. The *Two Elegies* of Op. 8b, written only one year later, express similar emotions while using a much more expansive romantic nineteenth-century approach to the keyboard. Bartók's *Four Dirges*, Op. 9a of 1909–1910, are stylistically more akin to Debussy, and look toward the elegy that Bartók wrote as a memorial for Debussy, included in his *Improvisations* of 1920. Even some of his little pieces from *For Children* also include several original mourning songs. These works differ stylistically in pianistic approach, but they share the profound emotions associated with mourning and loss. Bartók demonstrates with each individual lament that his music is indeed capable of touching the soul.

Bartók's piano music never hides its natural pianism. No matter which fork in the road he stylistically followed, his pianism always went along. It should be remembered that Bartók was practically born a pianist, starting at the keyboard at a very young age. As a composer, he had the courage to follow his intuition without fear of where it might lead. Down all those less-traveled roads, when composing for the keyboard, some variant of his nineteenth-century pianistic roots always went with him.

All art has the right, even the duty, of looking for links and lessons in preceding ages. Let us recall how many formulae J. S. Bach, the greatest of them, borrowed from his contemporaries and predecessors. The big test of a real talent will be the form he lends to this loan.[15]

ADDITIONAL REPERTOIRE TO EXPLORE

Rachmaninoff	*Preludes* Op. 23, Op. 32
Liszt	*Three Concert Etudes*
	Hungarian Rhapsodies
	Mephisto Waltz
	Totentanz
	Harmonies Poétiques & Réligieuses
	Nuages Gris
	"Liebestod" from Wagner's *Tristan und Isolde*
Strauss	*Burlesque*
	Thus Spake Zarathustra
	Ein Heldenleben
	Til Eulenspiegel's Merry Pranks
Franck	*Variations Symphoniques*
	Piano Quintet
de Falla	*Nights in the Gardens of Spain*
Dohnányi	*Capriccios*
	Rhapsody, Op. 1
Brahms	*Piano Sonatas,* Op. 1, 2, 5
	Piano Pieces, Op. 118
	Hungarian Dances
	Piano Quintet in F minor
	Piano Quartet in G minor
	Sonatas for violin & piano
Ravel	*Miroirs*
	Gaspard de la Nuit
Schubert	*Piano Sonatas* (A major D. 959; B-flat major D. 960)

Chopin   *Sonata* in B minor, Op. 58
Grieg   *Piano Concerto*
Wagner   *Tristan und Isolde*

NOTES

1. Béla Bartók, "Harvard Lectures" (1943), in *Béla Bartók Essays*, ed. Benjamin Suchoff (Lincoln: University of Nebraska Press, 1976), 383.

2. Béla Bartók, "Autobiography" (1921), in *Béla Bartók Essays*, ed. Benjamin Suchoff, 408.

3. Béla Bartók, "Folk Songs of Hungary" (1928), in *Béla Bartók Essays*, ed. Benjamin Suchoff, 333.

4. Béla Bartók as quoted by Agatha Fassett in *The Naked Face of Genius* (New York: Houghton Mifflin Company, Riverside Press, 1958), 357.

5. Béla Bartók, "Introduction to *Béla Bartók Masterpieces for Piano*" (1945), in *Béla Bartók Essays*, ed. Benjamin Suchoff, 433.

6. Béla Bartók, "Hungarian Folk Music" (1929), in *Béla Bartók Essays*, ed. Benjamin Suchoff, 4.

7. Randall Thompson, in *Bartók Remembered*, ed. Malcolm Gillies (New York: W.W. Norton, 1991), 171.

8. Béla Bartók in *Béla Bartók: Letters*, ed. János Demény, trans. by Péter Balabán and István Farkas, trans. rev. by Elisabeth West and Colin Mason (London: Faber & Faber, 1971; New York: St. Martin's Press, 1971), 105.

9. Béla Bartók, "Autobiography" (1921), in *Béla Bartók Essays*, ed. Benjamin Suchoff, 409.

10. Bartók, "Autobiography," 409.

11. Béla Bartók in *Béla Bartók: Letters*, ed. János Demény, 45–46.

12. The one-movement version is published by G. Schirmer in *Bartók: Selected Works for the Piano*, compiled by Ernö Balogh. Only its closing five measures differ from what is written in the extended composition.

13. Béla Bartók, "Introduction to *Béla Bartók Masterpieces for Piano*" (1945), in *Béla Bartók Essays*, ed. Benjamin Suchoff, 433.

14. Béla Bartók in *Bartók Béla Levelei*, (Béla Bartók Letters), ed. János Demény, (Budapest: Zenemükiadó, 1976), 68.

15. Béla Bartók, "*A 1932 Interview with Bartók* by Magda Vámos," in *Bartók Studies*, ed. Todd Crow (Detroit: Detroit Reprints in Music, 1976), 189. [This interview originally appeared in *The New Hungarian Quarterly* XIV/50 (Summer 1973).]

2

✢

A New Piano Style

Much has been said about the intimate relationship between mathematics and music. Whether this is mathematics or music, the most perfect form has been achieved when all that has to be said is said and not one iota more.

—Béla Bartók[1]

The *Bagatelles* of Op. 6, written in 1908, represent a critical juncture in Bartók's piano music; they signal the development of a new and uniquely individual compositional style. Revising these earlier piano works for a new edition during the last years of his life, Bartók had the special advantage of being able to look back and evaluate these pieces in relation to his complete piano repertory. Bartók wrote these words about the *Bagatelles* for the 1945 Boosey & Hawkes publication:

In these, a new piano style appears as a reaction to the exuberance of the romantic piano music of the nineteenth century, a style stripped of all unessential decorative elements, using only the most restricted technical means. As later developments show, the *Bagatelles* inaugurate a new trend of piano writing in my career, which is consistently followed in almost all of my successive piano works.[2]

Even the avant-garde composer-pianist Busoni, hearing these pieces for the first time in 1908, exclaimed, *"Endlich etwas wirklich neues!* [At last, something truly new!] I hold these pieces to be among the most interesting and original of our times; what the composer has to say is out of the ordinary and entirely individual."[3]

It was during these early years of 1906–1908 that Bartók seriously began to record and collect Hungarian peasant folk material with his friend and colleague Zoltán Kodály. In 1907, Bartók also accepted the position as Professor of Piano at the Budapest Academy of Music, mainly because this afforded him the financial security to nourish his passion for ethnomusicological folk research. His first real discovery in folk music, a study of Székely folk ballads, was published in 1908, and some of its material was used to complete his second orchestral *Suite,* which had remained unfinished for three years; this is the first work to reveal a glimpse of Bartók's new style. It was also in 1907 that his friend and fellow composer, Kodály, returned from a visit to Paris and brought back to Hungary the music of a new and interesting musician, Claude Debussy. By 1908, Bartók was well acquainted with the piano pieces *Images* and *Pour le Piano,* in addition to studying the scores of *La Mer* and the *String Quartet.* Bartók and Kodály also managed to acquire a manuscript of Schoenberg's first *String Quartet* and transpose it for four hands so both of them could read and study it at the keyboard. For Bartók, the Frenchman and the Viennese were among the most interesting of his contemporaries.

The prolific period of 1907–1908 gave birth to three piano cycles: *Three Hungarian Folk Songs from the Csík District* and the *14 Bagatelles,* Op. 6, composed in May, 1908, immediately followed by the *Ten Easy Pieces,* completed in June of 1908. These are all significant because they represent the first piano works to be born from a genuine folk idiom and molded into Bartók's new compositional style.

The economy and lack of filler, evident in Bartók's new style, is a strong reaction to all the excesses of the previous century. The modal nature of the folk melody provides the catalyst for a new harmonic language. The traditional nineteenth-century harmonization with its diatonic, triadic tonic/dominant relationships no longer works. Hence the need for a new syntax with which to set this original folk material.

In his introduction to the revised edition of the *Ten Easy Pieces,* Bartók explains his need for a new language by offering an example of the old language, an 1853 popular version of an original Slovak folk melody. (After 1919, this folk tune became the Czechoslovakian national anthem.)

Example 2.1: No. 16 from *l00 Magyar népdal,* collected by Ignás Bognár and harmonized by Füredi, reprinted in Dover (1981), p. x, introduction

Example 2.2: No. 8 from *Ten Easy Pieces* Dover (1981), p. 113, m. 1–10

Here, Bartók uses the same folk melody, but what a stunning difference his harmonic language evokes—giving further force to his dictum: "It is not so much the theme which matters but what the artist can make of it."[4]

Despite the prevailing and accepted opinions of many music theorists, Bartók's new harmonic language was neither atonal, bitonal, nor polytonal. According to Bartók: "An 'atonal' folk music, in my opinion, is unthinkable."[5] Bartók shared with his contemporary Arnold Schoenberg the belief in the equality of all twelve pitch tones; however, it was Schoenberg's absolute denial of the basic governing aural considerations that set these two composers poles apart. For Bartók, polytonality or atonality was nonexistent and impossible to achieve, except intellectually, because the ear naturally related every sound to those previously heard and then linked them together to a tonal center. Even though polytonality could be proven in theory and demonstrated by looking at the manuscript, the ear was always present to contradict the thesis. Bartók was not a theorist; he was a pianist as well as a composer. He was a concert performer whose occupation relied mainly on his trained ears and his ability to listen.

Observing the two different key signatures notated in the first *Bagatelle*, theorists have used this piece as their favorite example to advance the claim of two tonalities operating within one composition. However, it is quite amusing that Bartók himself makes fun of this theory and refuses to accept bitonality or polytonality as a serious option.

The first one bears a key signature of four sharps (as used for C-sharp minor) in the upper staff and of four flats (F minor) in the lower one. This half-serious, half-jesting procedure was used to demonstrate the absurdity of key signatures in certain kinds of contemporary music. After carrying the key-signature principle *ad absurdum* in the first piece, I dropped its use in all the other *Bagatelles* and in most of the following works as well. The tonality of the first *Bagatelle* is, of course, not a mixture of C-sharp minor and F minor but simply a Phrygian-colored C major. In spite of this, it was quoted as an "early example of bitonality" in the 1920's when it was fashionable to talk about bi- and polytonality.[6]

In the first mislabeled bitonal *Bagatelle*, the ear hears two different and unequal sound planes having a dialogue with each other; the *mf* right hand moves toward the E, and the *p* left hand descends to C. However it is the right hand that has the more dominant voice. Indeed, if the hands are heard separately, two separate tonalities do exist; however, when heard together, the ear naturally gravitates toward the E of the second measure and continues to hear the piece within the context of C major. The left hand's passing dissonances provide wonderful color contrasts while the *pp* C of the third measure serves to underscore the C tonal center. Tonal ambiguity produces dramatic effects; how satisfying Bartók makes the final measure's return to C. It is impossible to hear these two separate sound planes as equals; the ear will unconsciously make an aural judgment and go toward whichever tonal plane dominates.

Example 2.3: *Bagatelle* No. 1, Dover (1981), p. 69, m. 1–18 [Track 4]

Bartók, in his Harvard lectures of 1943, clarified and expanded his thoughts on atonality as well as on bitonality and polytonality:

> Real or "perfect" atonality does not exist, even in Schoenberg's works, because of that unchangeable physical law concerning the interrelation of harmonics and, in turn, the relation of the harmonics to their fundamental tone. When we hear a single tone, we will interpret it subconsciously as a fundamental tone. When we hear a following different tone, we will—again subconsciously—project it against the first tone, which has been felt as the fundamental, and interpret it according to its relation to the latter.[7]
>
> Polytonality exists only for the eye when one looks at such music. But our mental hearing again will select one key as a fundamental key, and will project the tones of the other keys in relation to the one selected. I will use a simile: Our two eyes cannot simultaneously perceive two totally different pictures; they have to concentrate their direction on one picture (the slight difference caused by the distance between the eyes is of no consequence). Similarly, our hearing cannot perceive two or more different keys with two or more different fundamental tones, as such; it will simplify matters by reducing the maze of keys to one principal key.[8]

The *Bagatelles* provide the proof of Bartók's words. Within the sixth, seventh, eighth, and ninth *Bagatelles*, Bartók purposely creates an impression of tonal ambiguity but, at the same time, states clearly in his introduction that these pieces were written in the keys of B major, D-sharp minor, G minor, and E-flat minor, and adds: "This information is addressed especially to those who like to pigeonhole all music they do not understand into the category of 'atonal' music."[9]

Any understanding of Bartók's music must be based primarily on listening. Granted, what had previously been labeled dissonance in the last century has now become consonance in Bartók's new harmonic language, but Bartók's expert use of repetition helps the ear to naturally adjust to this new vocabulary. Let's take a rather obvious example to demonstrate this repetitive technique: If one hears a new and uncomfortable sound such as buzzing, the ear will only begin to tolerate and accustom itself to the sound if it is kept constant. At a certain point in time, its startling effect will diminish, and the ear will even cease to hear it, or will certainly not hear it as strongly as when initially perceived. Bartók is a master of repetitive effects and combines these expertly with the art of contrast. Repetition is used by Bartók in the ideal minimalist sense: "to say what needs to be said and not one iota more."[10]

> In nearly every great modern musical work one may, in fact, perceive an effort toward clarity of construction, a rigorous severity of composition coupled with a tendency to do without flourishes. But modern simplicity is just a moment of condensations within a complex evolution.[11]

FOURTEEN BAGATELLES, OP. 6 (1908)

Bartók was expert at creating what was new and modern by using traditional tools. The pianistic effects honed from his study of nineteenth-century romantic piano music were adapted to the simplicity and economy of his new piano style. A solid foundation was firmly in place that gave Bartók the freedom to build, expand, and to soar! Bartók's title for these fourteen pieces recalls Beethoven's bagatelles, and his use of the old, original folk melodies in the fourth and fifth *Bagatelles* looks back even farther to the past. The thirteenth and fourteenth *Bagatelles* were directly inspired by Bartók's emotional relationship with Stefi Geyer, and the final *Bagatelle* was also orchestrated by Bartók in 1911 as the second "Grotesque" movement of his orchestral work *Two Portraits*, Op. 5. In this set of fourteen uniquely individual pieces, Bartók reveals all the necessary tools and equipment with which to go forward and adventurously embrace the twentieth century.

Bartók has left the pianist with certain instructions for playing his *Bagatelles* that also can be applied to all his other piano works:

1. Accidentals affect only those notes that are on the same line or in the same space, and within only one measure. An exception is made only when notes are tied over into the next measure.
2. Pedaling is indicated by the sign: /_____/.
3. Here and there a rest is placed above the bar line (e.g., No. 9 and No. 11). There we want a pause between the respective measures, whose duration is indicated by the value of the rest.
4. The word sostenuto indicates a sudden slowing down of the tempo; ritard. or riten., a gradual slowing down.

Bagatelle No. 1 [Track 4]

The first *Bagatelle* is the only piece of the set that makes use of key signatures: two different ones used simultaneously within the same composition! This is Bartók's private joke, his way of poking fun at the theorists who will spend their time analyzing his compositional techniques. Again he is saying here with his sharp sense of humor that he will not be beholden to key signatures nor amenable to categorization; it is the ear that must be trusted, and the ability to listen, well developed. This piece is written in two parts, relying on the binary structure of its oral folk model. This is not a study in bitonality but an exploration of the contrasting colors between two separate sound levels. Especially difficult to maintain are the independent voices of the final four measures that work toward the final C resolution (see example 2.3). The emotional effect of this simple one-page piece is startling and elusive.

Bagatelle **No. 2**

Prokofiev could have included the three-part second *Bagatelle* as one of his *Visions Fugitives* (*Visions*, Op. 22; Prokofiev's set of twenty piano pieces were written several years later, during the 1915–1917 period). Bartók's sharp, direct humor recalls Prokofiev's third *Vision*. This piece must be played as lightly as possible while also observing Bartók's sudden jabbing accents. Bartók indicates its key as D-flat major; the repetitive major seconds that open and close the piece are not heard as dissonance, but function here as consonance.

Example 2.4: *Bagatelle* No. 2, p. 71, m. 22–30

Bartók's metronome marking of 84 seems just a bit slow, and his own recording of this piece is indeed at a slightly faster tempo. His colleagues have suggested that the little metronome he constantly kept with him in his back pocket might not have been absolutely accurate. Here, just a few notches faster will work.

I should add . . . that in my earlier works MM signs are very often inexact, or rather they do not correspond to the correct tempos. The only explanation I can think of is that I metronomized too hastily at that time, and perhaps my metronome was working imperfectly.[12]

Bagatelle No. 3

The third *Bagatelle* recalls another Russian, Sergei Rachmaninoff, and his G-sharp minor Op. 32 *Prelude* (written two years later in 1910). An unchanging five-note chromatic ostinato figure appears in the right hand, while the left hand sings out a simple ABA melody constructed from only five notes that span the distance of a tritone. Bartók's extreme simplicity and economy are startling in their emotional impact. As in Rachmaninoff's writing, diatonic tonic-dominant relationships are preserved.

Example 2.5: *Bagatelle* No. 3, p. 72, m. 1–6

Attention to form is an essential ingredient in shaping this monothematic piece.

Bagatelle No. 4

Another Russian, Moussorgsky, could have inspired the fourth *Bagatelle*, even though the source of the melody is an old Hungarian folk song from the Transdanubian region. The form of the composition is derived from the verses of the folk song, with the first eight-syllable line repeated, followed by the repeat of the final sixteen-syllable lines. It is obvious that the original words of the folk song in no way influenced Bartók's grandiose setting of the melody. (*I was an old cowherd/I slept by my cows/I awoke in the night/Not one beast was in its stall.*) Another example of Bartók's sense of humor!

(Note: According to the draft of the *Critical Edition*, the correct metronome marking should be an eighth note equals 69, not a quarter note as it appears in the Dover edition. The original recording made by Bartók of this folk song, as sung by the peasants, supports this slower tempo.)

Bagatelle No. 5

Bagatelle No. 5, with its irregular phrase lengths, is based on an original Slovak folk song from Geimer County. The constant eighth notes should emerge as lightly and as evenly as possible. Even though the piece is marked *vivo*, the metronomic indication is not as fast as expected, which is a help in negotiating the sometimes awkward eighth-note chordal repetitions. (Here, as in No. 2, I believe that the metronome marking should be a few notches faster than indicated.)

Example 2.6: *Bagatelle* No. 5, p. 76, m. 42–47

Bagatelle No. 6

With his linear approach, Bartók forces the ear to follow the melodic line and also frees it from any reflexive, traditional diatonic harmonic thinking. In *Bagatelle* No. 6, Bartók plays with our ear, teasing it by presenting B major in only the opening chord and then traveling farther away from it. When B major does reappear, it is only in passing until this one-page piece comes to rest at the final cadence of the B major chord. Or is it B minor? Bartók is still playing, juggling the D-sharp and the D-natural and then resolving these to E-sharp. However, B major wins out because it remains in the ear the longest; it also is the key that Bartók has acknowledged as the tonal center of the sixth *Bagatelle*.

Example 2.7: *Bagatelle* No. 6, p. 78, m. 1–5, m. 16–25

Bagatelle No. 7 [Track 5]

The seventh *Bagatelle* surely must have influenced Aaron Copland's piano piece *The Cat and the Mouse*, as well as "From the Diary of a Fly" in Book VI of *Mikrokosmos*, and it also looks toward Bartók's third *Burlesque*. Bartók uses the key of D-sharp minor to anchor this rhapsodic three-part form. The certainty of the tonal center allows him to be heard at his most capricious. Sudden changes of tempo, shifting rhythms, plenty of rubato, and use of inversion and augmentation techniques create an exciting canvas, bustling with activity. The motto theme heard in the opening finally reappears to conclude the piece and rest on D-sharp.

Example 2.8: *Bagatelle* No. 7, p. 79, m. 6–11, m. 18–23

In this example from the opening section, Bartók seems to cloud the D-sharp tonality by shifting interest back and forth to the C-sharp. (The D of the inverted arpeggios in the right hand also adds some spice.) The left-hand motto is built in thirds, while the right-hand appogiaturas are constructed with fourths. Bartók seems to have fun stretching the ear, seeing how far it can travel, while still maintaining its tonal center. An impression of spontaneity should be projected by the performer while at the same time observing Bartók's detailed directions for rubatos and tempo changes. This piece is not easy to master; it is fragmented and needs to be held together. It should sound fresh, improvised, capricious, and funny. This *Bagatelle* is a wonderful example of Bartók's attempt to write out, with his indicated tempo and metronome changes, his exact definition of capriccioso. Of course, in performance, the seams must not be noticeable. Bartók's details function as helpful clues for the performer; when digested and naturalized, the piece's humor will emerge.

Bagatelle No. 8

The opening measures of *Bagatelle* No. 8 reveal how well Bartók knew the piano's color possibilities. He uses the technique of octave displacement for expressive and harmonic effect, disguising the appogiatura's unresolved chromatic dissonances and making them sound much more interesting and dissonant to the ear when written an octave apart in another register.

Example 2.9: *Bagatelle* No. 8, p. 83, m. 1–4

With such a minimum of material present in this short three-part form, maximum color contrast is essential to uncover its hidden treasures.

Bagatelle No. 9

Bagatelle No. 9 is meant to be a playful scherzo, performed by both hands in unison. However, unison writing does not reduce this composition's tonal ambiguity. This theme is varied rhythmically and also harmonically, finally reaffirming its tonal center of E-flat with its last note, but clouding it as well with its interval of the tritone. The form is unified by a motto theme that separates each of the three sections and also concludes the piece. Some of the seeds of Bartók's first *String Quartet* are already heard in this ninth *Bagatelle*.

Example 2.10: *Bagatelle* No. 9, three mottos: p. 85, m. 13–14; p. 86, m. 37–38; p. 87, m. 70

The key to the proper interpretation of this piece is grazioso.

Bagatelle No. 10

The tenth is the longest *Bagatelle* of the set, written in the heavy barbaroso style of the "Bear Dance," and clearly centered in the key of C. (This was also Prokofiev's favorite key, because it gave him so many possibilities for travel to distant places, far away from C.) Bartók manages to explore foreign territories, especially in the chromatic middle section, but strongly maintains diatonic tonic-dominant ties in the outer sections with left-hand ostinatos. Generous use of pedal is recommended to underline the C pedal points.

Bagatelle No. 11

The playful *Bagatelle* No. 11 looks forward to the second *Burlesque*, "A Bit Tipsy." Lightness of touch is essential for playing the consecutive staccato fourths and sevenths, as well as for helping to make the rhythm flexible and molto rubato, as Bartók indicates. The tonal center of A-flat is arrived at in the second measure and also at the end of the piece. Augmentation techniques heighten the contrasting middle section and coda. (Note: Erratum on p. 94, m. 50: bass line should move chromatically, going from D-flat to C-double-sharp to E-flat.)

Example 2.11: *Bagatelle* No. 11, p. 94, m. 44–51

Notice how Bartók uses the "above-the-measure" rest, which always appears just before the half note of the theme. It functions as a sixteenth-note breath/pause in the opening, and upon its return as a longer eighth-note breath.

Example 2.12: *Bagatelle* No. 11, p. 93, m. 1–8; p. 94, m. 69–76

Bagatelle No. 12 [Track 6]

Bagatelle No. 12 certainly reveals the expressive side of Bartók and looks toward his writing in the first *Elegy*, Op. 8b. This piece has been frequently compared to Schoenberg's early romantic compositional style in his Op. 11 piano pieces. Both sets were composed within the same time frame, and their crafting of motivic technique is similar. However, neither was directly influenced by the other. (Bartók states in his 1920 essay about Schoenberg that it was not until 1912, when one of his piano students brought him an unpublished score of the Op. 11 piano pieces, that he first became acquainted with Schoenberg's piano music. During this same time period, Schoenberg in his *Harmonielehre* (1911) also quotes from Bartók's tenth and fourteenth *Bagatelles*.) Bartók's writing is well grounded within tonality and governed more by aural considerations than by the specific formulae of compositional technique that Schoenberg later advocated. Opening with an improvised introduction imitating the sounds of the cimbalom, Bartók's B minor key is only briefly hinted at in the second measure.

Example 2.13: *Bagatelle* No. 12, p. 95, m. 1–7

This is followed by the poco più mosso section, which gives the impression of a pendulum swinging back and forth in strict rhythm. A variation of the improvised repeated A of the opening measures (A is the tone leading to the key center B) functions formally to introduce each section. There is also a wonderful coloristic effect of church bells heard over an A pedal in the middle section.

Example 2.14: *Bagatelle* No. 12, p. 96, m. 19–26

(Errata: At m. 9, the metronome marking should read 50 per dotted quarter, not per eighth note as written. This misprint is confirmed with the metronome indication at m. 26. Also, Bartók does not include a time signature for the opening measure or for any measures with the repeated note motive. For clarification, all these measures [1, 5, 22, 35] can be thought of in 4/4.)

An understanding of form within this freely improvised framework, as well as a rich color palette, is essential for a successful performance of this extremely difficult bagatelle.

Bagatelle No. 13

Bagatelle No. 13 commemorates February 14, 1908, the very day Bartók received the letter from Stefi Geyer breaking their engagement. Hence the title of this dirge: "She is Dead." Using the inversion of the Stefi motif in its opening measures, Bartók employs only two chords throughout but creates an emotional impact. Whenever Bartók uses the Stefi Geyer motif, he reveals a depth of soul that rarely surfaces with such direct force. He also makes use of repetition to heighten emotional intensity.

Example 2.15: *Bagatelle* No. 13, p. 98, m. 1–5

Bagatelle No. 14 [Track 7]

The final *Bagatelle*, "My Dancing Sweetheart," has the irony and dazed hysteria that one might encounter in a Fellini film. Using Stefi's leitmotif, this *danse macabre* projects an almost eerie and wild sense of desperation, combined with Bartók's humor and sarcastic wit. The piece is difficult but definitely must not sound that way. It is basically a waltz, played as if the record player has been set on the wrong speed.

(Errata: In some editions, Bartók's metronome marking has not been corrected. The correct marking reads: a dotted quarter note equals 120. Also, at m. 134 the accent on the first beat is misplaced and should appear on the first beat of m. 135.)

Note: Fragments of Stefi's leitmotif can also be found in *Bagatelles* Nos. 2, 5, 6, 7, 8, 9, 10, 11, and 12.

TEN EASY PIECES (1908)

Bartók wrote these pieces right after completing the *14 Bagatelles*. Perhaps a more appropriate title for this set might have been *Ten Easier Pieces*. Although they are certainly less difficult than the *Bagatelles*, these ten pieces are not easy. Even though originally conceived as teaching pieces, not all of them are suitable for young students. "Evening in Transylvania" (No. 5) and the "Bear Dance" (No. 10) became favorite encore pieces of Béla Bartók on his concert tours; he also orchestrated these pieces as the first two of the five pieces in his *Hungarian Sketches* of 1931. In the 1945 Boosey & Hawkes revised edition, Bartók wrote:

> The *Ten Easy Pieces*—with a "Dedication" as an eleventh—are a complement to the *Bagatelles*. The former were written with pedagogical purposes, that is, to supply piano students with easy contemporary pieces. This accounts for the still more simplified means used in them.[13]

These pieces function as a genuine series, with the tonality of the final "Bear Dance" relating back to the opening "Dedication." As in the Baroque suite, movements are contrasted by tempi, and folk material alternates with non-folk material.

"Dedication" sets the tone of the entire suite, but its mood is elusive and difficult to pinpoint. Based on the four notes of the Stefi Geyer chord, this freely improvised introduction, notated by Bartók without any tempo indications, is constructed on two separate sound planes; whole-note chords alternate with a parlando-rubato melody. Bartók creates the impression that these blocks of sound function quite independently; each retains its individual character and dynamic design. A dialogue does not occur, just an alternation of contrast, with neither seeming to be aware of the other. [Track 8]

Example 2.16: "Dedication" from *Ten Easy Pieces*, Dover (1981), p. 106, m. 1–18

Debussy could have penned this piece, and a rich and varied color palette is essential to bring the interesting canvas to life. Surprisingly, this is the most sophisticated composition of the entire set, and musically the most difficult; it was clearly not meant to be a child's piece. It is a real beauty, and well worth the time needed to live with it, to experiment with its sonorities, and to eventually arrive at a personal viewpoint.

"Peasant Song": This binary structure, based on folk material and written in unison, makes use of two different kinds of accents (^, >) plus the tenuto marking (-). When the tenuto is used, Bartók is asking for different tone quality with gentler emphasis and a separate downward motion given to each note.

"Frustration" is a three-part composition that, with its left-hand ostinato, is an easier version of the third *Bagatelle*.

"Slovakian Boy's Dance" is a setting of a folk melody, similar to the pieces that Bartók included in *For Children*.

"Sostenuto" uses a motto theme to open and close the work; this is a favorite formal device often used by Bartók in his suites.

"Evening in Transylvania":

> . . . an original composition, that is, with themes of my own invention, but the themes are in the style of the Hungarian Transylvanian folk tunes. There are two themes: the first one is in a parlando-rubato rhythm, and the second one is more or less the imitation of a peasant-flute playing. And the first one, the parlando-rubato, is an imitation of song, vocal melody. The form of it is ABABA.[14]

This is the expressive Bartók. Bartók recorded this piece several times; his performances are currently available on CD (Hungaroton HCD #12326/31).

"Hungarian Folk Song" is a simple two-part transcription.

"Dawn" could be viewed as a skeletal version of the opening "Dedication"; the Stefi Geyer leitmotif is hidden within its measures.

"Slovakian Folk Song" is an example of how Bartók set an original folk song. Bartók's comparison of a folk tune to a setting of a Bach chorale seems appropriate: "We may take over a peasant melody unchanged or slightly varied, write an accompaniment to it and possibly some opening or concluding phrases. This kind of work would show a certain analogy with Bach's treatment of chorales."[15] In the hands of a lesser composer like Füredi, harmonization is restricted by conventional triadic harmony (see examples 2.1, 2.2). Notice how Bartók highlights the familiar dominant-tonic cadence, setting it in bold relief by the modal harmonies that precede it. How obvious is the difference between a conventional rendering and the freedom of Bartók's harmonic imagination.

"Five Finger Exercise": Whole-tone scales provide the framework for this study, and are used to accompany the melody, which is linked to "Dedication." The closing thirds also recall the opening movement.

"Bear Dance" is a heavy, thumping dance; "Bear Dance" and "Evening in Transylvania" are the set's most significant and effective compositions. This piece is a prototype for the perpetuo mobile movements Bartók later developed into a more sophisticated form heard in the *Suite* Op. 14; the *Sonata*; and also the *Out of Doors*.

THREE HUNGARIAN FOLKSONGS
FROM THE CSÍK DISTRICT (1907)

These three early works were written just before the *Bagatelles* and are the first piano works to be completely based on original material collected by Bartók and Kodály. When Bartók tried to set these melodies, he immediately realized that the major and minor triads with their third intervals were no longer applicable; traditional harmonization and V–I cadences did not work. The first two folk melodies are written in parlando-rubato style, and the last melody in a tempo giusto dance rhythm. Bartók transcribed these pieces exactly as he heard them from the peasant's singing or flute playing; all the ornamental embellishments are present, and harmonies remain simple. His transcriptions capture the linear, freely improvisatory quality of these melodies and their constantly shifting meters. The folk tunes must be played with genuine simplicity, which is not easy to accomplish. Therefore, these pieces are only recommended for the student already familiar and comfortable with Bartók's folk idiom.

SEVEN SKETCHES, OP. 9B (1908–1910)

From the Boosey & Hawkes 1945 edition:

> The *Seven Sketches* are from the years 1908–1910 . . . they represent, on the whole, a similar trend to that observed in the *Bagatelles,* although in *Sketch* No. 4 there is a certain return to old-style technique (note the "decorative" broken chords there). *Sketch* No. 2 (which is not bitonal or polytonal, although it was quoted several times in the 1920's as an early example of bitonality) is indisputably a pure C major. *Sketch* No. 4: C-sharp minor; *Sketch* No. 7: B major.[16]

These are undiscovered gems. To learn Bartók's new language, the pianist must focus primarily on line. Only with a horizontal approach will the ear be freed of any preconceived harmonic expectations. The fifth *Sketch*, "Rumanian Folk Song," demonstrates Bartók's linear thinking; the twelve-measure original folk melody is repeated three times, but Bartók liberates the melody line completely from any harmonic expectations. Even when using repetition, Bartók is able to create surprise by rhythmic and harmonic variants. He constructs a perfect three-part form within the key of B major. Encompassing such a small time frame, the dynamic contrasts and the transposition of melody from the right hand to the left create an impact.

Bartók is able to write in a new language without sacrificing communication. Emotional content is pared down to essentials, without the grand gestures of the previous century. The first *Sketch*, "Portrait of a Girl," inspired by Marta Ziegler, expresses youth, innocence, and charm with simplicity of line and three-part form. However, perhaps his former love Stefi Geyer has not been completely forgotten, because her inverted motif is present in the final cadence. "Seesaw . . ." is the second *Sketch*, and its visual motion is communicated by its two-voiced piano writing. With the subtitle "In perpetual memory of the hours 6, 7, 8, 9, 10, 11 p.m., 16 Feb., 1909," Bartók seems to be laughing with his secret. (Notice how Bartók brings the seesaw motion to a stop in the last two measures.)

Example 2.17: MS version of "Seesaw," *Sketch* No. 2 ("with a 'perpetual' extension of the final unison") reprinted from Dover (1981), Introduction to Volume I

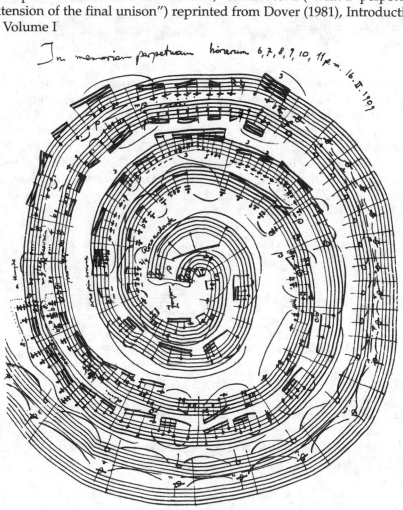

The third *Sketch*, dedicated to Bartók's good friends Kodály and Kodály's wife Emma Gruber, is written in C major. This piece demonstrates Bartók's liberation of line from any preconceived harmonic expectations. Contrast and rhythmic variation are achieved through repetition of minimal melodic motives. (Compare the return section variant with the opening material.) The C major final cadence delivers its emotional impact.

Example 2.18: *Sketch* No. 3, Dover (1981) p. 141, m. 21–26

Only the fourth sketch reverts back to Bartók's former Lisztian pianism, also heard in his two *Elegies*, Op. 8b, and this large canvas sounds as if it could have been written by Rachmaninoff. Pianism is used here to underline emotional content and to create a poignant statement. A heaviness of soul lies just beneath the sixteenth-note passagework, which also recalls what an excellent pianist Bartók was. The third *Bagatelle* is the skeletal model for this enlarged *Sketch*; however, the *Bagatelle* is much leaner, with no trace of the fat and extra calories included here (see example 2.5).

Example 2.19: *Sketch* No. 4, p. 143, m. 12–14

The sixth *Sketch*, "In Walachian Style," based on original folk material, is similar in its approach to the fifth Rumanian folk melody and the spare writing found in the *Bagatelles*. It shows what Bartók can achieve with minimal material and variation. The final piece, which Bartók titles "In B Major," opens with the B major triad and concludes the set with three ambiguous cluster chords, all in B major.

To forge his new style, Bartók needed to shed all traces of the romantic pianism he had known and inherited, the pianism associated with showmanship, bravura, verbosity. Why use so many words to express something that could be stated much more succinctly, and certainly more directly? The *Bagatelles*, Op. 6, represent Bartók's severe reaction to excess. They provide the skeletal models and clearly demonstrate a principle to which Bartók would adhere throughout his composing life: Nothing should ever be written (nor said) that is not necessary and meaningful.

Later in life, Bartók was able to look back and describe the journey he had taken in search of his own voice, how the old peasant music had forged and shaped his new "modernism":

> We all have to begin somewhere before finding our own place, choosing to follow the footsteps of someone perhaps far back in the past, or another no more than an arm's length away from us in the present. And only after trying out both can we make our final choice; at least, that was the course I myself followed, getting my first real push from the Richard Strauss tone poem, *Also Sprach Zarathustra*, but not satisfied there I turned in the opposite direction, hurling myself all the way back to the beginning. Through searching for my own path to follow, I came to believe one thing: that only from the entirely old can the entirely new be born. For all those complications that have been occurring in between the two were only obstructions standing in the way at the many forks of the crisscross road. And after those first confusing steps, I finally found my way through, bypassing all those shapes and forms of growth that wedged themselves in between the past and the present, cutting away everything between myself and that original strong, arrow-straight root, disregarding all the branches that sprouted from it at one time or another.[17]

ADDITIONAL REPERTOIRE TO EXPLORE

Rachmaninoff	*Preludes*, Op. 23, Op. 32
Moussorgsky	*Pictures at an Exhibition*
Prokofiev	*Visions Fugitives*, Op. 22
Copland	*The Cat and the Mouse*
Ginastera	*Twelve American Preludes*
Debussy	*Pour le Piano*
	Images

                          La Mer
                          12 Etudes
Schoenberg   *Piano Pieces*, Op. 11
                          String Quartet No. 1

NOTES

1. Béla Bartók, "*A 1932 Interview with Bartók* by Magda Vámos," in *Bartók Studies*, ed. Todd Crow (Detroit: Detroit Reprints in Music, 1976), 186. [This interview originally appeared in *The New Hungarian Quarterly* XIV/50 (Summer 1973).]

2. Béla Bartók, "Introduction to *Béla Bartók Masterpieces for Piano*" (1945) in *Béla Bartók Essays*, ed. Benjamin Suchoff (Lincoln: University of Nebraska Press, 1976), 432.

3. Bartók to Etelka Freund (1908) in *Béla Bartók: Letters*, ed. János Demény, trans. by Péter Balabán and István Farkas, trans. rev. by Elisabeth West and Colin Mason (London: Faber & Faber, 1971; New York: St. Martin's Press, 1971), 83.

4. Béla Bartók, "*A 1932 Interview with Bartók* by Magda Vámos," in *Bartók Studies*, ed. Todd Crow (Detroit: Detroit Reprints in Music, 1976), 189. [This interview originally appeared in *The New Hungarian Quarterly* XIV/50 (Summer 1973).]

5. Béla Bartók, "On the Significance of Folk Music" (1931), in *Béla Bartók Essays*, ed. Benjamin Suchoff, 345.

6. Béla Bartók, "Introduction to *Béla Bartók Masterpieces for Piano*" (1945), in *Béla Bartók Essays*, ed. Benjamin Suchoff, 433.

7. Béla Bartók, "Harvard Lectures" (1943), in *Béla Bartók Essays*, ed. Benjamin Suchoff, 365.

8. Bartók, "Harvard Lectures" (1943), 365–66.

9. Bartók, "Introduction to *Béla Bartók Masterpieces for Piano*" (1945), in *Béla Bartók Essays*, 433.

10. Béla Bartók, "*A 1932 Interview with Bartók* by Magda Vámos," in *Bartók Studies*, ed. Todd Crow (Detroit: Detroit Reprints in Music, 1976), 186. [This interview originally appeared in *The New Hungarian Quarterly* XIV/50 (Summer 1973).]

11. Béla Bartók, "*A 1932 Interview with Bartók* by Magda Vámos," in *Bartók Studies*, ed. Todd Crow (Detroit: Detroit Reprints in Music, 1976), 183. [This interview originally appeared in *The New Hungarian Quarterly* XIV/50 (Summer 1973).]

12. Béla Bartók to Max Rostal in *Béla Bartók: Letters*, ed. János Demény, 218.

13. Bartók, "Introduction to *Béla Bartók Masterpieces for Piano*" (1945), 432.

14. From Bartók's Introduction to the 1945 edition, *Piano Music of Béla Bartók*, Series I, ed. Benjamin Suchoff (New York: Dover, 1981), p. x.

15. Béla Bartók, "The Influence of Peasant Music on Modern Music" (1931), in *Béla Bartók Essays*, ed. Benjamin Suchoff, 341.

16. Bartók, "Introduction to *Béla Bartók Masterpieces for Piano*" (1945), 432.

17. Béla Bartók, as quoted by Agatha Fassett in *The Naked Face of Genius* (New York: Houghton Mifflin Company, Riverside Press, 1958), 346.

3

+

Bravura,
Virtuosity, and Pianism

By the way: I cannot play the three Études! I haven't played them—ever
or anywhere—since 1918. (1919)

—Béla Bartók, from a letter to Ernö Südy, January 20, 1934[1]

ETUDES, OP. 18 (1918)

Even Bartók, as pianist and interpreter of his own music, knew how difficult his *Etudes* were to play. How reassuring this information has to be
for any performer practicing these demanding pieces! I recall experiencing a
similar feeling after reading a letter written by Sergei Prokofiev just before
he embarked on a concert tour with his formidable second *Piano Concerto*; he
was complaining to a friend that if he didn't spend many hours each day, including every day of his vacation, practicing the difficult first-movement cadenza, he would never be able to play his concerto in public. It's good to
hear that the composers responsible for writing such challenging repertoire
are also obliged occasionally to do their own homework at the keyboard. Actually, Bartók did play the first performance of his *Etudes* in Budapest in
1919, and after performing the entire set, immediately came back onstage to
play the three again—a good warm-up, not only for the pianist but also for
the audience, who must have been shocked by what they had heard.

Written in the same period as his *Fifteen Hungarian Peasant Songs*, the
Etudes represent a digression from Bartók's new compositional style. The
leanness and simplicity of the folk tune has been replaced here by "big-time"

pianistic virtuosity and tonal and musical complexity. Bartók revels in the pianism, the huge sonorities, and the piling up of dissonances. By 1918, Bartók had already become acquainted with Schoenberg's Op. 11 *Piano Pieces* as well as Debussy's *Etudes*. Years later in 1928, he would admit: ". . . there was a time when I thought I was approaching a species of twelve-tone music. Yet even in works of that period the absolute tonal foundation is un-mistakable."[2]

Bartók stretches the boundaries of tonality to its limits, especially in the second *Etude*, but ultimately acknowledges the domination of the ear over the twelve-tone row. In this composition, he comes closest to Schoenberg's music but decides not to follow that path.

Bartók's set of études continues the pianistic tradition of writing stud-ies or exercises whose primary purpose is to focus on a specific technical aspect of playing the piano. Bartók joins a long list of composers who also wrote studies for the keyboard: Czerny, Scarlatti, Alkan, Hummel, Chopin, Liszt, Mendelssohn, Scriabin, Schumann, Saint-Saëns, Rachmani-noff, Szymanowski, Debussy, Prokofiev, and Stravinsky, among others. Like the best of these, Bartók goes beyond virtuosity to arrive at another level tonally, harmonically, and musically. In these sophisticated études, technical facility is developed into bravura playing, and the ears as well as the fingers increase their flexibility.

Pianistically, each étude concentrates on a different and extremely difficult technical problem. It is reasonable to conclude that a pianist who can get through any one of these études will have solved the problem upon which the composition is based. For example, the first étude (which could almost be an exercise in preparation for the boogie-woogie piano style) focuses both hands on the irregular distances between consecutive sevenths and ninths. Using octave displacement, Bartók has taken a rather simple unison melody, recalling the theme from the finale of Chopin's B-flat minor *Sonata*—

Example 3.1: Chopin *Sonata* in B-flat minor, Op. 35, Dover (1981), Presto, p. 143, m. 1–6

—and made it even more difficult to play because of its unequal leaps.

Example 3.2: *Etude* No. 1, Boosey & Hawkes (1939), p. 3, m. 1–6

Had Bartók written only a few measures using this pattern, it certainly would not be as challenging as playing the entire allegro molto five-page composition.

The second *Etude* continues the grand romantic pianistic style heard in the *Elegies*, Op. 8b, but musically and tonally goes way beyond nineteenth-century pianism. This *Etude* is one of Bartók's tonal experiments. The musical language sounds much more foreign than the other two compositions of the set, and here Bartók manages to stretch the ear to its limits. However, despite its harmonic ambiguities, it still remains within the tonal realm with B as its tonal center. The pianistic focus here is on leggiero, sixteenth-note figures, recalling Debussy's or Ravel's piano writing. This étude also could function as a study in color and pedaling techniques and concentrated listening.

The final *Etude* of the set focuses technically on the problem of leggiero, capriccioso left-hand playing within constant changing meters. This is Bartók's version of "Scarbo," and the goblin is acting as mischievous as usual. Only in the middle section does Bartók divide the problems between both hands, recalling the rhythmic motion of Chopin's first *Prelude*.

Similar to Chopin's Op. 10 and Op. 25 *Etudes* and Liszt's *Transcendental Studies*, these compositions go beyond sheer pianism and technical exercises to emerge as superbly crafted and well-structured musical compositions, all written in three-part form. The real jewel of the group, and the most advanced harmonically, is certainly the middle étude. When played as a complete set, this work becomes the central focus, prepared by the contrasting, more extroverted rhythmic energy of the outer movements.

Etude No. 1

This étude is the most difficult to play in terms of sheer physical energy and stamina, mainly because its rhythmic energy never lets up. It is essential that the étude be played without tiring. If the pianist gives even a hint of sounding tired or of pushing, the *Etude* will fall flat. The pianist should be able to recognize, when looking at a passage, what physical motion is required to overcome the technical difficulty. Here, a rotation technique must be incorporated in the third measure, using the middle of the forearm as the axis for this movement; an arch motion between leaps will shorten the distance the hand must travel. Absolutely no tension or tiredness should ever be felt in the arms. (Practicing the piano does not mean working like an athlete in order to build muscle strength and endurance.)

Bartók indicates breathing points for the pianist by adding commas within the demanding outer sections, and he also slows down the motion in the transition to the middle section (see example 3.3). He continues using the rotating figuration in the middle section; he alternates this passagework between the two hands so the pianist will be able to catch his breath—but not for long (see example 3.4). When the opening material returns, the two hands are no longer written in unison (see example 3.2) but in more difficult parallel and contrary motion (see example 3.6).

The difficulty is enhanced by the rhythmic irregularity and variants of the pattern, and by its perpetuo mobile effect of carrying the technical problem through the entire design of the composition, so the motion actually never ceases. Bartók might alter the character of the transition to the middle section by changing tempo and articulation, but basically the same pattern and rotation motion are used throughout.

Example 3.3: *Etude* No. 1, p. 4, m. 35–42

The middle section is contrasting in character, but the pattern continues in the right-hand accompaniment to the declamatory brass instruments of the left hand. (The chords played by the left hand are condensed vertical reductions of the striding, horizontal motif.)

Example 3.4: *Etude* No. 1, p. 5, m. 63–70

The return section brings back the original material, although no longer piano or in unison and much more difficult to play up to tempo. Notice Bartók's use of a one-accent indication (^) for the first two notes. The effect desired here is not the equivalent of separate accents for each eighth note. Each must be stressed, and at the same time connected to each other. As a pupil of Bartók explained: "This is not so much a marcato as a stress of an agogic, emphatic, espressivo character."[3] This dual accent also marks the arrival of the final section, and the following sets of accents are used as punctuation marks for this material. (Liszt also used the dual accent marking in "Harmonies du Soir," one of his *Transcendental Studies*.)

Example 3.5: Liszt *Harmonies du Soir*, Dover (1988) p. 242, m. 99–101

Example 3.6: *Etude* No. 1, p. 7, m. 105–12

The *fff* climax of the piece occurs in the middle section and is again re-called in the coda.

The pianist must play through this piece allegro molto, while observ-ing Bartók's overall dynamic design. The ability to perform this first étude up to tempo without tiring will indicate that the problem of rotat-ing the arm properly in order to negotiate the awkward leaps has been mastered.

This étude recalls the martellato style of the 1911 *Allegro Barbaro*, taken to its extreme. It's easy to understand why Bartók stopped playing these pieces in concert; they demand a concentrated effort and plenty of time to prepare adequately.

Suggestions for Performance

Rhythms are tricky; observe accents only where Bartók indicates. They are irregularly placed to highlight shifting rhythms, dissonances, and phrase structure. Of course, the pulse is at all times maintained, which means also having a slight accent at the beginning of measures.

Example 3.7: *Etude* No. 1, p. 3, m. 11–18

Think of the first three measures in example 3.7 as one six-beat measure, followed by three-beat measures. Bartók's rhythms will make better sense, aiding in memorization. (Try using formulas like this throughout.)

Example 3.8: *Etude* No. 1, m. 11–18 (rebarred to clarify phrasing)

Take advantage of the time changes in the transition before the return section to rest and calm down (Bartók indicates più tranquillo). Note Bartók's use of accents over two notes at the return section. This two-note motif has been repeated in the four measures immediately prior to the return; the double accents on this motif signal its formal return. (Liszt frequently used this marking in his piano writing; see example 3.5.)

Bartók marks allegro molto as the opening tempo; each pianist must find whatever tempo giusto works best, without pushing and losing control! (Note: Bartók's indicated metronome marking of 132 seems much too fast[4]—almost unplayable; my suggested tempo would be around 126. Every time Bartók returns to the a tempo, it has another metronome marking. His use of the a tempo marking is occasionally confusing; see the note for the fifth *Improvisation*, discussed in chapter 4.)

Etude No. 2 [Track 9]

When I first began learning this *Etude*, its opening pages left me with the feeling that Bartók had somehow lost his way. Later, I came to the conclusion that he just wanted to see where his harmonic wanderings would lead him, asking the pianist to go along and trust that eventually the destination would be reached. The problem for the performer is how to reveal the structure and give shape to the many notes housed within. Only with complete understanding of Bartók's harmonic journey and larger formal design will the pianist be able to gain a perspective on the work. Because of Bartók's formidable technique at the keyboard, he is able to extract and retain the best of nineteenth-century bravura pianism and to use its tools to write a composition that sounds new and experimental, even by today's standards.

Under both French and Viennese influences, Bartók combines elements of the coloristic piano writing of Debussy and Ravel with harmonic allusions to the Schoenberg/Webern school—an interesting and quite unusual casserole. A clearly delineated three-part sectional mold gives outline and shape to this harmonically ambiguous material, which sounds at first to be just a free improvisation at the keyboard. Gradually the veil is slowly lifted as the B tonal center comes more sharply into focus. After several attempts at going forward and pulling back with lovely color contrasts in between, including trills underlining the B tonality, Bartók continues the momentum till the end of the opening section, and prepares the contrasting meno mosso section with a molto allargando. This middle section resembles a recitative, and needs to be declaimed and played with as much rubato as possible without losing sight of its shape and direction. Bartók writes out a nineteenth-century virtuosic cadenza based on the three-note motif heard earlier (example 3.13). With the return section, tempo giusto, Bartók finally clarifies all, even revealing in a three-phrase sequence the twelve pitches used in the melody line, which is the closest Bartók ever gets to a twelve-tone row.

Example 3.9: *Etude* No. 2, reduction of 12-tone melody at tempo giusto, p. 14, m. 35–43

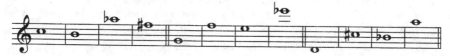

The sixteenth-note figurations that were first heard in the opening measures now function as sound filler, played by both hands in contrasting motion. This sounds like Bartók's *Hommage à Webern*. The final six measures still mask the tonality of the composition and also reflect the ambiguity of the *Etude's* opening, but the ear eventually will come to rest at the B tonal center, surrounded and prepared by its subdominant, E and E-flat.

The first page of this étude will be the most difficult for the performer to understand and shape. With its opening measures, the listener is suspended inside an impressionistic wash of sound.

Example 3.10: *Etude* No. 2, p. 9, m. 1–4

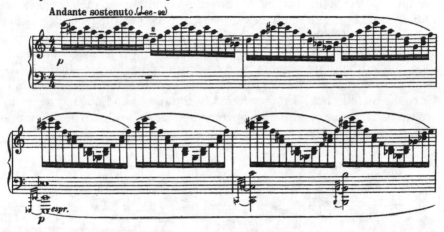

These first two measures should not be interpreted as a separate introduction. Bartók uses them to outline the chordal harmonic skeleton and then continues by extending and dovetailing this line into the left-hand E-flat of the third measure. Progressing from the second to the third measure must sound as seamless as possible. A rhythmic pulse should be maintained, even though the effect desired here is one of free improvisation, which can be achieved only within a strict rhythmic structure.

Example 3.11: *Etude* No. 2 (chordal outline of m. 1–3)

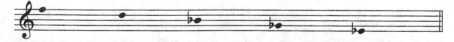

The reason these opening measures sound so dissonant and foreign to the ear is because of the minor seconds. Not only is the E-flat bass entirely surrounded by minor seconds, but the passagework constantly clashes with conflicting half-tones.

Example 3.12: *Etude* No. 2 (chordal reduction of clashing seconds, m. 1–3)

The ear must be flexible and prepared to go wherever Bartók takes it har-monically; a resting place will eventually be found. Even though not per-ceived till the second page because the composition begins on the sub-dominant, Bartók is heading toward the tonal center of B, suggested initially only in the eleventh measure and affirmed by the repetition of the three-note motif in the following bar. (Any allusion to B prior to this point, as in measures 4 and 6, had only a passing tone function.) From the begin-ning, the left-hand melody has been one continuous line; the first rest oc-curs only in measure 12, emphasizing with repetition the three-note motif. Once the melody has been transferred to the right hand, the ear seems to have a better sense of where the opening section is headed. The difference in perceived dissonance with this change of register is stunning.

Example 3.13: *Etude* No. 2, p. 10–11, m. 12–13

Now that the ear is focused on B, Bartók uses repeated trills and tremolos to reaffirm the key center. Yet at the same time he also disguises it, sur-rounding it with dissonance and ambiguity. During this strange harmonic journey, Bartók occasionally conveys the impression that even he might not know where his wanderings will lead; the wash of sounds is wonderfully French, floating in and out of the canvas. The sudden color contrasts (the *p* dolce subito of measure 18, the subito *p* of measure 20), the push/pull feel-ings of the sempre agitatos, and the molto ritardandos are quite grand, even excessive, in their bravura romantic pianism. Experimentation with color and pedaling effects, including the use of the middle sustaining pedal for maintenance of the melodic line at the return, is essential.

From a technical standpoint, every sixteenth-note figure in the *Etude* is a variant and should be treated melodically. Occasionally more time will be needed because of harmonic considerations, as in the beginning of the fifth measure. The fingering of these arpeggiated passages can be awkward, as seen in the third measure where the use of the fourth finger requires extra preparation. (The piece will be impossible to play if the wrist remains fixed; this will only produce tension and inhibit the sound-color desired. The elbow should be used to guide the hand up and down the keyboard, but at no time should the elbow maintain a rigid position close to the body.) In addition to focusing on lightness of touch and leggiero playing, this *Etude* is a concentrated study in hand, wrist, finger, and arm flexibility, focusing the ear on color and on pedaling techniques.

Within the middle section, Bartók writes an elaborate virtuosic cadenza on a three-note motif. This is a separate mini-étude on the playing of parallel fourths, to be played espressivo and with expansive, romantic bravura. The variants within this recitative cadenza should sound freely improvised and declaimed as clearly as speech. Here Bartók uses the melodic motive introduced earlier in measure 11 in the left hand, repeated and then transferred to the right hand in measure 13 (see example 3.13).

Example 3.14: *Etude* No. 2, p. 13, m. 29–30

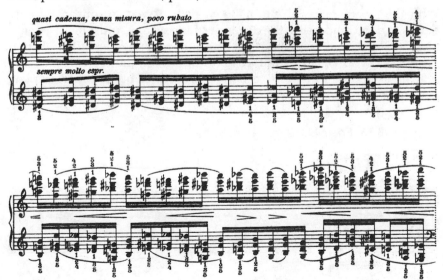

The last two measures of the middle section are difficult; experimentation is needed here with pedal vibrato and color effects. This passage begins softly and decreases in sound with its accelerando. The impression should be that the sounds just disappear into vaporous air before the return section, but they must vanish with all their notes intact!

Example 3.15: *Etude* No. 2, p. 13–14, m. 32–34

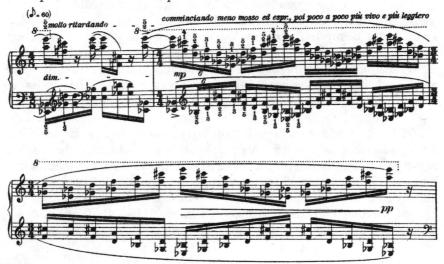

With the return material, the melody, now played in unison by both hands and encompassing the distance of the tritone, must be differentiated by touch and color from its sixteenth-note leggiero filler. This is Bartók's bow to Webern and the Viennese school; the French sixteenth-note passages of the opening section have changed both in character and nationality.

Example 3.16: *Etude* No. 2, p. 14, m. 35–38

Use of the middle pedal to maintain the melody will be helpful, and Bartók indicates the rubato desired. Translating the phrasing of this return section, Bartók writes three four-measure phrases, followed by the three-measure più lento coda.

This *Etude* will take plenty of time to digest and understand, but it remains an undiscovered gem. Careful study will certainly stretch the fingers and ears and keep them in shape. Be assured that the more time spent with this *Etude*, the more the ear will come to appreciate and enjoy its mysterious ambiguity.

Etude No. 3

This *Etude* recalls the capriciousness of the seventh *Bagatelle* and the third *Burlesque*. In addition to concentrating on the left hand's lightness of touch, the third *Etude* is also a study in rhythms, as well as an excellent exercise in the use of pedal vibrato. Bartók indicates capriccioso and proceeds to write out detailed instructions in every measure to achieve this playful mood. (The pianist must observe these markings; they reveal Bartók's phrasing and sense of direction but at the same time should sound improvised.)

An understanding of the *Etude's* formal structure is essential to the shaping of the work. A six-measure introduction, played within one pedal, prepares the twelve-measure opening section. Rhythmic development follows with sudden syncopations and jabbing accents and also includes a rhythmic paraphrase *à la Chopin* that dramatically prepares the return. An underlying rhythmic pulse propels and drives the return section, and the rubato two-measure concluding cadence is a reflection of the étude's opening measure.

Suggestions for Performance

The two-measure transition between the four-measure introduction and the tempo giusto should be as seamless as possible; good pedal vibrato will help. This passage needs to be played with a true freedom of rubato.

Example 3.17: *Etude* No. 3, p. 16, m. 1–7

Bartók makes use of irregular syncopated rhythms throughout this final *Etude* (11/16, 10/16, 9/16, 7/8, 6/8). A particularly difficult patch occurs in the middle developmental section. Make sure all accents and sudden jabs are observed by both hands, as Bartók indicates. Notice that in the second sequence the accents are varied and move from the left hand to the right; Bartók's use of accents adds to the momentum of the sequences.

Example 3.18: *Etude* No. 3, p. 17, m. 27–32

This last sequence, which acts as a transition to the Chopin *Prelude* paraphrase, must be well paced. Make sure the left-hand melody line is not lost.

Example 3.19: *Etude* No. 3, p. 18, m. 36–42

The return section is held together by its rhythmic pulse, onward momentum, and ever-increasing dynamics. Make sure to observe the specific accents marked in the left hand. Bartók varies these between one and two to a measure in order to propel the excitement.

To achieve accuracy and the lightness required, slow practice is highly recommended.

These three *Etudes* are difficult but wonderfully effective pieces, suitable only for the very advanced pianist with a solid technical foundation. Certainly, there is a very good reason why most pianists do not attempt to play these studies; they require many concentrated hours of practice at the keyboard. However, these pieces need to be practiced in the *right* way—without any trace of tension—or possible damage to the hands could occur; they are not studies of painful endurance, but require the relaxed coordination of all technical "equipment." When performing these works, it should never be forgotten that the real purpose of an étude is to master all the difficulties so that they will sound easy in performance. Although pianistically awkward, their musical rewards are worth the struggle.

TWO RUMANIAN DANCES, OP. 8A (1910)

These two dances are outstanding bravura concert pieces with which to close or to end the first half of a recital. It is preferable to perform these dances as a set because of their contrasting and complementary qualities, but they also work quite well individually. While not up to the level of difficulty encountered in the three *Etudes*, each dance, because of its three-part

structure, well-crafted motivic developmental technique, and difficult piano writing, also functions as a mini-étude.

These dances—the first based on completely original material and the
second recalling a Rumanian folk tune—capture the popular folk-music
idiom, with their infectious rhythmic vitality, duple rhythms, and open-
fourth sonorities. Written in three-part form, both compositions rely heavily on repetition, ostinato effects, and pedal points that imitate the original folk instrumental accompaniment of the bagpipe drone. Because of
the economy and simplicity of the repetitive material, Bartók takes full
advantage of contrast in all guises: dynamics, color, articulation, shifting
registers, and harmonic changes. The second piece, containing extended
rondo-like episodes within its three-part structure, formally contrasts the
clear, even, square, three-part sectional form of the first dance movement.
Tonality is straightforward in both compositions: C minor and G minor.
Bartók's pianistic effects are clearly based on Lisztian foundations.

Example 3.20: *Rumanian Dance* No. 1, Editio Musica Budapest (1950),
Rózsavölgyi (1910), p. 7, m. 64–65 (from middle section)

Example 3.21: *Rumanian Dance* No. 2, p. 18, m. 110–16

By using constant repetition with simple motivic material, the rhythmic motoric energy builds to a driving momentum, enhancing the pianistic bravura that gives real definition and true character to these dances. These solo piano compositions are much akin in spirit to the two *Rhapsodies* for violin and piano, written in 1928 and based on folk material. (Bartók transcribed the first Rumanian dance for orchestra in 1911.)

Rumanian Dances, No. 1

Suggestions for Performance

A tempo giusto must be found and overpedaling avoided when beginning this dance. Think of the bass rhythm in the outer sections as the constant unchangeable factor of this composition.

All accents, variations of accents, and pedal indications must be carefully observed.

Example 3.22: *Rumanian Dance* No. 1, p. 4, m. 26–31

Bartók makes use of commas to indicate breathing spaces for the performer. In addition to those indicated, I also add a comma before the second 4/4 return when the left hand takes up the theme, and also eight measures after that, right before the leggiero section.

Make sure the transition passage to the middle cimbalom section (example 3.20) is well prepared. Because of the strong sectional nature of this dance, seams should be guised to avoid fragmentation.

The middle section must possess an improvisatory feeling. Bartók is imitating the cimbalom here. Tasteful use of rubato is called for, especially at the beginnings of phrases.

The transition section after the grand middle section must be paced dynamically and tempo-wise to feel the *ff* arrival of the E-flat section, but enough energy must be saved for the *fff* of the next E minor section.

Concentrate on the pacing of the final vivo section. The rhythm should be established immediately, aided by the left-hand accompaniment. In the final five measures, experiment with gradations of forte. Try to exploit the orchestral sonorities of the keyboard.

This first dance is a wonderful example of Bartók's less-is-more craftsmanship. Basically, two motifs are used: the even eighth-note motif, and the two sixteenths followed by an eighth note.

Rumanian Dances, No. 2

This is technically the more difficult dance of the two. Its contrasts occur more quickly and are not as predictable as in the first dance. Bartók asks for a complete separation of the two hands, with the left hand carrying most of the burden. This dance could certainly function as an excellent study for developing stronger left-hand technique.

Example 3.23: *Rumanian Dance* No. 2, p. 15, m. 49–52

Because of its many episodes and the repetitiveness of material within this tempo giusto rhythm, there is once more the danger of sectional fragmentation. Attention to the overall three-part structure will help to delineate and shape this effective bravura composition.

Suggestions for Performance

Bartók's indications of tempo changes help delineate and shape the form. Maintaining the poco allegro tempo of the entire first section will aid in creating the contrast of the più mosso (b) theme. Remember, the tempo here is only a little faster. Save the faster tempo for later.

Within its opening measures, three voices are presented; each must retain a different color.

Example 3.24: *Rumanian Dance* No. 2, p. 13, m. 1–4; p. 14, m. 37–40

The melody must always be clearly heard, even though this passage is a little awkward with its shifting of hands.

Example 3.25: *Rumanian Dance* No. 2, p. 17, m. 85–87

Observation of the commas in the score is essential and extremely helpful in performance. In this difficult passage, Bartók uses the commas for emphasis as well to give the performer a little more time to lean forward to play the octaves.

Example 3.26: *Rumanian Dance* No. 2, p. 18, m. 103–9

This is a particularly difficult octave passage. Crescendos, accents, forward momentum: all must be present.

Example 3.27: *Rumanian Dance* No. 2, p. 20, m. 152–62

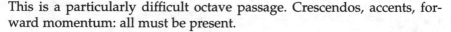

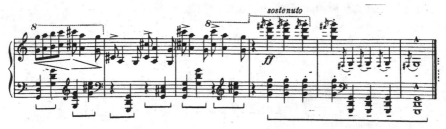

These compositions contain numerous examples of Bartók's variants of staccato, tenuto, and sforzato.

Variants of staccato: Staccatissimo ('''), indicated by a wedge marking, is the shortest type of staccato, implying a more percussive and sharper touch than the staccato (''') played at half the value of the given note.

Variants of tenuto: Tenuto (- - -) is used to emphasize the note and give it greater weight, color, and melodic importance; each note has a separate downward motion. The note is held for its full value but the sound is not as closely connected as a legato. The sound ends when the finger is lifted off the key, producing a slight disconnection between the notes. The dampers fall freely. (The dampers fall slowly when playing legato.) Tenuto does not necessarily indicate an added accent, just an added stress. Frequently Bartók uses the tenuto along with an accent marking ^ ^ ^. When the tenuto appears above the note in a slurred passage ⌒, Bartók is asking for "a gentle emphasis, by means of a different tone quality."[5] The dotted tenuto ⁻ ⁻ ⁻ is a shorter and more detached tenuto, also using a separate downward motion on each note. It should be held longer than half its value. The portato ⌒ creates a different color, making use of pedal vibrato to alter the touch. A vertical wrist motion on each note and gentle finger activity help achieve the proper sound. In both tenuto and portato there is a slight disconnect between every note, but the difference rests with the dampers. Lifting the dampers gently separates them gradually, creating a sound palette different from the one achieved by the sudden up-and-down damper motion of the heavier-weighted tenuto.

Variants of sforzato: Sforzato (*sf, sff*) is the strongest accent. Marcatissimo (^ ^ ^) is less strong than sforzato and is used expressively for emphasis. Marcato (> > >) is less strong than marcatissimo but also used as an added stress to the note.

The preparation of the *Two Rumanian Dances* Op. 8a will be beneficial for the advanced student. Observing what Bartók is able to achieve with repetitive rhythms, limited thematic material, contrasting variants, and orchestral sonorities, while confined to a three-part formal structure, will heighten appreciation of his craftsmanship. Shaping the form and pacing its momentum are the crucial issues in interpreting these *Rumanian Dances*, which are great fun to practice and even more enjoyable to perform.

(Note: In Volume I of the Dover collection, the earlier unrevised version has been printed, which should not be learned. Substantial harmonic differences exist, especially in the last two pages of the second dance and in the piano writing in the middle section of the first dance. Look for the Kalmus, the Boosey & Hawkes, or the Hungarian edition when studying these works.)

ALLEGRO BARBARO (1911) [TRACK 10]

This composition has greatly contributed to Bartók's stereotype as the twentieth century's pianist barbaroso. According to Kodály (as told to

Denijs Dille, the former director of Boosey & Hawkes), it came to be written as the result of a bad review by a French critic. On March 12, 1910, Bartók played a recital in Paris with a program of the *Bagatelles* and the first *Rumanian Dance*. The reviewer wrote that Bartók was one of the *"jeunes barbares hongrois* (young Hungarian barbarians)." Bartók's response was to write his *Allegro Barbaro* of 1911.

The *Allegro Barbaro* consists of more than just percussive piano playing; it is a very well-crafted composition. As in the *Two Rumanian Dances*, Bartók shows what he is able to do with very minimal material while working within a basic three-part design, using the alternating and contrasting principles of rondo form. Within the sameness of consistently repetitive rhythms and heavy reliance on forte dynamics, boundaries are overlapped and themes become dramatically transformed. The performer must work at shaping the piece to heighten contrast. It is quite surprising that within this driving motoric work, Bartók gives the pianist many opportunities to stretch the rhythmic structure and to make use of rubato. Listen to one of his own recordings, which capture his romantic interpretation of this composition (see chapter 11).

The recordings show that Bartók played the piece a bit faster than his metronome marking and frequently varied the numbers of repeated measures, playing as many measures as needed to descend from *f* to *pppp*. (He used the marking 0-0 in his second *Elegy* to show this possibility.) In one of the first editions of this composition, the metronome indication specified Bartók's tempo per quarter note, instead of per half note as he had intended. As a result of this oversight, a transcription of this composition that he had approved for a military band became known as his "adagio barbaro." This embarrassment was sufficient to convince the composer to note the duration of each work so that any future similar mistakes might be avoided.

A connection between the theme of the *Allegro Barbaro* and Scarbo's theme from Ravel's *Gaspard de la Nuit,* which Bartók performed in concert in 1911, has been pointed out by the Hungarian musicologist Ferenc Bónis.

Example 3.28: *Scarbo,* Dover (1986), m. 52; *Allegro Barbaro,* Dover (1998), m. 5–11

The *Allegro Barbaro* proves to be a very effective virtuosic encore and was a consistent favorite of the composer. It served as the prototype for the quick movements of some of Bartók's later compositions: the *Sonata*, the *Out of Doors*, and the *Suite* Op. 14. Many twentieth-century composers were influenced by this piece, imitating its percussive and primitive piano style; there are well-known examples by such composers as Alberto Ginastera in Argentina, Aaron Copland and Samuel Barber in America, and Francis Poulenc in France.

Suggestions for Performance

The opening *sff* chord must stand apart from what follows. A short pedal on the first chord will be helpful, followed by a sudden drop in dynamics with a pedal for every beat. (Pedal vibrato might also be necessary.)

Observe that Bartók does not include an accent over the fifth melody note of the first theme (see example 3.28, *Allegro Barbaro*). It is treated the same way on every recurrence. Make sure the melody stands out in bold relief from its steady eighth-note accompaniment. At the closing theme of the first section, differentiate between the *sff* on the third and fourth beats.

Example 3.29: *Allegro Barbaro*, m. 34–37

Pay attention to transition sections; pacing of dynamics is essential. At the transition prior to the middle section, dynamics must descend to *pppp*. Orchestrate the B section and imagine it played on brass instruments.

Example 3.30: *Allegro Barbaro,* m. 58–61

The middle section must sound improvised; Bartók indicates poco sosten.
I found it helpful in the initial learning process to think of this as written
not in two beats, but in a combination of 3/4 and 2/4 measures, as rebarred in example 3.32. Rubato used wisely is a necessity here.

Example 3.31: *Allegro Barbaro,* m. 112–23

Example 3.32: m, 112–23 (rebarred)

Bartók imitates antiphonal choirs, both singing *ff,* but answering each other from different parts of the cathedral.

Example 3.33: *Allegro Barbaro,* m. 131–44

At the meno sost. that follows at m. 152, continue using this antiphonal technique until Tempo I. Pace the return of the theme, beginning at *pp* for its arrival at the *fff* chord. This repetitive section increases in dynamics, rhythm, and momentum.

The closing octave A should be held with sustaining pedal, while pedaling every beat. Bartók indicates senza ped. four measures from the end. Observing this marking immediately produces a wonderful contrasting color effect; I also use a very short pedal on the final forte chord for added color.

Example 3.34: *Allegro Barbaro,* m. 210–24

senza Ped.

(Note: A revised edition of the *Allegro Barbaro* was issued by Universal in 1992, with corrections to the original edition by Peter Bartók.)

The initial aim of writing études or studies is to achieve technical mastery at the instrument. In all of the above compositions, Bartók has combined a pianistic challenge with a uniquely personal compositional style to produce musical statements that go beyond the realm of technical expertise. His primitivism cuts away all that is superfluous, going back to the essential rhythms of the drums, recalled with a child's simplicity and directness. What is revealed, even in Bartók's easier and simpler children's pieces from the *Mikrokosmos*, is that he is consistently an original. A simple folk tune in his hands is transformed to yield a concentrated personal statement, outside the current mainstream of musical composition. What always remains is the fact that all his music was written by someone who knew the instrument, had mastered it, and loved and respected what the piano could do.

NOTES

1. Béla Bartók to Ernö Südy in *Béla Bartók: Letters*, ed. János Demény, trans. by Péter Balabán and István Farkas, trans. rev. by Elisabeth West and Colin Mason (London: Faber & Faber, 1971; New York: St. Martin's Press, 1971), 227.

2. Béla Bartók, "Folk Songs of Hungary" (1928), in *Béla Bartók Essays*, ed. Benjamin Suchoff (Lincoln: University of Nebraska Press, 1976), 339.

3. Lajos Hernádi, "Bartók—Pianist and Teacher" in *Bartók Studies*, ed. Todd Crow (Detroit: Detroit Reprints in Music, 1976), 153. [This article originally appeared in *The New Hungarian Quarterly* IX/30 (Summer 1968).]

4. According to László Somfai, head of the Bartók Archives in Budapest, Bartók's personal copy of the first edition by Universal included the duration marking of 2'10 for the *Étude*, No. 1. Also at m. 38, the metronome marking of 70 was changed to 80.

5. László Somfai, *Béla Bartók: Composition, Concepts, and Autograph Sources* (Berkeley: University of California Press, 1996), 265.

4

✢

Folk Music:
The Perfect Union

Folk art cannot have a fertile influence on a composer unless he knows the peasant music of his native country as thoroughly as he does his mother tongue. In this way folk music will flow through the veins of the composer and the idiom of peasant music will have become his own musical language, which he will use spontaneously, involuntarily, and naturally, just as a poet uses his mother tongue.

—Béla Bartók[1]

The Op. 1 *Rhapsody* was the last piece written by Bartók for solo piano that was not influenced by his extensive folk-music research. By the time he again composed for the piano, he and his friend, composer Zoltán Kodály, had traveled throughout the Hungarian countryside gathering hundreds of peasant tunes. (In addition to 3,700 Hungarian folk songs, Bartók collected more than 3,500 Rumanian folk tunes; 3,223 Slovakian; 89 Turkish; 65 Arabic; and more than 200 Ruthenian, South Slavic, and Bulgarian.) Bartók's early *Three Hungarian Folk Songs* of 1907 were based on folk tunes he had heard in the county of Csík and transcribed for piano. By 1920, with the publication of his eight *Improvisations on Hungarian Peasant Songs,* Bartók had succeeded in creating his own musical language; the old original Hungarian peasant tunes had become the catalyst for a uniquely personal idiom.

Why was collecting native folk music so important to Bartók and Kodály? Together their words provide the most convincing explanation of their search for historical continuity. Kodály believed that the collection and study of folk material was essential to the foundations of a Hungarian school of composition. His words could also be applied to other small East-ern European countries searching for their own musical traditions. (Kodály, unlike Bartók, confined his studies only to Hungarian folklore; Bartók branched out to embrace other cultures and even began studying the ballads native to West Virginia during the period he was in residence at Columbia University.) Kodály explains:

> So little of written old Hungarian music has survived that the history of Hungarian music cannot be built up without a thorough knowledge of folk music. It is known that folk language has many similarities with the ancient language of a people. In the same way, folk music must for us replace the remains of our old music. Thus, from a musical point of view, it means more to us than to those peoples that developed their own musical style centuries ago. Folk music for these peoples became assimilated into their music, and a German musician will be able to find in Bach and Beethoven what we had to search for in our villages: the continuity of a national musical tradition.[2]

Living in a small country such as Hungary heightened Bartók's personal awareness of the need for musical roots and an identifiable national tra-dition, as distinct from the venerable German musical legacy:

> The work of Bach is a summing up of the music of some hundred-odd years before him. His musical material is themes and motives used by his prede-cessors. We can trace, in Bach's music motives, phrases which were also used by Frescobaldi and many others among Bach's predecessors. Is this pla-garism? By no means. For an artist it is not only right to have his roots in the art of some former times, it is a necessity.[3]

Both Bartók and Kodály were committed to finding the true source of their musical heritage. Some nineteenth-century composers, Brahms and Liszt among them, had inaccurately labeled as Hungarian folk music what was in actuality popular music written by amateurs. Bartók's early piano works, including his Op. 1 *Rhapsody* and the last of the *Four Early Pieces* for piano of 1903, have more in common with this popular type of folk-writing than with the Hungarian peasant melodies he and Kodály heard directly from the peasants in the countryside.

> What is usually called Gypsy music—that is, tunes played by Gypsy bands—are mostly compositions by dilettante members of the Hungarian middle class, town dwellers, or landed gentry. At most one could add that this mu-sic is played "*à la tzigane*," which seems to be the only original element con-tributed by the Gypsy nation to Hungarian art music composed in the pop-ular fashion. It is absolutely obvious that the melodies featured in Liszt's *Hungarian Rhapsodies* and Brahms' *Hungarian Dances* are not Gypsy products

but melodies of popular amateurs; in most cases, we are acquainted with the name of these composers—educated dilettantes.[4]

What Bartók and Kodály set out to do had never been done before with their level of passionate commitment and rigorous scholarship. In a 1928 lecture, Bartók openly shared his personal feelings about these field trips:

> It would probably be difficult for you to imagine the great amount of toil and labor connected with our work of collection. In order to secure musical material, uninfluenced by urban culture, we had to travel to villages as far as possible removed from urban cultural centers and lines of communication. In order to obtain older songs—songs perhaps centuries old—we had to turn to old people, old women in particular whom, quite naturally, it was difficult to get to sing. They were ashamed to sing before a strange gentleman; they were afraid of being laughed at and mocked by the villagers; and they were also afraid of the phonograph (with which we did most of our work), as they had never in their life seen such a "monster." We had to live in the most wretched villages under the most primitive conditions, as it were, and had to make friends of the peasants and win their confidence. And this last, in particular, was not always easy, for in previous times the peasant class had been too thoroughly exploited by the gentry, and, in consequence, was full of suspicion where those who appeared to belong to this class were concerned. Yet despite all this, I must admit that our arduous labour in this field gave us greater pleasure than any other. Those days which I spent in the villages among the peasants were the happiest days of my life . . . it was of the utmost importance that we do our collecting ourselves, and did not make the acquaintance of our melodic material in written or printed collections. The melodies of a written or printed collection are in essence dead materials. It is true though—provided they are reliable—that they can acquaint one with the melodies; yet one absolutely cannot penetrate into the real, throbbing life of this music by means of them. In order to really feel the vitality of this music, one must, so to speak, have lived it—and this is only possible when one comes to know it through direct contact with the peasants. In order to receive that powerful impression of this music, which is needed if it is to exert a proportionate influence on our creation, it is not enough merely to learn the melodies. It is just as important, I might almost say, to see and to know the environment in which these melodies have their being. One must have witnessed the peasants' changes of features when they sing; one must have taken part in their dance entertainments, weddings, Christmas festivities, and funerals of the peasants, for on all these occasions quite special melodies, often characteristic in the highest degree, are sung . . . in our case it was not a question of merely taking unique melodies in any way whatsoever, and then incorporating them—or fragments of them—in our works, there to develop them according to the traditionally established custom. This would have been mere craftsmanship, and could have led to no new and unified style. What we had to do was to grasp the spirit of the hitherto unknown music and to make this spirit (difficult to describe in words) the basis of our works. And, just in order to rightly

grasp the spirit of this music, was it so supremely important for us to be able to carry on the collection of these melodies ourselves, in person.[5]

The key phrase in Bartók's vivid description of his field work is "to have lived it," to try to feel what the peasants were able to communicate. Bartók's observations resemble the philosophy of the Dutch painter van Gogh, who also spent much of his time living among the peasants. As he wrote in his letters to his brother Theo, his pictures of peasants only worked "when the diggers dig." Bartók's music can come to life only when the performer is able to capture its true folk origins and the spirit in which it was conceived. From the sowing of folk tunes, Bartók was able to reap art songs!

Bartók's deep immersion into the folk music of other cultures combined intense concentration with discipline. Not only was he fluent in many languages, but he also had studied Arabic, Rumanian, and Slovak, and was learning Turkish in preparation for an in-depth exploration of its folk music. An amusing anecdote, indicative of Bartók's seriousness and rigorous scholarship, is told by a former student who had met Bartók at the Hungarian Academy of Sciences while the composer was studying the Bulgarian folk music collections: "'What is Bulgarian folk music really like?' I asked. To which he replied: 'I can't answer that question yet, for I have seen only five thousand Bulgarian folk songs so far.'"[6]

Bartók was in search of a new idiom to replace the overblown language of the previous century. Sense had to be made from the musical chaos he perceived all around him: ". . . various trends, explorations, efforts, experimentations. Mere fumbling. There is but one trait which seems to be clearly outlined: a total rejection of the nineteenth century."[7]

Folk music provided him with freedom and structure and became the catalyst from which he could develop a new harmonic language. The modal patterns of the folk tune could not be harmonized by the functional tonic/dominant system of triads and chromatic harmonies used by the romantic composers; more importantly, what had previously been considered as dissonance within nineteenth-century harmonic language could now be accepted as consonance within the modal folk idiom.

> The outcome of these studies was of decisive influence upon my work, because it freed me from the tyrannical rule of the major and minor keys. The greater part of the collected treasure, and the more valuable part, was in old ecclesiastical or old Greek modes, or based on more primitive (pentatonic) scales, and the melodies were full of most free and varied rhythmic phrases and changes of tempi, played both rubato and giusto. It became clear to me that the old modes, which had been forgotten in our music, had lost nothing of their vigor. Their new employment made new rhythmic combinations possible.[8]

Example 4.1: Ancient modal scales

Example 4.2: Pentatonic modes built on five-octave segments of a hemi-tone pentatonic row

Every musical element that Bartók respected was embodied in folk music: clarity, economy, directness—nothing extraneous or excessive. The superficial emotionalism from the previous century, erroneously associated with the *tziganes*, was completely banished.

> . . . a genuine peasant melody of our land is a musical example of a perfected art. I consider it quite as much a masterpiece, for instance, in miniature, as a Bach fugue or a Mozart sonata movement is a masterpiece in larger form. A melody of this kind is a classic example of the expression of a musical thought in its most conceivably concise form, with the avoidance of all that is superfluous . . . we have what is only fundamentally essential . . . from this music, we have learned how best to employ terseness of expression, the utmost excision of all that is nonessential—and it was this very thing, after the excessive grandiloquence of the Romantic Period, which we thirsted to learn.[9]

The simplicity of melody initially attracted Bartók to folk material, and Bartók's sense of melodic line remains the true key to understanding his music. No matter how complex the texture might become, how many parallel planes might concurrently be in motion, Bartók never loses sight of the line. Occasionally, it might be difficult to determine which voice carries the line and then to extract and underline its prominence, but ultimately, this becomes the function of the performer and the performance. As Bartók frequently stated:

> Melody is still the body of work just as it was with the old masters. Those who speak of poverty of invention and poverty of melody are mistaken. Despite the arrival of the machine age, the powerful stream of music throbbing with life's eternal rhythm will never dry up. And the source of this stream—particularly in the countries devoid of musical traditions—will always be found in folk music.[10]

The simplicity of the folk tune served as the foundation for Bartók's complex harmonic language. The first of Bartók's eight *Improvisations* (1920) provides an excellent example of Bartók's use of harmonic variation: A simple folk tune is repeated three times. With each successive repetition the harmonic changes mask the sameness of melodic content, and the dramatic contrasts among the three phrases are highlighted. Bartók learned from the study of folk material the importance of variation; an idea can never repeat in exactly the same way. Written into the repetition is also the rubato of its musical line; Bartók even notates the breath of the singer within the score.

> . . . the simpler the melody the more complex and strange may be the harmonization and accompaniment that go well with it . . . these primitive melodies, moreover, show no trace of the stereotyped joining of triads. That again means greater freedom for us in the treatment of the melody. It allows us to bring out the melody most clearly by building round it harmonies of the widest range varying along different keynotes.[11]

In Bartók's hands, the melody and its harmonies are indivisible and seem inevitable.

Example 4.3: *Improvisation* No. 1, Dover (1998), p. 89, m. 1–16 [Track 11]

(attacca:)

Bartók's principle of never repeating a musical idea unchanged was certainly directly related to the performances of folk tunes he heard from the peasants. The composer never presumed to have found the one correct version of a melody. That would have been impossible, against all his values as a performer whose job was to bring music to spontaneous life every time his hands touched the keys.

> A folk melody is like a living creature; it changes minute by minute, moment by moment. One should never state, therefore, that a certain melody is as notated on the spot, but rather was such during the time it was notated—assuming, of course, that the melody was correctly notated. (By the way, this interpretation of folk music is very similar to the interpretation of great artists: There is no set uniformity; there is the same diversity in perpetual transformation.)[12]

As meticulous as Bartók was when in the field gathering folk material from the peasants, he demonstrated great flexibility as a composer when using this material. The folk tunes in Bartók's compositions assume many guises. In earlier works, a tune might be quoted exactly as he had heard it sung by the peasants, to which might be added a simple harmonic accompaniment "of secondary importance, a frame in which we insert the peasant melody, like a precious stone in its setting."[13] To this category belong *Three Hungarian Folk Songs from the Csík District* (1907), discussed in chapter 2; *Three Hungarian Folk Tunes* (1914–1918); *Rumanian Christmas Carols* (1915); and *Rumanian Folk Dances* (1915).

A more elaborate working out of the original tunes is provided in the *Sonatina* (1915) and the *Fifteen Hungarian Peasant Songs* (1914–1918). Here the peasant melody is the motif and catalyst for what is going on around it. In the *Two Rumanian Dances* of Op. 8a, no original folk material was used in the first dance, and the second alludes to a popular Rumanian folk tune, but the authentic Rumanian rhythms and folk-tune style heard in Transylvania (which had belonged to Hungary prior to 1920) are imitated faithfully throughout. The spirit of the folk dance became Bartók's inspiration. Only years later did Bartók take the leap from excellent craftsman, completely comfortable with his material, to fully formed musical personality, able to incorporate and assimilate folk music into a truly personal idiom as demonstrated by the *Improvisations* of 1920. "I reached the extreme limit in adding most daring accompaniments to simple folk tunes."[14]

Bartók and Kodály were targets of much criticism because of their folkloric studies. Many music critics of their time were inclined to dismiss compositions based on peasant tunes as not being in the same serious realm as completely original work.

> Many people think it is a comparatively easy task to write a composition round folk melodies. A lesser achievement at least than a composition on "original" themes. Because, they think, the composer is relieved of part of the work: the invention of themes. This way of thinking is completely erroneous. To handle folk melodies is one of the most difficult tasks; equally difficult if not more so than to write a major original composition. If we keep in mind that borrowing a melody means being bound by its individual peculiarity we shall understand one part of the difficulty. Another is created by the special character of a folk melody. We must penetrate into it, feel it, and bring it out in sharp contours by the appropriate setting. The composition round a folk melody must be done in a "propitious hour" or— as is generally said—it must be a work of inspiration just as much as any other composition.[15]

According to Bartók's *Autobiography*, his works from Op. 4 (his second orchestral *Suite* was the first in which he used folk material) and later were greeted in Budapest with animosity and a total lack of musical understanding. What the critics were unable to grasp initially was the realization that the simple folk melody was Bartók's foil, used to veil an introspective emotional complexity. (Bartók's own performances of his piano works are good proof of this thesis, revealing the secret emotional world that exists behind the simple folk melody.)

Here are some general guidelines that may be extracted from the study of the solo piano compositions that make use of folk idioms:

1. Relationship of Hungarian language to rhythm: First, in accordance with the accentuation found in the Hungarian language in which the first syllable carries the tonic accent of the word, the musical phrase of the folk tune almost never begins with a weak beat.

   > There are no upbeats; it is a music rhythmically based on starts with an arsis, as a contrast to Western European, Russian, modern Greek, and

Arab music—all based rhythmically on starts with a thesis (but of course with numerous exceptions). And when we say that our art music is based mainly on a similar arsis principle, then this statement must be taken again *cum grano salis* (with a grain of salt)! It does not mean that we never use upbeats; on the contrary, we rather frequently use them. It means only a general outlook, a general point of view, a general spirit concerning rhythm.[16]

Similarly, the dotted rhythmic patterns that are part of the natural rhythm and accentuation of the Hungarian language are also characteristic of Hungarian folk music.

Example 4.4: Dotted Rhythmic Patterns

(The rhythmic pattern used by Brahms in *Hungarian Dance* No. 1 is cited by Bartók as being an anti-Hungarian rhythm!)

From the metrical point of view, the vowels of our language divide into two groups: short vowels and long vowels. The discrimination in the pronunciation of the two kinds is very marked, very distinct, especially in emphatic speech; the long vowels have approximately double the length of the short ones. Blurred, mute vowels do not exist; this circumstance is an intrinsic difference between the vowel sound system of the English, French, and German languages, and the Hungarian and some other Eastern European languages. The discrimination between short and long vowels is perhaps less perceptible when the words are spoken at normal speed. In slower and more emphatic pronunciation, however, it immediately appears and creates the peculiar dotted rhythm, even in common speech.[17]

2. Tempo giusto and parlando-rubato: Bartók's peasant folk tunes fall into two general categories: tempo giusto, usually reserved for melodies connected to body motions such as working and dancing, which have regular, straightforward rhythms; and parlando-rubato style, containing a freer rhythmic outline, related to speech and the syllabic structure of the lyrics, and usually punctuated with fermatas, or commas at the end of each line, to enable the singer to take a breath. In the latter, the rhythm of the words takes

precedence over the rhythm of the dance. Bartók also frequently used a third "hybrid" type, with rhythmic patterns evolved from the parlando-rubato method of performance but written in tempo giusto for the purpose of dancing.

3. Meter changes: As is generally true of most twentieth-century repertoire, metrical changes between measures are common.

> I also mention the quite incredible rhythmic variety inherent in our peasant melodies. We find the utmost conceivable free, rhythmic spontaneity in our parlando-rubato melodies; in the melodies with a fixed dance rhythm the most curious, most inspiring rhythmic combinations are to be found. It therefore goes without saying that this circumstance pointed the way to altogether novel rhythmic possibilities for us.[18]

4. Accompaniment of folk tunes: Most of these tunes were originally sung to the accompaniment of folk instruments: the peasant fiddle, the droning bagpipe, the alpenhorn, the flute/pipe, the drums, the cimbalom or dulcimer, and so forth.

5. Tonality and key center: These tunes were modal and always written around a key center; they cannot be classified as atonal.

> One point, in particular I must again stress: our peasant music, naturally is invariably tonal, if not always in the sense that the inflexible major and minor system is tonal. (An "atonal" folk music, in my opinion, is unthinkable.)[19]

6. Equality of twelve tones: In the majority of these modes, the fifth degree of the scale does not have the same role as within the major/minor system. A functional hierarchy no longer exists; therefore, the traditional tonic/dominant cadence does not exercise the dominance that it had previously. The third, fifth, and seventh degrees of the scale have been freed to function as equals.

> This new way of using the diatonic scale brought freedom from the rigid use of the major and minor keys, and eventually led to a new conception of the chromatic scale, every tone of which came to be considered of equal value and could be used freely and independently.[20]

7. Consonance and dissonance: The modal diminished seventh is now heard as a consonant interval. What was previously heard as dissonance in the major/minor system might now be used by Bartók as an ostinato accompaniment to a folk tune and also found in the final cadence.

Example 4.5: *Improvisation* No. 8, p. 100, m. 1–6 [Track 15]

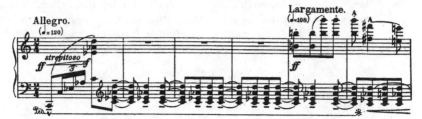

Example 4.6: *Bagatelle* No. 5, Dover (1981) p. 75, m. 1–5

Example 4.7: *Bagatelle* No. 5, p. 77, m. 84–90 (final cadence)

This fact, as early as 1905, led me to end a composition in F-sharp minor with the chord F-sharp/A/C-sharp/E (*Suite* No. 2). Hence, in this closing chord, the seventh figures as a consonant interval. At the time a close of this kind was something quite out of the ordinary; only in works of Debussy of approximately the same period could a parallel case be found. It is true, at the time in question I was not as yet acquainted with these Debussy compositions.

... This result is obtained by a logical process, and not, as many objectors believed, through sheer whimsicality. The incentive to do this was given by these pentatonic melodies. When the consonant form of the seventh was established, the ice was broken: From that moment the seventh could be applied as a consonance even without a necessarily logical preparation.[21]

8. The perfect fourth: In old melodies, the skip of the perfect fourth frequently occurs and also finds its way into the harmonic vocabulary, with chords constructed of perfect fourths.

We have simply projected onto a vertical plane what used to follow in a horizontal one. Through inversion, and by placing these chords in juxtaposition one above the other, many different chords are obtained and with them the freest melodic as well as harmonic treatment of the twelve-tones of our present-day harmonic system.[22]

Example 4.8: *Bagatelle* No. 4, p. 74, m. 1–4 (folk song from Transdanubian region)

Example 4.9: *Improvisation* No. 3, p. 93, m. 37–46 [Track 12]

9. The tritone: Frequent use is made of the tritone (the augmented fourth/the diminished fifth).

Example 4.10: *Bagatelle* No. 9, p. 87, m. 66–70 (final cadence)

Example 4.11: *Bagatelle* No. 10, p. 88, m. 5–14

10. Homophonic texture: Contrapuntal techniques are not found in most original folk material; the folk tunes are usually homophonic, consisting of melody plus accompaniment. "We found no contrapuntal progressions in our peasant music, and perhaps it is due to this that our works, in general, are homophonic in character."[23]

IMPROVISATIONS ON HUNGARIAN PEASANT SONGS, OP. 20 (1920)

These eight pieces, based on Hungarian folk songs, provide substantial proof for Bartók's words: "It does not matter what themes we use: It is the form into which we mold them that provides the essence of our work, revealing the knowledge, the creative power, and the individuality of the artist."[24]

The *Improvisations* of 1920 have earned the right to stand alongside the *Sonata, Out of Doors*, and the *Suite* Op. 14 as masterworks of the twentieth-century piano repertory.

Bartók restricts each improvisation to the working out of one folk melody, repeated with variants three or four times. (The original folk songs from Nos. 1, 3, 4, 6, and 8 are listed as Nos. 37, 40, 244, 64, and 46 respectively in Bartók's *Hungarian Folk Music* [1931].) The seventh piece of the set was the first to be completed, and was originally written for a special issue compiled by *La Revue Musicale*, entitled *Tombeau de Debussy*. Various composers contributed to this memorial album, dedicated to the composer whom Bartók so greatly admired. The piece includes no original quotes from Debussy's music, but the harmonies recall the gamelan's sound and the composer's modal approach, and rich and varied color palette. The *Improvisations* conclude with a virtuosic finale based on the lyrics of a bawdy folk song, which Bartók seems to have enjoyed, judging by his antics all over the keyboard.

Each of these original melodies was meant to be sung. Bartók often indicates commas (,) or breaks (/) to mark the end of the line, as in the first *Improvisation* (first two parts of example 4.3), and to indicate where the singer is supposed to breathe. In a 1939 letter to his editor at Boosey & Hawkes, Bartók explained that he used the comma "to mean not only an interruption, but also an additional rest (*Luftpause*): and the break (/) to mean only an interruption (division of sound) without extra rest."[25] (In the first *Improvisation,* both the comma and break appear together.)

Bartók is meticulous with every performance direction. He is able to write out, with precision, how a rubato should be paced. It becomes the responsibility of the performer to observe Bartók's markings and at the same time to make them sound freshly improvised. Bartók is fond of the marking capriccioso, as used in the second, fourth, and sixth pieces, where all the tempo changes must make logical sense in relation to the total movement's structure. Abrupt changes of tempi function here as exclamation points—interjections among the four lines of the folk tune.

Example 4.12: *Improvisation* No. 2, p. 90, m. 1–17

The third piece is an excellent example of the quasi-parlando style, as are the first and seventh. The melody is recited three times, with digressions placed in between. The atmosphere is quite special, inspired by the original folk song's lyrics: *"Wait, thou raven, carry greetings to my father, my mother, and my bride. If she asks how I am, tell her I fain would rest in the churchyard at Győr."* This third improvisation assumes a character similar to a Chopin nocturne. One hand maintains the rhythm, while the other plays the melody as freely as possible.

Example 4.13: *Improvisation* No. 3, p. 92, m. 1–10 [Track 12]

The fourth piece, marked allegretto scherzando, resembles the second with its written-out rubato. Bartók's use of accents and tempo changes contributes to its scherzando mood. The fifth piece demonstrates Bartók's ability to use a minimum amount of thematic material to create a varied composition. Subtle changes of harmonies, dynamics, rhythm, and tempi are employed for maximum effect.

In the sixth piece, the pianist must imitate the sounds of the cimbalom and show extreme tempo flexibility.

Example 4.14: *Improvisation* No. 6, p. 96, m. 1–6 [Track 13]

In the seventh improvisation, marked *à la mémoire de Debussy*, the line, once found, must never be lost; what is foreground and what is filler or background should be differentiated and colored accordingly.

Example 4.15: *Improvisation* No. 7, p. 98, m. 1–6 [Track 14]

Lusty lyrics must be implied in the performer's devil-may-care approach to the finale's technical difficulties. *"To plough in winter is hard work, one can hardly hold the plough; 'tis better to remain abed disporting with a young woman."*

Example 4.16: *Improvisation* No. 8, p. 102, m. 69–82 [Track 15]

From original folk material, Bartók builds a multifaceted structure whose form is determined by the stanzas of the individual folk songs and unified by the contrasting (sometimes alternating) slow/fast movements, reminiscent of the Baroque suite. (Bartók's attacca markings between movements should be observed.) The tonal center throughout is C, but Bartók shows great freedom and sometimes much ambiguity in his travels away from and back to the key center. Tonality is not based on original source material, but chosen for purely musical considerations and organized into four key centers beginning in C (Nos. 1, 2), moving to G (Nos. 3, 4, 5), descending a third to E-flat (No. 6), and returning to C (Nos. 7, 8)—all outlining the C tonality. Bartók's writing forces the pianist to shed the vertical, harmonic approach that so dominated the nineteenth-century repertory and to concentrate more on the horizontal line of each voice's unique character and identity. Each piece unmasks another atmosphere, and Debussy's coloristic influence pervades all of the *Improvisations*, not only the one dedicated to his memory.

Suggestions for Performance

No. 1: The opening line of the melody should emerge from a distant place, as if played by panpipes or a wooden flute (first part of example 4.3); it returns to that place with its final C. Each line of this folk song must have a different color and dramatic intent. In addition to the break and comma marked at the conclusion of each of the first two lines, Bartók also indicates a rallentando at the end of these two phrases (first two parts of example 4.3). With the third statement, Bartók extends the theme and writes out a gradual slowing down by augmentation, substituting half notes at the final cadence; no extra ritardando is needed. Make sure enough time is taken with the dramatic arpeggiated left-hand harmonies (third part of example 4.3).

No. 2: Clarify the punctuation and distinguish what is interjection and what is folk tune (example 4.12). Color the tranquillo section and keep the

A-flat pedal points held. (Bartók is imitating the drone pipe of the bagpipe here.) This section should remain all piano, no crescendos.

Bartók's use of expressive accents helps to define the capriccioso character of the folk melody; observation of his markings explains the rubato desired.

No. 3: The metronome indication of 96 seems to be too fast and not in keeping with the lento character of the piece; a tempo of 76 makes better sense overall, supported by Bartók's subsequent metronome markings at più lento and ancora più lento (example 4.13). Although there is no recording available of Bartók playing this improvisation, a corrected manuscript in Peter Bartók's possession includes Bartók's timing of 2'42.

The use of pedal color effects will define the nocturnal mood of this improvisation. The pedal is a necessity to create the hazy but seamless droning ostinato accompaniment.

At the beginning of the second statement of the theme, I find that a rebarring of these irregular measures is helpful. Instead of 4/4 followed by 5/8—

Example 4.17: *Improvisation* No. 3, p. 92, m. 19–22 [Track 12]

—try thinking of 7/8 followed by 6/8:

Example 4.18: *Improvisation* No. 3, p. 92, m. 19–22 (rebarred)

As in No. 2, distinguish throughout what is interjection. At the second episode with the F pedal point, make sure the F rings through the decrescendo. Experiment with varied pedaling but, ultimately, learn to listen and trust the ear.

Example 4.19: *Improvisation* No. 3, p. 92–93, m. 26–36

No. 4: Observe the allegretto indication: not too fast and as light as possible. Work out the last two lines; each voice must go its own way. The left hand descends to *p* while the right hand crescendos to *f*. Be aware that the F natural sforzato in m. 38 resolves in the last measure to the G key center. (I find it easier to play the F natural sforzato with the left hand.) The four-measure ending should sound humorous. Strong contrasts in touch, accents (three varieties), and dynamics will be helpful.

Example 4.20: *Improvisation* No. 4, p. 94, m. 33–40

No. 5: Note: The metronome marking for the a tempo is confusing at m. 27 and 34. This is not the tempo of either the four-measure introductory Allegro molto or the Allegro (84 per half note) that follows. Bartók's own recording confirms that the a tempos are to be played at a new and

slightly faster tempo of 92. His use of the phrase a tempo is occasionally misleading because in several pieces, a tempo will not refer back to a previously established tempo.

The left-hand grupetti of the second-line statement will need a little more time for articulation. Make sure the concluding canon is properly paced to move ahead and arrive at the two final chords.

No. 6: Make the tempo changes natural and seamless, as if improvised. The rests in the first two measures will help keep the improvisatory effect, and strong accents on the right-hand tremolos will imitate the cimbalom (example 4.14).

Experiment with the color possibilities of the poco rubato section. It should be awash in pedal. Make sure the expressive accent markings in the left-hand accompaniment are observed; they help define the rhythmic contrast between sections.

Distinguish between the interjecting episodes and the principal theme; this will help shape and clarify the structure. The whole-note C of m. 19 is a bridge or transition to the final statement. Make sure the rolled chords at the più sostenuto are rolled slowly. The last few measures are particularly difficult; hands must function independently and all accents should be observed.

(Erratum: In the fifth measure, the change of meter to 5/4 in the Boosey & Hawkes edition is incorrect. There is no change of meter. It remains in 4/4. See example 4.14.)

Example 4.21: *Improvisation* No. 6, p. 98, m. 27–32 [Track 13]

No. 7: Separate the voices and make sure each has its own identity throughout. Distinguish which material is sound and color filler and what should be made more prominent and brought to the foreground (example 4.15). (I use sostenuto pedal in m. 2, 5, and 11 to catch the tied half-note.

Bartók wants these notes to sound through the next measures. At the end of m. 3 and 6, he marks an eighth-note rest, a short breath before beginning the next statement. The sostenuto pedal used to catch the C in the next-to-last measure is also effective.) The five-measure coda reaffirms the C key center.

Pay attention to the arrival of the last C: How low in dynamics can you descend and peacefully arrive and rest on the C, before attacking the fortissimo opening of the finale?

(Erratum: The metronome indication at molto tranquillo, ten measures from the end, should read an eighth note instead of a quarter.)

No. 8: Divide the opening chords of the first four measures between the two hands. Not only is this easier, but it will help create the strong forte sound desired. Carefully pace the capriccioso section; it should sound "a bit tipsy," as in the second *Burlesque*.

The canon must be carefully paced, beginning very slowly and growing in speed to vivo. Memory can be tricky here. Don't confuse quarter notes with eighth notes in the right hand.

Example 4.22: *Improvisation* No. 8, p. 101, m. 58–63 [Track 15]

The ending contains difficult piano writing. Remember to make this sound like the conclusion to the entire suite. Some pedal at the beginning of the final measure will help; release pedal immediately after the last *sfff* chord.

As Beethoven did, Bartók has left the performer his urtext edition with specific directions to follow: tempo indications, exact metronomic markings and duration timings, accents, written-out rubatos, etc. When asked by his colleague, violinist Josef Szigeti, his reasoning for adding specific duration timings to his pieces instead of just approximate timings, Bartók answered: "It isn't as if I said: 'This must take six minutes, twenty-two seconds,' but I simply go on record that when I play it, the duration is six minutes, twenty-two seconds."[26] Bartók allows the performer more flexibility, within reason, than these markings might indicate. In addition, the pianist must understand the reasoning behind every marking. Often what appear to be arbitrary indications are the insights of an experienced pianist sharing his performance secrets.

However, when played, this music should embody the fresh, simple spirit of the original peasant folk tunes.

> These melodies are the classical examples of the art of expressing any musical idea with the highest perfection, in the shortest form, and using the simplest and most direct means.[27]

OTHER SOLO COMPOSITIONS USING FOLK MATERIAL

Three Hungarian Folk Songs from the Csík District (1907)

These three pieces are discussed in chapter 2.

Sonatina in Three Movements (1915)

This work is based on five of the Rumanian folk tunes that Bartók collected from 1910–1914 from the peasants in a Transylvanian village. (The original melodies can be found in Bartók's study, *Rumanian Folk Music*, listed as Nos. 42 and 639 of Vol. I [first movement]; No. 171 of Volume IV [second movement] and Nos. 107 and 7 of Volume I [finale].) This work was later transcribed for orchestra in 1931 as *Transylvanian Dances*. According to the composer:

> The *Sonatina* was originally conceived as a group of Rumanian folk dances for the piano; the three movements were selected from the group and given the name *Sonatina*. The first movement, "Bagpipers," is a dance—these are two dances played by two bagpipe players, the first by one and the second by another. [Also described in original version as *ardeleana*, a round dance in two parts, usually performed by two women and a man.] The second movement is called "Bear Dance"—this was played for me by a peasant violinist on the G and D strings, on the lower strings in order to have it more similar to a bear's voice. Generally the violin players use the E string. And the last movement contains also two folk melodies played by peasant violin players.[28]

(The first dance of the finale is also described in its original version as a *turca*, danced by a man wearing a peculiar type of animal head with a moveable beak; as he dances, he operates the beak with a string, which produces a clattering sound made in the rhythm of the dance. This dance was traditionally performed during the winter solstice.)

The joyful and playful folk character of this music must be captured by the performer without apparent effort. The piano writing is very Lisztian, especially in the finale. Large contrasts are called for in the first and last movements. In the first movement, Bartók carefully indicates the pedaling desired for maximum effect; these long pedals highlight the droning sound of the bagpipes. A significant difference should be heard between the two bagpipers, and attention must be given to the final forte statement with its offbeat accents. In the second dance, the offbeat accents of the left hand are crucial, underlining the heaviness and humor of this movement. In the finale, careful study of the variants of the theme is required; every time it is stated Bartók changes something in the bass line. Also, following the gradual tempo changes that Bartók writes in the second theme of the finale will keep the music natural and seamless.

Rumanian Folk Dances (1918)

All the six pieces of this set are based on collected fiddle tunes, and all are written in 2/4 except for the fourth piece, which is in 3/4, and the fifth, which makes use of both rhythms. Bartók transcribed these dances for chamber orchestra in 1922.

The first of the six, *Joc cu Bâta,* is a dance with sticks. The left hand maintains the strict rhythm, while the right hand sings out a syncopated folk tune. The second, *Brâul,* is a waistband dance, performed by couples with a cloth belt held between them. In *Pe Loc,* the stamping dance, the dancers remain in the same spot. This slow, steady rhythmic dance was accompanied by bagpipes. The expressive *Buciumeana,* or hornpipe dance, is the only piece of the set completely in 3/4 rhythm.

The fifth piece, *Poarcă Românească,* is a Rumanian polka—a fast children's dance in which the melody is divided rhythmically into consecutive groups of three beats, three beats, and two beats. The final *Mâruntel* or quick dance uses very small steps and quick movements.

These folk dances are a natural introduction to Bartók's folk language and are fun to learn. All are cast in binary form and written in strict rhythmic tempo giusto style.

(Note: In 1993, Universal issued a new edition by Peter Bartók of this work.)

Rumanian Christmas Carols (Colinde) (1915)

These two series of ten carols each are based on original vocal material and are meant to be played continuously, without interruption. With their irregular, asymmetric rhythms, the contrast between music meant only for singing, compared with the dance tunes of the *Rumanian Folk Dances,* is clearly marked. In his study of Rumanian folk music, Bartók writes:

> We must not think of the *colinde* in terms of the religious Christmas carols of the West . . . (some of) the most important parts of these texts have no connection with Christmas . . . here are texts preserved from ancient pagan times . . . Caroling usually takes place in the following custom: After several weeks of "study" (choral singing in unison) of the *colinde,* a group of eight or ten boys,

under the leadership of a chief, set out for the performance itself. They stop in front of each house and ask whether the hosts will receive them. Once inside the house, the group sings four to five carols in antiphonal fashion.[29]

These Christmas carols are an excellent introduction to Bartók's piano music. Bartók's unpredictable rhythms and uneven stanza lines prove liberating for the pianist, who will not be able to rely on any preconceptions about rhythm, melody, or harmony. (These *colinde* were my first introduction to Bartók's music when I began my studies at the University of Michigan with Hungarian pianist György Sándor, who was a Bartók student.)

Three Hungarian Folk Tunes (1914–1918)

These three popular folk tunes, "The Peacock," "At the Fair Grounds of Jánoshida," and "The White Lily," are all related tonally to the key center of G. These are easy pieces, quite suitable for the beginning student, although some of the *Ten Easy Pieces* or compositions from *Mikrokosmos* (Volumes IV–VI) might be of more interest.

Fifteen Hungarian Peasant Songs (1914–1918)

This set of folk songs provides the transition between the early transcriptions of original folk tunes and the compositional level reached in 1920 with the *Improvisations*. As preparation for learning the *Improvisations*, it is recommended that the pianist first be acquainted with this work.

The fifteen songs are arranged by their titles into four sections: four old tunes, scherzo, ballad, and old dance tunes. The entire set can be structured to fit the older model of a four-movement composition, with an opening movement (Nos. 1–4), scherzo (No. 5), slow movement (No. 6), and finale consisting of the old dance tunes (Nos. 7–15).

Occasionally, only the old dance tunes are performed independently, and these also adjust to a four-movement form: fast (7–10), slow (11), and fast (12–14), ending with the dance finale (15). In 1933, Bartók orchestrated Nos. 6–12 and 14–15 for large orchestra.

The finale, inspired by bagpipers, contains the only genuine example of instrumental writing. Using open fourths, Bartók exploits the overtones of the keyboard with virtuosic pianism; he makes us hear the bagpipers and the "crazy fiddlers" and imagine the wild dancing. (According to Bartók, Hungarian bagpipe music was transcribed, unaltered from a phonograph record, for the last dance and provided with an accompaniment.)

The first three sections of the set—four old tunes, scherzo, and ballad—were meant to be sung, and are written in homophonic style. The ballad functions as the entire composition's focal point, with its theme followed by nine variations. Bartók sets a twenty-three-strophe ballad about a fallen girl whose story ends in tragedy, as heard in its last measures. Starting with a unison theme in 7/8 meter, Bartók is not limited by the simple folk material. The key ingredient in the ballad and throughout the entire work is contrast in color, timbre, and articulation, achieved with an economy of material. Bartók's superb craftsmanship keeps repetition from sounding repetitive. In this set, vitality of spirit mixes with the melancholic nostalgia for rural life.

Six Dances in Bulgarian Rhythm (from *Mikrokosmos*, Vol. VI) [Track 16]

These six dances must be included in any discussion of folk idiom in Bartók's piano works. (In chapter 10 the complete *Mikrokosmos* as a teaching tool is discussed, and this set of pieces is analyzed from a pianistic viewpoint.) These are difficult but very effective concert pieces. Bulgarian rhythm can be defined as irregular, asymmetrical rhythms, the most usual being 5/16 (3&2 or 2&3), 7/16 (2&2&3), 8/16 (3&2&3 or 3&3&2), and 9/16 (2&2&2&3 or 4&2&3):

> . . . that in which the quantities indicated in the irregular time-signatures are exceptionally short (MM 300–400) and in which these very short, very basic quantities are not evenly—that is to say not symmetrically—grouped within larger quantities.[30]

Bartók tells the story of a famous musician who first heard these rhythms and cried out, "What! Are the Bulgarians all lame, that their songs have these limping rhythms?"[31] A further explanation of the irregular rhythm, as in 2&2&3, could be that the extra beat was originally needed to prolong duration and act as a breathing point written out at the end of the measure. Bartók believed that the teaching of Bulgarian rhythms should be part of every child's musical education, beginning ideally at an early age. (Two pieces in Bulgarian rhythm are also included in Volume IV of *Mikrokosmos* and provide a good introduction for the student to these irregular rhythms.)

Bartók stated that these dances were not based on Bulgarian folk songs but only on the Bulgarian rhythm:

> These are not Bulgarian folk songs, merely rhythms, the so-called Bulgarian rhythm. They are original compositions and contain no folk melodies . . . Incidentally, many of the pieces in Bulgarian rhythm are not of Bulgarian character, and indeed some of their melodies are like the Hungarian grafted onto Bulgarian rhythm.[32]

In this age of political correctness, which includes the questioning of basic established premises, it indeed could be possible to imagine a future reevaluation and reinterpretation of Bartók and Kodály's place in twentieth-century music, addressing the central role folk music played in their work. A revisionist scenario might substitute for the musical reasons discussed in this chapter a historical, political explanation of extreme Hungarian nationalism and chauvinism. Bartók's reply, in defense of his folk-music research, might read as follows:

> . . . I extended my interest and love also to the folk music of the neighboring eastern European peoples and ventured into Arabic and Turkish territories for research work. In my works, therefore, appear impressions derived from the most varied sources, melted—as I hope—into unity. These various sources, however, have a common denominator, that is, the characteristics common to rural folk music in its purest sense . . . the complete absence of any sentimentality or exaggeration of expression. It is this which gives to rural music a certain simplicity, austerity, sincerity of feeling, even grandeur—qualities in which the works of lesser composers become more and more deficient during the Romantic period of the nineteenth century. Apart from the great lessons we acquired from the classics, we learned most from those uneducated, illiterate peasants who faithfully kept their great musical inheritance and even created, in a so-to-speak mysterious way, new styles.[33]

What Bartók discovered and confirmed, with his extensive field work to many remote areas around the globe, was the existence of universal patterns. The Bulgarian rhythms did not appear only in Bulgaria, but were also found in the folk tunes of the Turks and the Rumanians. The origin of the *cântec lung* (the long song) was not clear, as Bartók also had observed the same melodic type in Persia, Iraq, Algeria, Rumania, and the Ukraine. Could each of these peoples, by some strange coincidence, have produced the same melodic form around the same time period, quite independently of each other? Bartók concluded that the field of folk song research could be reduced to several universal primitive forms and styles for classification. Bartók extended these universals beyond the geographical areas of his folk-music research. In his *Autobiography* (1921), Bartók expresses surprise at discovering in Debussy's work

> "pentatonic phrases" similar in character to those contained in our peasant music. I was sure these could be attributed to influences of folk music from Eastern Europe, very likely from Russia. Similar influences can be traced in Igor Stravinsky's work. It seems therefore that, in our age, modern music has developed along similar lines in countries geographically far away from each other. It has become rejuvenated under the influence of a kind of peasant music that has remained untouched by the musical creations of the last centuries.[34]

Accepting that folk material can transcend national boundaries, then, a specific, politically based reevaluation of Bartók's work seems unjustified. Although Béla Bartók's music was undeniably shaped by his Hungarian roots and Eastern European heritage, he transcended those parameters and spoke with a universal tongue. The composer rightly concludes:

> Even the greatest performing artists could draw inspiration from them (the musical performances of the unspoiled rural people) concerning methods of expression as well as technical devices. As the French say, *"Les extremes se touchent."* The highest degree of perfection is to be found, on the one hand, in the achievement of a great artistic genius, and on the other hand, in the creations of the illiterate peasant, as yet untouched by urban civilization.[35]

NOTES

1. Béla Bartók, *"A 1932 Interview with Bartók* by Magda Vámos," in *Bartók Studies*, ed. Todd Crow (Detroit: Detroit Reprints in Music, 1976), 186. [This interview originally appeared in *The New Hungarian Quarterly* XIV/50 (Summer 1973).]

2. Zoltán Kodály as quoted by Béla Bartók, "On the Significance of Folk Music" (1931) in *Béla Bartók Essays*, ed. Benjamin Suchoff (Lincoln: University of Nebraska Press, 1976), 347.

3. Bartók, "On the Significance of Folk Music" (1931), 346.

4. Béla Bartók, "Hungarian Folk Music" (1921), in *Béla Bartók Essays*, 70.

5. Béla Bartók, "The Folk Songs of Hungary" (1928), in *Béla Bartók Essays*, 332.

6. Sandor Veress in *Bartók Remembered*, ed. Malcolm Gillies (New York: W.W. Norton, 1991), 160.

7. Béla Bartók, *"A 1932 Interview with Bartók* by Magda Vámos," in *Bartók Studies*, ed. Todd Crow (Detroit: Detroit Reprints in Music, 1976), 183. [This interview originally appeared in *The New Hungarian Quarterly* XIV/50 (Summer 1973).]

8. Béla Bartók, "Autobiography" (1921), in *Béla Bartók Essays*, 410.

9. Bartók, "The Folk Songs of Hungary" (1928), 333.

10. Béla Bartók, *"A 1932 Interview with Bartók* by Magda Vámos," in *Bartók Studies*, ed. Todd Crow (Detroit: Detroit Reprints in Music, 1976), 183. [This interview originally appeared in *The New Hungarian Quarterly* XIV/50 (Summer 1973).]

11. Béla Bartók, "The Influence of Peasant Music on Modern Music" (1931), in *Béla Bartók Essays*, 342.

12. Béla Bartók, "Why and How Do We Collect Folk Music?" (1936), in *Béla Bartók Essays*, 10.

13. Béla Bartók, "The Relation between Contemporary Hungarian Art Music and Folk Music" (1941), in *Béla Bartók Essays*, 351.

14. Béla Bartók, "Harvard Lectures" (1943), in *Béla Bartók Essays*, 375.

15. Bartók, "On the Significance of Folk Music" (1931), 345.

16. Bartók, "Harvard Lectures" (1943), 383.

17. Bartók, "Harvard Lectures," 384–85.

18. Bartók, "The Folk Songs of Hungary" (1928), 338.
19. Bartók, "The Folk Songs of Hungary" (1928), 338.
20. Bartók, "Autobiography" (1921), 410.
21. Bartók, "The Folk Songs of Hungary" (1928), 335.
22. Bartók, "The Folk Songs of Hungary" (1928), 338.
23. Bartók, "The Folk Songs of Hungary" (1928), 338.
24. Bartók, "On the Significance of Folk Music" (1931), 346.
25. *Béla Bartók: XVII and XVIII Century Italian Cembalo and Organ Music Transcribed for Piano,* ed. László Somfai (New York: Carl Fischer, 1990), vii.
26. Josef Szigeti in *Bartók Remembered,* ed. Malcolm Gillies, 122.
27. Béla Bartók, "*A 1932 Interview with Bartók* by Magda Vámos," in *Bartók Studies,* ed. Todd Crow (Detroit: Detroit Reprints in Music, 1976), 185. [This interview originally appeared in *The New Hungarian Quarterly* XIV/50 (Summer 1973).]
28. From Bartók's radio interview of July 2, 1944, during the "Ask the Composer" concert broadcast from the Brooklyn Museum, recorded by WNYC, New York, as quoted in *Piano Music of Béla Bartók,* Series II, ed. Benjamin Suchoff (New York: Dover, 1981), xxiv.
29. Béla Bartók, "Rumanian Folk Music" (1933), in *Béla Bartók Essays,* ed. Benjamin Suchoff, 120.
30. Béla Bartók, "The So-Called Bulgarian Rhythm" (1938), in *Béla Bartók Essays,* ed. Benjamin Suchoff, 44.
31. Bartók, "The So-Called Bulgarian Rhythm" (1938), 47.
32. Béla Bartók, Introduction to *Mikrokosmos,* Boosey & Hawkes, 1944.
33. Béla Bartók, "Hungarian Music" (1944), in *Béla Bartók Essays,* ed. Benjamin Suchoff, 395.
34. Bartók, "Autobiography" (1921), 410.
35. Bartók, "Hungarian Music" (1944), 395.

5

✛

Form and the Sonata

In music it is the thematic material that corresponds to the story of a drama. And in music, too, as in poetry and in painting, it does not signify what themes we use. It is the form into which we mold it that makes the essence of our work. This form reveals the knowledge, the creative power, the individuality of the artist. This process of molding is the part of the composer's work which proves his creative talent.

—Béla Bartók[1]

Bartók's musical material found its own form; the formal design was never predetermined or superimposed by rigid structural restrictions. Using his innate craftsmanship and musical intuition, Bartók allowed form the freedom necessary to emerge and give shape to the musical material. For Bartók the composer, musical meaning was defined by form; for Bartók as a performer/pianist and interpreter of his own music, the elucidation of form was a prerequisite for clarification of musical meaning.

It is essential for the performer to initially comprehend the large formal structure into which Bartók pours his material. Because of the vast detail contained within Bartók's formal mold, each individual marking must be evaluated in terms of function and significance within its larger formal context. When first approaching a major work such as the piano *Sonata*, it is natural to be overwhelmed by its complexities and the detailed markings that jump out from every page. However, be certain that behind each mark exists a musical reason. Ultimately, the performer must find a way to understand the logic behind these specific performing directions. Only then can the pianist arrive at an interpretation, a viewpoint based as closely as possible on how the composer crafted the work.

For Bartók, the essence of the composer's craft was revealed through form and structure, and the *Sonata* in B minor of Franz Liszt represented the "perfect form."[2] It had taken Bartók many years of studying Liszt's compositions to see beyond the technical bravura and appreciate the craftsmanship. Certainly Bartók was true to his own dictum; he did not judge Liszt by the choice of his thematic material but by the way this material was shaped and molded. The crafting of motivic material, thematic transformation, use of motto themes, fugal writing, economy and unity of design—all are legacies of Liszt that Bartók himself employed in his *Sonata* of 1926. Liszt and Bartók evolved from the same pianistic tradition. Evidences of Liszt's bravura pianism are clearly visible in Bartók's piano writing, even though the sentimental excesses of romanticism have been honed into a more percussive style. However, the pianistic technique required to master and approximate Bartók's color and sound imagery would be impossible to achieve without Liszt's pianistic foundations, his technical expansion of the keyboard and its sonorities. Bartók extracts the essence of Liszt the composer and discards the excesses of Liszt the virtuoso.

The year 1926 was a fruitful year for Bartók's piano compositions; the necessity of having to compose new repertoire for his first concert tour, scheduled in the United States during 1927, forced him to focus on the keyboard once again. To program earlier works, such as the *Rhapsody* Op. 1 for piano and orchestra or some of the early piano pieces, was unacceptable to the composer; by now, his romantic nineteenth-century pianism had evolved into the more percussive/martellato style first heard in his *Allegro Barbaro* of 1911. In 1926 Bartók produced not only the piano *Sonata* but also the first *Piano Concerto*, the *Out of Doors* suite, and *Nine Little Piano Pieces* (discussed in later chapters)—certainly enough repertory for his American tour.

SONATA (1926)

The three-movement piano *Sonata* of 1926, dedicated to his second wife, pianist Ditta Pásztory (Bartók and Marta Ziegler were divorced in 1923), is one of Bartók's major works for the solo repertoire. Along with the five *Out of Doors* pieces, it is one of Bartók's most difficult works for solo piano. Each movement presents the pianist with different problems. Musically speaking, the second movement is probably the most difficult to understand and shape. The finale seems to play by itself once its technical pianistic problems are overcome; certainly it is the most demanding physically, requiring proper pacing of energy and plenty of stamina to perform it up to tempo. The first movement contains many of the same problems in evidence in the other movements. However, it is the only movement to be cast in sonata-allegro form, and certainly ranks as the best-crafted movement of the *Sonata*. As with the *Sonata*'s classical models, form is clearly delineated in all three movements; repetition is frequent and contrast essential for a convincing performance.

(Note: Boosey & Hawkes has published a new 1992 edition of the *Sonata*, revised by Peter Bartók. This edition was prepared by comparing the previously printed Boosey & Hawkes edition with the following available manuscript sources, cited in the introduction to the new edition: a manuscript, apparently intended as a final copy, on deposit at the Szécheny Library in Budapest, also published in facsimile by Editio Musica, Budapest; the manuscript that was the source of the first engraving by Universal Edition, apparently hand-copied by the composer from the above, with a few minor alterations; and a printed copy corrected by Bartók.)

I have compared both Boosey & Hawkes editions and agree with most of the added markings, which are mainly confined to sforzatos, accents, or octave indications that had previously been overlooked. However, several additions to this edition are questionable because of their musical implications, and it is my opinion that Bartók had deliberately deleted these for just that reason from his corrected printed copy. These will be specifically cited within the discussion of the separate movements of the sonata so that the student will be able to study the sonata using either one of the Boosey & Hawkes editions.

First Movement: *Allegro moderato* [Track 17]

Formal structure: Sonata-allegro form

Exposition:

- First theme: m. 1–43

  Example 5.1: *Sonata*, Universal (1927), Boosey & Hawkes (1955), p. 3, m. 1–6

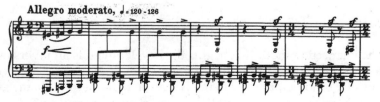

- Transition material: m. 44–75

Example 5.2: p. 4, m. 44–46

- Second Theme: m. 76–115

Example 5.3: p. 6, m. 76–86

- Inversion variant of second theme: m. 116–34

Example 5.4: p. 7, m. 116–20

Development: m. 135–81

- The interjection motif that begins the development is an inversion of the first two notes of the first theme (example 5.1) and also inverts the interjection motif used in the transition to the second theme at m. 70. It is also the inversion of the second theme (example 5.3).

Example 5.5: p. 8, m. 135–39

- False Recapitulation: m. 176–81

Recapitulation:

- First theme: m. 182–210
- Return of second theme: m. 211–22
- Closing section: material of first theme, m. 222–34
- Extended coda: m. 235–68

Concentrating first on the larger outlines of the exposition, it is important to see what Bartók does with very limited thematic material and how this is altered before reaching the transition to the second theme at m. 44. From the opening measures, Bartók chooses to exploit the dark, hammerlike, repetitive, primitive, and percussive qualities of the keyboard. Only at m. 36 (example 5.6) with the arrival of the C-sharp, followed by an eight-measure preparation before the transition material to the playful, coquettish second theme, is there a brief letup from an extreme martellato style and repetitive eighth-note rhythm. The transition material at m. 44 (example 5.2) is reminiscent of the naïve and simple folk song quality heard in Bartók's first *Rondo*.

Bartók exploits one motif made up of two components: the three-note motif (G-sharp/A-sharp/B) covering the interval of the third, and the last note of that motif, B, which forms the basis of the repetitive motif (example 5.1); at m. 7 this is sequenced beginning on C-sharp, with the last note of that motif (E) being repeated and heading toward the G sforzato; from there it goes toward the C-sharp, which becomes the pedal of the transition at m. 44. In the larger design, it could be reduced to these tonal center points and analyzed in terms of second and tritonal relationships:

G-sharp/<u>B</u>
     C-sharp/<u>E</u>/<u>G</u>/<u>C-sharp</u>
(Recap: A-sharp/C-sharp
        B/D
            C/E-flat
                C-sharp/E/<u>G</u>/<u>B-flat</u>/<u>B</u>)
                    G/E/B/<u>E</u>

This is significant for the performer of this work, because Bartók's use of repetition must be understood in order to give shape and direction to the material. Form provides the outline and supplies the boundaries within which direction must be paced. Ultimately, the B, E, and G and the C-sharp must be emphasized so that they will emerge in relief, apart from the other printed notes of the opening pages. The performer must know his destination; only then will he be able to decide the most direct route.

What stunning effects and contrasts Bartók achieves with an economy of material. Further analyzing the first theme, it is built primarily upon one note (B) repeated on every eighth-note beat for at least the first thirteen measures, with occasional jabbing sforzatos for effect (example 5.1). That's a total of fifty-three times using the same note; it's never boring, because it's constantly in a state of change. Notice that the transition is also derived from the repeated one-note motif (example 5.2), and observe the second theme's repetitive quality (example 5.3). Bartók employs the technique of repetition not as an end in itself, as does minimalist Terry Riley in his *Composition in C*, but always to serve the formal, structural, and dramatic needs of the composition. The constant repetition of the B in the opening pages creates excitement, momentum, and the cumulative tension to drive the phrase forward to the C-sharp, the next harmonic juncture, which also functions as the pedal of the transition section leading to the second theme.

Example 5.6: p. 4, m. 31–40

With so much repetitive thematic material, how is contrast possible? Contrast is built into the *Sonata's* formal structural mold. Even though the material of the second theme is organically derived from the opening measures, its character is not at all percussive or driven but is playful, coy, and rather funny (example 5.3). (The humor written into Bartók's work is frequently ignored, the assumption being that everything must be played loudly and aggressively.) Two basic ostinato accompaniments (G/F-sharp/E/F-sharp and E/D/C/D) to this simple folklike melody are combined and sound more complex because of their shifting registers. From Bartók's complexity, a simple repeated four-note motif in thirds emerges (example 5.3). The middle-section development (example 5.5) becomes a contrast in texture with fugal imitative voices and sudden interjections. The mood has suddenly shifted, and the writing has become angular and jagged, exploiting the instrument for maximum dynamic and color effects. Notice how the craftsman Bartók prepares the return section. The opening motif creeps in at m. 176. After several false starts and sudden interjections, Bartók finally delivers the recapitulation. Its arrival isn't fully confirmed until the G sforzato in m. 187:

Example 5.7: p. 10, m. 172–87

How effective the regular, repetitive eighth-note rhythms now sound after the sudden interjecting outbursts of the middle section. Even though Bartók changes the mood with the introduction of the second theme, notice that there are no tempo changes indicated in the first movement until the più mosso of the coda. Repetition and constant eighth-note rhythm are the driving forces here. The excitement of the closing section and coda result from the cumulative rhythmic momentum building straight to the last measure.

Suggestions for Performance

The tempo giusto must be found and then maintained. Bartók indicates allegro moderato, and the chosen tempo should underscore the moderato aspects of the allegro. Bartók indicates 120–126; I gravitate towards the 120 tempo, which allows the movement not to sound too harried or pushed. Constant repetition at the same tempo will create inner tension and drive and will contribute to a more effective and exciting performance. Continuous drumming in the left hand is responsible for the hypnotic rhythm. In the opening measures, a clear distinction must be made between the accents indicated on the offbeats and the sudden sforzatos. Even though the same pitch, B, is repeated, the character of its different accents must be distinguishable (example 5.1).

Attention must be paid to all two-note interjections; they are like outbursts, exclamation points, on and off the beat. Make sure they possess a different color; they must stand out in relief (examples 5.2, 5.5, 5.7). The three-note melody that emerges in m. 13–14 after the repetitive chords must be heard clearly, and the line should not be broken. Make sure both voices of the G unison are held over in the right hand.

Example 5.8: p. 3, m. 13–20

At m. 30, the pattern previously set up by the sforzato accents is changed. Now the sforzato also appears unexpectedly on the last beat of m. 30 in the right hand, and the syncopated C-sharp sforzatos in m. 36 are also jarring. Bartók, like Haydn, frequently delivers surprises.

Example 5.9: p. 4, m. 26–30

(In the original Boosey & Hawkes edition, only one sforzato is marked in m. 30 and appears on the last beat; an accent in the left hand's third beat is missing. However, in the recapitulation at m. 196, Bartók indicates two sforzatos for emphasis on the last two beats; also, at m. 203, a passage similar to m. 30, accents occur on the first two beats. This obvious misprint at m. 30 has been corrected in the 1992 revised edition: a *sf* has now been added to the left hand's third beat.)

Example 5.10: p. 10, m. 193–96

Example 5.11: p. 11, m. 202–6

At m. 38, the three-note opening motif should be more playful, played with a little rubato. Because of its formal function as preparation for the transition, Bartók alters its original character. The left-hand accompaniment should resemble a light snare drum (example 5.6).

Contrast is essential; exploit fully all changes in dynamics, accents; follow every marking that Bartók indicates (subito *p* at m. 38, 59, and 119). Many performances of this movement suffer from too much heaviness and never seem to get off the ground.

At the inversion of the second theme (m. 116), bring out the thumb of the right hand to keep the continuity of the line (example 5.4). Starting at m. 135 of the development, attention must be paid to each interjecting motif and to the dynamic spiraling of the successive sequences going toward the F-sharp sforzato on the last beat of m. 155. (Notice how the 3/8 measures at m. 138 and m. 145 with their sforzato exclamation points disrupt the regularity of rhythm and prepare the next sequence.) A short pedal on the last beat of m. 155 will delineate the F-sharp and add to the feeling of arrival. Make sure all the three-note motifs in the left hand are underlined.

Example 5.12: p. 9, m. 151–55

After three sequential statements of the three-note opening motive, the sforzato G in m. 187 (example 5.7) confirms the final arrival and tonal resting place of the recapitulation. It might help to take a little breath before m. 186 and prepare the crescendo. Make a difference between m. 176 (the false recap) and m. 182 (the real one).

The second theme in the return section is briefly interrupted by a two-measure interjection; the melody should continue as if nothing unexpected had occurred. (At m. 223, the left- and right-hand divisions that Bartók has indicated in the score might prove awkward for a small hand. I find it easier not to divide the hands.) Before m. 211, at the return of the second theme, I insert a comma, a slight breath before beginning the measure.

M. 225–end: The sudden accents are important and contribute to ongoing forward motion. At m. 234, try playing the last beat with two hands, which will make the leap to m. 235 easier. The listener must recognize that the conclusion has been reached with the glissando to the final sforzato chord. (The finale of *Out of Doors* also ends abruptly. Perhaps Bartók's frequent abrupt endings were influenced by the unprepared endings of the many peasant tunes he transcribed.)

The following measures have been corrected with the 1992 edition:

1. M. 30 and 35: Add *sf* to left-hand second beat.
2. M. 47: Add accent marking (^) to left-hand first beat.
3. M. 87: Right hand G-sharp should be an octave higher.
4. M. 121: Add *sf* to right-hand second beat.

I question the addition of an accent on the fourth beat of m. 158; this was not indicated by Bartók in the corresponding passage of the exposition. What is wanted here is the effect of equal and percussive forte eighth notes; an expressive accent will be made naturally because of the direction of the melody line.

(Erratum not addressed in new edition: In the development at m. 146, it is my opinion that Bartók forgot to indicate the *p* in the left-hand accompaniment; this dynamic pattern is confirmed by previous and subsequent sequential phrases.)

This opening movement, superbly crafted, exploits minimum material for maximum contrast. Bartók brings to the technique of repetition an economy related to structural function and design, and he demonstrates that contrast can be achieved effectively within the repetitive context. As technically difficult as the movement might seem, it always remains pianistic, clearly written by a pianist who possessed a formidable technique and knew the instrument's vast color possibilities. First become familiar with Bartók's vocabulary, sentence structure, and punctuation, and then use the piano's colors to carve out this movement's design and illuminate its meaning.

Second Movement: *Sostenuto e pesante* [Track 18]

Formal Structure: Three-part form

- First section: m. 1–30; repeat with variants of first section: m. 15–29; closing section: m. 24–29
- Middle section: m. 30–41
- Return of opening material: m. 42–52; closing section: m. 48–52
- Coda: m. 53–62

Certainly the middle movement qualifies as the most elusive movement of the entire *Sonata*. It stands apart from the two outer, more extroverted movements and seems on first hearing to be written in a completely different language. There is less to grab onto here: None of the rhythmic momentum of the other two movements propels it forward. In other words, this movement will not play by itself; it needs more time to be digested, in order to be defined by the performer. Even though its three-part form is clearly delineated and its tonal center of E/E-flat firmly established by repetition in the opening bars and confirmed with its final chord, the harmonies here sound more foreign and the phrase structure much more angular and irregular. It's as if there is a dialogue going on between two or more parties but no one is listening or answering the other; each operates on separate and distinctly different sound planes. These independent sound planes at first appear unrelated, but the ear intuitively links these lines together and does make the aural connection.

This movement is derived from only three motifs, all interrelated and each undergoing transformation throughout the movement:

1. Repetitive motif: The rhythmic, repetitive Es of the right hand clash with the repeated chords of the left, forming the E–E-flat second and underlining the tonal center E–E-flat by its very repetition.

Example 5.13: p. 14, m. 1–6

Motif #1 recalls the first movement's opening repetitive motif and its clash of the repeated B and A-sharp (example 5.1).

2. Chords and fourth motif: The chords are derived from the repeated chord of example 5.13 but are transposed and expanded to form tritones with open fourths and fifths. The fourth functions not only harmonically but also linearly. The melody line is built in fourths, and this motif is extended horizontally in m. 8–12. At m. 13, it is inverted and augmented rhythmically in the left hand to span the interval of the tritone. At m. 19, it expands linearly into a sequencing pattern of fourths and fifths.

Example 5.14: p. 14, m. 7–8

Example 5.15: p. 14, m. 8–12

Example 5.16: p. 14, m. 13–14

Example 5.17: p. 14, m. 17–20

3. Third diatonic motif. These three notes, encompassing the interval of the third that first appears in m. 7–8 (see example 5.14), were already suggested in motif #1 with the appearance of the D in m. 6 (example 5.13). The motif also appears in augmentation in the middle section at m. 30, becoming the basis for sequential development. The right-hand melodic line spans the distance of the third, and the sequencing in thirds is present in the tenor voice as well.

Example 5.18: p. 15, m. 30–33

It functions as a closing motif—

Example 5.19: p. 15, m. 24–29

—and returns before developing into an ostinato in the coda.

Example 5.20: p. 16, m. 50–62

The last chord of the second movement is derived from this motif and recalls the first movement's opening bars (example 5.1), which also underscore this third interval.

Because of the minimal material used, contrast is achieved not by in-
troducing new ideas, but by transformation of material for maximum
dramatic effect. Bartók is intrigued with the planing of sonorities, suddenly changing dynamics, displacement of octaves, interchanging of

material between hands, and vertical and horizontal motion. This economy of means, without any unnecessary filler, not only produces contrast but also provides unity. Listen to the startling, sudden color change Bartók evokes with pedal effects in the middle section while also slowing down the harmonic rhythm. The terrace dynamics of forte and piano of the opening are effective, as well as the contrasting repeat of this material at m. 15. A simple device, such as transposition of hands while also changing dynamics, disguises the original material (m. 42–47).

Confining analysis to only the opening section, which is more fragmented and extended than the middle and return sections, it will be helpful to examine phrase structure now that the motivic material has been identified:

- The first three-measure phrase is repeated with contrasting terrace dynamics, altering the last repeated tone at m. 6 to include D, in preparation for the germination of the diatonic-third motif #3 (example 5.13).
- M. 7–8 (example 5.14) might be interpreted as an interjection, in preparation for the dialogue of the four separate horizontal voices in m. 9 (example 5.15).
- M. 9–12 is an internal dialogue, in horizontal motion of interchanging voices using all three motifs. Each voice needs to retain its separate identity (example 5.15).
- M. 13–14 shows vertical and horizontal interjection of motifs #2 (inverted) and #1. M. 13 is reduced to the skeletal harmonic outline of m. 12 and also rhythmically prepares the return opening material.
- M. 15 shows contrasting repeat of opening measures (example 5.13) but in retrograde, beginning with the D on the last beat of m. 14 and extended imitatively. In m. 17–21, motif #2 provides the material for each measure to expand a little further than previously (example 5.17).
- In m. 22–23, the two-measure summation before the closing section is derived from diatonic motif #3.
- In m. 24–29, closing section, there is imitative sequencing of two motifs (#3 & #2).

This movement might be titled, "The Conflicts that Exist between Seconds and Tritones," but to me this first section conveys the impression of a conversation with many participants. They politely await their turn to answer; when they finally speak, they do so without reacting to what has previously been said, even though sharing similar material. Each seems to talk only to itself, and each retains a separate and individual sound plane. With the arrival of the middle section and the pedal point of D, harmonic motion becomes static and conversation is suspended. At m. 42, a false recapitulation, the conversants start up again. At. m. 43 there is another speaker, as in m. 44 and 45, and finally, at m. 46, the last and loudest voice has the final say. The closing section begins with m. 47, with the concluding coda at m. 53. At m. 59, with the appearance of the opening motto, the conversation has been brought to its conclusion; it has come full circle, back to where it began originally. It is the form that gives definition to this dialogue.

When the ear accepts the repetitive and static aspect of this material, it unconsciously adjusts to it and makes concessions. The dissonant seconds of E/E-flat of the opening, because of their repetition, eventually come to be heard as consonance within this specific context. The ear is forced to accept the parameters Bartók imposes.

More than any of the other movements of the *Sonata*, this second movement seems to be most influenced by compositional techniques used by Liszt in his B minor *Sonata*. The opening measures function formally as a quasi-ritornello, similar to the opening measures in the Liszt composition. In both compositions, a motto theme opens and closes the work and is used as punctuation between contrasting material and to delineate its formal outlines.

Example 5.21: Liszt *Sonata* in B minor, Dover (1990) p. 1, m. 1–7

Suggestions for Performance

From the very first notes of the opening measures, the proper character must be established; Sostenuto e pesante is a good description of what Bartók wants. There is a weariness of soul to be captured within this movement. At times it sounds like a dirge, a funeral processional. Bartók's metronomic indications will provide excellent guidelines for finding the right tempo; avoid any pushing forward of the tempo (example 5.13).

Erratum: In m. 4, the piano dynamic indication should begin with the left hand, on the second beat (example 5.13) and not later as in the earlier editions. (This has been corrected in the 1992 edition.)

In the right hand of the opening, each repeated E-natural is played slightly differently, and shape and direction derived from its place within the phrase (example 5.13).

Rests are vital to Bartók's irregular phrase structure and must be observed. They function as punctuation.

At m. 9, make the distinction between four separate voices. Experiment with voicing. Remember that even though separate, the voices are not equal (example 5.15).

At m. 15, with the repeated opening measures, make sure the focus is on contrast; the character here is markedly different.

Experiment with dynamics. The forte marking in m. 1 should be a different quality of forte from that played in m. 42. The opening is strongly stated, but m. 42 must be declaimed.

At m. 30, either make use of the middle, sustaining D pedal throughout this section, or play it with pedal vibrato. I prefer to use pedal vibrato because it gives more color flexibility and allows the use of the left pedal, which is necessary here. If using the sustaining pedal, lift at m. 43. Gradually increase dynamics within each phrase (each sequence).

What Bartók has written at m. 49–51 is impossible to play on the modern Steinway. Bartók composed this work on his own Bösendorfer, which had an extended lower bass. He was looking for a certain quality of sound for rhythmic emphasis and punctuation, and he chose the timbre of the lowest octave in which the pitches are barely distinguishable. Therefore, I recommend playing this passage at the lowest octave on the piano for effect, while retaining only one note of the original octave as indicated in the score. The ear will not be able to decipher the low pitch, so the effect will be similar to what Bartók has written. Keep the three voice planes separate, observing a separate set of dynamics and touch for each line.

Example 5.22: p. 16, m. 46–53

To be played:

From m. 52–58, continue each voice line with a separate identity. The coda begins with the last two beats of m. 52 (example 5.20). At the last chord of m. 62, play the E-natural with the right hand and try taking a little time before the triad for dramatic effect. Bartók indicates a crescendo as well as an expressive accent on this final chord (example 5.20).

In this movement Bartók defines musical meaning by form and not by the quality of thematic material. He makes even one repeated pitch interesting, meaningful, and profound.

Finale: Allegro molto

Formal structure: extended rondo with ritornello (large three-part structure)

Opening section:
- A theme: ritornello m. 1–19

Example 5.23: p. 17, m. 1– 12

- B theme: m. 20–39

Example 5.24: p. 17, m. 20–24

- Transition: m. 40–52
- A theme variation #1: m. 53–80
- Transition: m. 81–91
- Ritornello A theme (closing): m. 92–110

Middle section:
- B variant (inversion): m. 111–37
- Transition: m. 137–42
- A theme variation #2: "Musette's theme" m. 143–56

Example 5.25: p. 22, m. 143–48

Return:
- Ritornello A theme: m. 157–74
- Return of B theme: m. 175–92
- Transition: m. 192–204
- A theme variation #3: "Fiddler's theme from Transylvania" m. 205–26

Example 5.26: p. 25, m. 205–8

- Ritornello A theme (extended): m. 227–61
Coda: m. 262–81

Even though not based on original folk material, this movement has the true feeling of a peasant folk dance. It is extroverted music, meant to be enjoyed, and except for its extended formal structure, it is rather uncomplicated music. According to Bartók's original manuscripts, this movement's material underwent many revisions and cuttings. The A theme (variation #2) from the middle section ("Musette's theme," example 5.25) seems to be a variant of some of the material Bartók used in the *Out of Doors*, written during the same time period. What Bartók originally cut from one of the finale's episodes later became the third movement ("Musettes") from *Out of Doors*. The A theme (variation #3, example 5.26) was inspired by the shifting-rhythm style of the wild peasant fiddlers from Transylvania. (Similar material can also be found in the finale of the *Piano Concerto* No. 1, also written in 1926.)

This finale resembles other perpetual motion movements that conclude several of Bartók's larger works, such as the *Out of Doors*, or are included as one of the middle movements, such as the third movement of the Op. 14 *Suite*. Motion and energy never let up and must be sustained from beginning to end. Considering the similarity of material both in character and rhythm, sectional contrast is necessary and provides the formal mold into which the material can be shaped. However, because of its extended sectional form, there is the danger of making this movement sound too fragmented. The performer must always be conscious of the larger three-part form.

Breathing spaces are important in this movement. The opening eight bars (example 5.23) resemble the first line of a folk song; a natural breath is required before playing the octave repetition of the same line at m. 9. Notice that the line is going toward the second B in m. 16; what follows in the next two measures is rhythmic sound filler. A breath is also required before starting the next section at m. 20 (example 5.24). These small breaths and sudden interjections (m. 38) should not disrupt the driving pulse, which is headed for m. 110, the conclusion of the first large section.

The pianistic trouble spots that require special attention are concentrated at measures 49–92, 143–56, and 205–26. Pulse must be maintained, and the performer should try to avoid having these sections sound too heavy-handed or labored. Some of these passages will be awkward for the pianist with a smaller hand and indicate that Bartók must have had a large hand span at the keyboard. The octaves and sixths of m. 28–40 will also need additional practice.

Example 5.27: p. 18, m. 31–41

Suggestions for Performance

Bartók indicates a metronome marking of 170, not found on most metronomes. This might be a misprint; Bartók probably meant to indicate 176, which works for this movement. (At the più mosso at m. 192, Bartók indicates 194 and probably means 192.) Observe all accents that Bartók indicates. At m. 16, make a difference in the two accents on B.

Try using this fingering at m. 36–37 (example 5.27).

At m. 40, make sudden dynamic contrasts without losing the pulse.

At m. 111, a change of touch and timbre is called for; try the fingering Bartók indicates. At m. 113–14, I revert to normal fingering but try to imitate the sound of the thumb playing each note.

M. 119: Remember here to keep the right hand legato.

M. 143 (example 5.25): Try imitating the bird chirpings that Bartók also uses in *Out of Doors*; touch must be kept light.

Starting at m. 186, the new 1992 edition includes these additional markings:

Example 5.28: p. 24, m. 184–95

At m. 205 (example 5.26), keep in mind that Bartók is depicting a mad fiddler trying to play as fast as he can.

At m. 281, a feeling of conclusion must be felt with the last chord; take a little time before the final chord.

The 1992 edition adds some markings to the finale movement, which musically seem questionable.

Example 5.29: p. 19, m. 71–82

The inclusion of this accent is similar to what was questioned in the first movement at m. 58. The expressive accent will be made naturally by the direction of the melodic line. I feel that Bartók had deleted it because it was not necessary and altered the effect of the even eighth-note rhythmic motion.

Example 5.30: p. 21, m. 133–37

Here the inclusion of accents will impede the driving crescendo. Again, I do not think that it was Bartók's intention to include these; they alter the effect of the stringendo and affect the momentum.

At m. 251, the top note of the second beat chord in the right hand has been corrected in the new edition to D, replacing C.

With the *Sonata* of 1926, one of Bartók's most effective works for solo piano, proof is present that form is the most essential ingredient in understanding Bartók's musical compositions. However, Bartók never follows an academic, conventional approach to structure; he never knows in advance what form will manifest itself. (As part of his Harvard Lecture Series of 1943, Bartók had hoped to deliver a lecture entitled, "Every Piece Creates Its Own Form," but because of ill health was forced to cancel the remaining lectures.) He has the courage to take the leap of faith that allows the material to combine with creative intuition in order to shape the structure, thus creating its own form. Bartók, like Beethoven and Mozart before him, knew that form needs the freedom to proceed unencumbered in order to find its own way.

Bartók's *Sonata* left its mark on many later twentieth-century composers, and created a wide group of imitators. Bartók's pianistic influence is unquestionable in Alberto Ginastera's well-known 1952 *Piano Sonata*.

Example 5.31: Ginastera, *Sonata* No. 1, 2nd mvt., Barry (1954), p. 9, m. 35–39

Example 5.32: Ginastera, *Sonata* No. 1, 3rd mvt. p. 20, m. 61–69

Compare these passages to example 5.27.

(Note: Even in Ginastera's more mature works, Bartók's influence is evident. The finale of Ginastera's *First Piano Concerto*, written in 1961, is based on the same motif as the opening theme from the finale of Bartók's *Second Piano Concerto*.)

SONATA FOR TWO PIANOS AND PERCUSSION (1937)

This unique composition, the only sonata scored for two pianos and percussion instruments alone, qualifies not only as one of the great masterworks but also as one of the most effectively written and exciting compositions of the twentieth century. Originally commissioned by the Basel chapter of the International Society of Contemporary Music, it was underwritten personally by the conductor Paul Sacher, an old friend of Bartók's. Sacher also was responsible for commissioning two other masterworks by Bartók, *Music for Strings, Percussion, and Celeste* (1936) and the *Divertimento* (1939).

In 1938, Bartók wrote about the *Sonata*:

> I already had the intention years ago to compose a work for piano and percussion. Gradually, the conviction grew stronger in me that one piano would not be in satisfactory balance in relation to the often penetrating timbre of the percussion instruments. The plan was therefore altered to the extent that two pianos instead of one would oppose the percussion instruments. When the ISCM of Basel requested last summer that I compose a work for their Jubilee Concert on January 16, 1938, I gladly accepted the opportunity to realize my plan. The

seven percussion instruments—timpani, bass drum, cymbals, gong, snare drum, tenor drum, xylophone—require only two players; one of them at no time plays the xylophone, the other one never the tympani. These two percussion parts are fully equal in rank to one of the two piano parts. The timbre of the percussion instruments has various roles: In many cases it only colors the piano tone, in others it enhances the more important accents; occasionally, the percussion instruments introduce contrapuntal motives against the piano parts, and the tympani and xylophone frequently play themes even as solos. The formal structure of the work can be related as follows:

Assai lento; Allegro molto

"The first movement begins with a slow introduction, in which a motive of the movement is foreshadowed.

Example 5.33: *Sonata* for two pianos and percussion, Boosey & Hawkes (1942), p. 5, m. 1–5

[This theme strongly resembles Liszt's theme from his second concert étude, *La Leggiereza*, a composition Bartók had studied and also performed.]

Example 5.34: Liszt, *Concert Etude* No. 2, Dover (1988), p. 152, m. 11–14

The allegro movement itself is in C and is in sonata form. In the exposition, a main theme group is announced, consisting of two themes (of which the second has already been alluded to in the introduction),

Example 5.35: *Sonata*, p. 9, m. 32–40

Example 5.36: *Sonata,* p. 10, m. 41–46

after which follows the secondary (contrasting) theme.

Example 5.37: *Sonata,* p. 15, m. 84–90

Out of this a codetta develops on rather broad lines [exploiting the interval of the sixth, which will be further developed fugally in the closing section at the end of the movement],

Example 5.38: *Sonata,* p. 17, m. 105–9

at the end of which a brief reference to the contrasting theme occurs by way of conclusion.

Example 5.39: *Sonata,* p. 21, m. 161–65

The development, after a short transition of superimposed layers of fourths, consists essentially of three parts. [These consecutive fourths are difficult and must be played with a leggiero technique.]

Example 5.40: *Sonata,* p. 23, m. 186–88

The first one, in E, employs the second theme of the main theme group as an ostinato motive over which the first theme of the main group proceeds in the form of imitatively treated interpolations.

Example 5.41: *Sonata,* p. 24, m. 196–203

The second part is in the nature of a short interlude . . .

Example 5.42: *Sonata,* p. 26, m. 217–19

... after which the first part—with the ostinato in G-sharp and inverted—
is repeated in a much altered form.

Example 5.43: *Sonata*, p. 29, m. 231–34

In the recapitulation there is no proper closing section; it is replaced by a
rather extensive coda (with a fugato beginning) built on the closing theme."[3]

Example 5.44: *Sonata* p. 40, m. 332–40

This large and difficult first movement, twelve minutes in duration and comprising nearly half of the three-movement sonata, is the central focus of the entire work. Here Bartók proceeds to stretch the boundaries of classical sonata form as far as possible, while still maintaining structural balance. Everything is expanded in this movement. It begins with an extended introduction; the presentations of the exposition's first two themes are imitatively stretched over three sections; this tripartite design also is applicable to the appearance and return of the second theme after the closing motif. The exciting virtuosic development section is also constructed in three parts, and a case could be made for the tripartite structure of the recapitulation of the first and second themes and also a tripartite fugal closing section. (In the recapitulation, the head motif of the subsidiary first theme [example 5.36] originally heard in the introduction [example 5.33] now becomes the counterpoint accompaniment to the second theme.) Bartók's extraordinary craft has been learned through apprenticeship with two great masters of sonata form, Beethoven and Liszt.

Lento, ma non troppo

"The second movement in F is in simple song form, ABA."[4]

This movement resembles Bartók's other night movements: the fourth movement of the *Out of Doors*, the second movement of the second *Piano Concerto*, the slow movement in *Music for Strings, Percussion, and Celeste*. However, here Bartók has the additional advantage of the percussion instruments to contribute to the unique color effects. The middle section gradually builds and recedes in dynamic and emotional intensity, with the percussion participating as equals in this constant surging dialogue. The pianistic effects—recalling the piano writing of Debussy, Ravel, and Liszt—are stunning, and the ending of the movement is unique in its extended drama. Bartók uses repetition and augmentation techniques to create intensity and excitement. Even when taken out of the context of the total sonata, this slow movement qualifies as a masterwork of color and effect.

Allegro non troppo

"The third movement, in C, presents a combination of rondo with sonata form. Between the exposition and the recapitulation a new thematic group appears, wrought of two parts of the first theme treated in imitation. A coda fading away pianissimo brings the movement and the work to a close."[5]

This exuberant, extroverted dance finale recalls and magnifies the folk spirit of the 1926 *Sonata*'s last movement. After the pianissimo conclusion of the slow movement, the introduction to the finale is startling, and Bartók uses the xylophone to introduce the primary thematic material.

Example 5.45: *Sonata*, p. 65, m. 1–14

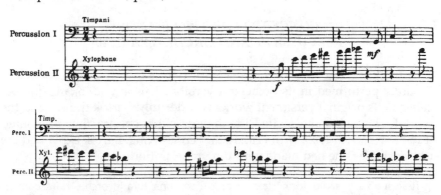

The second contrasting theme has a touch of Gershwin about it (bits of *An American in Paris?*).

Example 5.46: *Sonata*, p. 71, m. 101–5

The fugal, imitative writing has become even more sophisticated than that in the 1926 solo *Sonata*; in addition, imitation is now spread over four hands at two pianos, plus the voice of the xylophone.

This movement should be studied as an example of Bartók's highly developed motivic technique. From a simple tune played by the xylophone, Bartók crafts a complex formal structure and exploits all the participating instruments for their maximum sonorities and color effects.

This sonata is one of Bartók's most difficult performance works; it asks for four performers of comparable professional abilities to come together and become a unified ensemble. Because of its unique medium, this chamber work is not frequently heard; however, for the performers involved, it is a joy to prepare and to play, in spite of its many technical difficulties.

CONCERTO FOR TWO PIANOS, PERCUSSION, AND ORCHESTRA (1940)

This work is a rescoring of the *Sonata* for two pianos and percussion and is rarely performed in its orchestral version. This is understandable because in its original version, it works wonderfully. Bartók transcribed the work for himself and his wife Ditta to play with orchestra; they premiered it in New York in 1943, with Fritz Reiner conducting. Bartók explained the minor changes he had made with the orchestration:

> It seemed advisable, for certain technical reasons, to add orchestral accompaniment to the work, though, as a matter of fact, it gives only color to certain portions of the work. The two-piano and percussion parts remain practically unchanged, except for some of the climactic parts, which are now taken over from the two pianos as tuttis by the orchestra.[6]

That concert was the last public appearance Bartók made before his death in 1945.

NOTES

1. Béla Bartók, "On the Significance of Folk Music" (1931), in *Béla Bartók Essays*, ed. Benjamin Suchoff (Lincoln: University of Nebraska Press, 1976), 346.

2. Béla Bartók, "Liszt's Music and Our Contemporary Public" (1911), in *Bartók Studies*, ed. Todd Crow (Detroit: Detroit Reprints in Music, 1976), 122. [This article originally appeared in *The New Hungarian Quarterly* II/1 (January 1961).]

3. Béla Bartók, "About the Sonata for Two Pianos and Percussion" (1938), in *Béla Bartók Essays*, ed. Benjamin Suchoff, 417–18. The author's comments appear in brackets.

4. Bartók, "About the Sonata for Two Pianos and Percussion" (1938), 418.

5. "About the Sonata for Two Pianos and Percussion" (1938), 418.

6. Béla Bartók, as quoted in Halsey Stevens, *The Life and Music of Béla Bartók*, 3rd ed., ed. Malcolm Gillies (New York: Oxford University Press, 1993), 244.

6

+

The Evolutionary:
Out of Doors (1926)

Let me say in advance that revolution in art (for instance, in music) in its strict sense would signify the destruction of every previously used means and a new start from almost nothing—a setback of several thousand years. Complete revolution in art, therefore, is impossible or, at least, is not a desirable means to an end. Evolution, on the other hand, means development by natural process from something that existed before; that is, a change by degrees. In art there is only slow or rapid progress implying in essence evolution and not revolution.

—Béla Bartók[1]

Written during that fruitful year of 1926, the five "soundscapes" of the *Out of Doors* evolved from various sources to emerge as one of Bartók's most original compositions for solo piano; certainly it qualifies as one of his most difficult. This is music created from an impressionist's color palette and inspired by the Baroque dance suite. (In 1926, Bartók was also editing keyboard music by Couperin, Scarlatti, Zipoli, and Frescobaldi for a Hungarian music publisher.) These pieces anticipate the percussive, repetitive techniques exploited by the later minimalists and also recall the individual character pieces of the nineteenth century. Thus, *Out of Doors* reveals Bartók the modernist and Bartók the traditionalist, coexisting peacefully.

The *Out of Doors* suite is all about sound and color; certainly, only a master pianist with thorough knowledge of the instrument's technical and coloristic possibilities could have written these five pieces. Each movement, bearing a descriptive title, emerges as an individual sound canvas, unified by compositional techniques and a unique coloristic focus. From the opening bars of each piece, the ear is forced to adapt to the sound plane on which the structure is built and is asked to learn Bartók's direct but limited vocabulary. The listener is required to accept very specific parameters. What Bartók is doing here is analogous to the mime who communicates with the audience without speaking. In both cases, the restriction is part of the agreement between composer/performer and audience. It works successfully only when the terms are understood and accepted by both parties. Once again, Bartók proves his own dictum that it is not the quality of material that is important but how the composer shapes and molds this material. Economy is essential to Bartók's craft, with each piece of the set being crafted from minimal thematic material while at the same time exploiting the techniques of repetition, variation, and contrast.

Acting as middleman and translator, the performer must make the music live; recreate the colors and sounds with which to paint the scene; and at the same time highlight for the listener, as directly as possible, a personal point of view based on careful study of the composer's score. However, the pianist must never forget that this is primarily music to be heard and must transform intellectual discovery into a lucid musical statement.

Form, above all, provides the stable foundation for an understanding of Bartók's music; it is the structural mold into which this minimal material will be poured. A thorough analysis of Bartók's restricted vocabulary for each piece, how this material is transformed by its specific place within the formal design and then further altered by using the compositional devices of variation and contrast, will influence all performance decisions, such as how much sforzando or crescendo should be used, how much ritardando, etc. Some performance decisions do work better than others; therefore, it is helpful if these choices are based on a firm foundation of musical reasoning. The performer of Bartók's music, as compared to the first-time listener, has already learned the language and become comfortable with Bartók's material; the constant challenge is to shape the work and make it convincing aurally, both as an individual piece and within its relationship to the entire suite.

Although the five movements can function independently, they are definitely linked by contrast and key relationships, and it is recommended that the suite be performed in its entirety. Bartók creates an overall arch form from the set, based upon the key relationships (EGAGE). Their structure and progression seem inevitable, beginning with a bare-bones skeletal outline of drums and pipes followed by the calm, rhythmic but irregular patterns of the Barcarolle, the duple dissonant droning of the Musettes, and the intricate weavings of the memorable nocturne movement that Bartók makes the major focus of the entire suite. The finale, a perpetual motion chase, exciting from first note to last, becomes the culmination and the working through of what is only a rhythmic suggestion in the first piece. Thus, with the *Out of Doors*, Bartók has constructed a perfectly balanced and well-rounded form.

Because of the pianistic and musical difficulties inherent in this master-work, an in-depth analysis—including some of my personal experiences while learning the *Out of Doors*—will be outlined in the following pages. A work of this stature needs to be wrestled to the ground; the pianist must fight a personal battle with it during the courtship period when both the performer and the work are learning about each other and understanding the problems involved in their relationship. Complexities must be ana-lyzed and objectively understood, then digested and absorbed completely at the keyboard, so the pianist will be able to convey the assurance of hav-ing become fluent in Bartók's native tongue. The *Out of Doors*, in the same way as other piano masterworks such as Beethoven's Op. 106 and the Liszt *Sonata*, can serve as a barometer for measuring the musical and technical growth of the performer. Never fear, the pianist who returns to these pieces time and again will, with every successive visit, make an-other discovery.

(Note: A new and revised edition by Peter Bartók of the *Out of Doors* was published by Universal in two volumes: Vol. I, Nos. 1–3 (1990), and Vol. II, Nos. 4–5 (1996). Bartók's manuscripts, including an earlier sketch and two of what he called his "final copies," were compared to the last printed Boosey & Hawkes edition, and necessary corrections were noted.)

"WITH DRUMS AND PIPES" [TRACK 19]

In these first measures of the *Out of Doors*, Bartók provides the percussive outline of what will be filled in later with the finale movement. In the opening section he exploits the lowest register of the piano and, by using irregular rhythms and accents, makes this percussive repetition sound in-teresting. Here is Bartók the craftsman, the economist, the minimalist at work. (A comparison of these opening measures with those of the piano *Sonata* of 1926 shows a strong similarity to its skeletal structure.)

Example 6.1: *Out of Doors*, 1st mvt., Boosey & Hawkes (1927, 1954), p. 3, m. 1–15

Example 6.2: *Sonata*, Boosey & Hawkes (1955), p. 3, m. 1–6

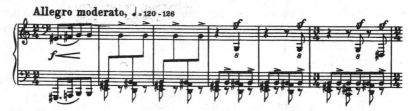

Everything in this three-part movement will evolve from the material of these opening measures. Bartók forces the listener and the pianist to accept his limited parameters and adjust to a limited color range. All performance decisions will be relative to these restricted boundaries.

The basic vocabulary is rhythmic: variation of eighth-note rhythm using minimal melodic material. As with the *Sonata*, the melody line basically encompasses the interval of a third on either side of the tonal center E. The thematic material of the middle section (example 6.4) is derived from the inversion of the sequential motifs from the opening section (example 6.3).

Example 6.3: *Out of Doors*, 1st mvt., p. 4, m. 20–34

Example 6.4: *Out of Doors,* 1st mvt., p. 4, m. 40–44

(Erratum, m. 42: It is my opinion that the accent marked in the left hand on the second beat should appear not over the A, but under the G, thus conforming to the sequential patterns that follow and highlighting the linear line [G/F#/E/D]. [This has not been addressed in the new edition.])

When using such a minimal amount of material, how is contrast effectively achieved? Because of the economy of material, the most subtle change can now create an impact. Listen to the second variant of the opening material (example 6.3). The addition of the F-sharp second to the cluster chord and the hands playing an octave higher after all the opening bass rumblings is an effective contrast; this F-sharp, the neighboring tone of the key center E, will also effectively return as the last note in the final cadence. Contrast is usually built into a three-part formal structure. Here, the vertical motion of the opening drums is replaced by an immediate feeling of horizontal line and the sweeter color of the pipes in the middle section (example 6.4); no vertical drumbeats here except for rhythmic interjections between phrases that signal the return.

It is always essential to start with an understanding of the larger form and then place the many details that fit into this structure. With Bartók's music it is impossible to work any other way; imagine not being able to grasp the vastness of the forest because of concentrating on one small leaf. Certainly every detail is significant and has a solid reason for existence, but all of Bartók's materials must be evaluated as part of the complete structure. Only then will the interpreter be able to understand the reasoning behind the composer's markings and be able to translate and share this with the listener. I strongly believe that music from every historical period should be studied in this way. However, because of the complexity of Bartók's compositional style, this approach is mandatory with his music. After all the homework has been done, the performer must be able to shape a phrase with the knowledge of its function within the larger structure. The following examples illustrate the importance of formal evaluation of material as it affects performance decisions.

Example 6.5: *Out of Doors,* 1st mvt., p. 4, m. 35–44

At the close of the first section, these three measures need to be emphasized and highlighted as the final cadence before the contrasting middle section.

Example 6.6: *Out of Doors,* 1st mvt., p. 5, m. 60–69

At the close of the middle section, before the first section material returns at meno f, a slight breath is needed, more like a period, which will help delineate the structure. A breath is also necessary before the final meno mosso that presents the closing epigram and final summation of this first movement.

Suggestions for Performance

Delineate the three-part structure to understand the mold into which the material is being poured:

- Opening section: 1–40
- Middle: 41–67
- Return: 68–87
- Coda: 89–114

Analyze the phrase structure of each section: The first four measures function as introduction and establish the drumbeats. Notice that Bartók contrasts two different bass drums here. Melodic material is introduced in m. 5 (example 6.1); m. 13 begins a variant of that material; and m. 24 (example 6.3) begins sequential treatment, developed harmonically, ultimately leading to the closing three measures of the first section, which should be emphasized (example 6.5).

At m. 25 maintain a strict tempo, as the 2/3/2/3/2 syncopations will be more effective within a tight rhythmic framework (example 6.3).

Keep the line going in the middle section, and make sure that at m. 42 the dotted quarter note is played so that it can sound through the next measure (example 6.4). The line stops only for drumbeat interjections; those are the only rests indicated from m. 41–48. The entire middle section provides good evidence that complete separation of hands is an absolute necessity. At m. 50, Bartók allows the left hand to go its own way, but its constant return to the F in the bass line, starting at m. 57, focuses attention on the importance of the independent left-hand line.

With the three accents on the F beginning in m. 57, Bartók prepares the arrival of the *sf* D (example 6.6), further emphasizing the third interval relationship of the opening measures. At m. 80, make sure to maintain the melody line.

Careful pacing of the stringendo and crescendo at the coda is necessary for an effective performance. It might be helpful to organize this passage into a four-measure group, followed by four two-measure units, three one-measures, and ending with one five-beat measure that will make sense of the patterning of Bartók's accents. These accents are used to write out the accelerando to m. 105, which must feel like the point of arrival.

Example 6.7: *Out of Doors,* 1st mvt., p. 6–7, m. 89–106

Meno mosso: This is Bartók's epigram, his summation of this movement, and it must be presented in direct relief to everything heard previously. The key center is not stated directly but alluded to with the final F-sharp, a neighbor-tone to the E tonal center that will prepare the G tonal center of the second piece.

"BARCAROLLA"

Following the aggressive, percussive rhythms of drums, the calm of the water is a welcome contrast. In this second piece, Bartók creates the illusion of a Venetian boat song. Rocking back and forth on the water, the listener is forced to accept the continuous eighth-note rhythmic pattern. (Bartók visited Venice with his wife Ditta in 1924 and was inspired by the gondolas there.) However, this movement is not about the regular rhythms of Chopin's *Barcarolle* or *Le barque sur l'ocean* of Ravel. Bartók writes in irregular measures, alternating 5/8, 9/8, 4/8, and 7/8 with 6/8, but these are all meant to be played in a flowing, constant manner. Bartók writes out the rubato desired within the strictness of these irregular but constant eighth-note rhythms, similar to normal breathing and speech patterns, but he also acknowledges that the water in the stream never flows without an occasional unexpected surprise, as Chopin had claimed.

Contrasting touches and colors are called for to define and delineate the separate lines and layers that begin to appear over the steady eighth-note rhythm: the cantando melody, which emerges first in the right hand; the staccato dissonant seconds heard under the melody; the pedal points of the melody line, which must sound through; the accents and sforzatos that occur in the development. All these separate lines weave in and out over a regular rhythmic pulse.

Example 6.8: *Out of Doors,* 2nd mvt., p. 8, m. 11–20

Development occurs in the middle section (m. 49–79): Perhaps a crack of thunder or a surprise encounter with a log on the water creates this agitato feeling, heightened by the appearance of C-flat sforzandos, but eventually the restful waves do return.

(Erratum: At m. 83, the bass note should be F, not A. [Corrected in 1990 edition.])

This movement, especially its return material, provides an excellent example of the formula that must be applied to the study of Bartók's music. To understand the rhythmic variants and their complexities, these must be analyzed, dissected, organized, or reorganized into phrase structures or accessible patterns that the brain can decipher. In example 6.10, I have rebarred some of these passages in order to make logical sense of the variants to facilitate my own memorization. Once the complexity has been mastered, the performer must then make these rhythmic variants sound as natural as possible. However, it is necessary to start from complexity to achieve this overall ease of effect.

Example 6.9: *Out of Doors,* 2nd mvt., p. 12, m. 106–14

Example 6.10: *Out of Doors,* 2nd mvt., p. 12, m. 106–14 (rebarred)

Suggestions for Performance

In the introduction, make sure there is a difference dynamically between the three Fs that prepare the G of the opening material.

Example 6.11: *Out of Doors,* 2nd mvt., p. 8, m. 1–10

(At m. 5, I find it easier to play the low G with the right hand.)

With the opening material, make sure the left hand is even and reliable. Coloring each line is essential (example 6.8).

The harmonic language used in this piece is that of the traditionalist: tonic/dominant; dominant of dominant relationships. Notice that the final F-sharp of the first movement prepares the G tonal center of the "Barcarolle"; the tritone final chord (G/C#/D) of the "Barcarolle" moves up a whole tone to prepare the opening chord of the "Musettes" (A/D#/E).

Example 6.12: *Out of Doors,* 2nd mvt., p. 12, m. 113–14; 3rd mvt., p. 13, m. 1–2

The four-note cluster chord of the fourth movement shares the second interval (G#/A) from the last chord of "Musettes."

Example 6.13: *Out of Doors,* 3rd mvt., p. 19, m. 126; 4th mvt., p. 20, m. 1

The F tonal center of the finale is prepared by the final sounds of the "Nocturne" movement (E#/F#/G/G#/A).

Once the syntax has been learned and all the details analyzed according to their places in the structural design, an overall unity of sound and color is required to evoke a water "soundscape." The performer must strive for the appropriate touch and pedaling; a great deal of control at the keyboard is necessary to paint this larger canvas.

"MUSETTES"

Bartók imitates the droning sound of the bagpipes, complete with their characteristic squeaks and burps. Using duple slurs to represent the in-and-out bellowing of the three sounding pipes of each instrument, the piano's harmonies become compatible with the construction of the folk instrument: the drone pipe, maintaining the same fundamental tone; the middle pipe, usually at more or less a fifth above, give or take the quarter and semitones; and the third, the chanter, responsible for the melody. From the opening measures, the ear is forced to accept Bartók's parameters and adjust to the tritones and dissonant seconds of these instruments. In the context of this movement, the dissonance, because of its repetition, is now heard as consonance. Within such a limited soundscape, it is extremely important to vary color and dynamics to achieve maximum contrast. Bartók remains faithful to the terrace dynamics of the Baroque. (Notice that the first fourteen measures do not exceed *mp*; at m. 15, the volume is suddenly turned up to *mf*. The subito *mp* should be observed at m. 23.) Occasionally, as in m. 30, the dynamics need to be organized on two separate sound planes to be understood. Bartók makes use of more than one set of bagpipes here.

Example 6.14: *Out of Doors,* 3rd mvt., p. 14–15, m. 27–34

The diminuendo is taking place on two different levels (*f* to *mf* to *mp; mp* to *p*).

The structural delineation of the three-part form inherently provides for a contrasting middle section, even though this più mosso material also happens to be derived from duple slur droning. Bartók does not rely on the simple three-part structure used in the first two movements; here the form is enlarged, resembling more the extended binary form found in a Scarlatti sonata. (Bartók also was editing Scarlatti's music in 1926.)

It is interesting that the dynamic climax of the piece occurs in the ad libitum section at m. 80. (John Cage surely must have been influenced by Bartók's use of this technique, which was also used as early as 1908 in his second *Elegy*.) Here, Bartók wants the sound prolonged for dramatic effect.

Example 6.15: *Out of Doors*, 3rd mvt., p. 17, m. 75–81

Bartók is meticulous with his score notations, and there seems to be a logical reason for every marking. I question the following measures, which might contain errors that occurred in the process of copying the manuscript:

Possible errata (Boosey & Hawkes score):

- M. 17: Tenuto marking missing on second beat of right hand. (Corrected in new edition.)
- M. 69: Left-hand tenuto marking should also be marked on every beat, as in the previous and following measures (not addressed in new edition).

- M. 91: There should be a left-hand tenuto marking on the first beat of the measure. Also, there seems to be no reason why Bartók did not add these markings for similar emphasis to the left hand in measures 88 and 90 (not addressed in new edition). Perhaps this is a copying error. Do add them for delineation, but be sure to avoid overthickening the texture.
- M. 95: Restore tenuto indication on second beat in left hand; also in m. 112 (restored in m. 95 in new edition; m. 112 not addressed).

Suggestions for Performance

Bartók uses many notes to prolong the dissonant droning and in-and-out breathing of the bagpipes; each figure must be thought out within its structural and dynamic context. What is not wanted is a notey, pedantic performance. The notes are written for a certain color effect, and the pianist's ear and imagination will ultimately remain the best judge of sound. Using the middle sostenuto pedal will help to maintain the sound and concentrate on the top voice line (see example 6.15). The following passage is especially awkward because of its stretch.

Example 6.16: *Out of Doors,* 3rd mvt., p. 18, m. 94–99

The coda at m. 105 coincides with the return of the tonal center. The panpipe melody in the right hand, derived from the duple più mosso material of the middle section, should sound playful. Make sure at m. 119 that the eleven-note group crescendos emerge as separate interjections.

The danger when performing this movement is in allowing the texture to become too thick; voicing to bring out the top note of the cluster on each beat is necessary. Remember that Bartók is after a certain sound effect here but needs to write out all these thirty-second notes to achieve it. Be careful that the overall design of the piece does not become bogged down by the many notes. A solidity of tempo will enhance the structural design, highlight the regular exhale/inhale quality of the pipes, and help create the overall unity desired. (This movement had been originally included as one of the episodes in the 1926 *Sonata* finale.)

"MUSIQUES NOCTURNES" [TRACK 20]

The real masterwork and central focus of the entire suite is the "Night Sounds" movement, which Bartók dedicated to his wife. (Bartók uses similar material in the slow movement of his third *Piano Concerto*, which was also dedicated to Ditta.) It is a good idea for the pianist beginning an in-depth study of the complete *Out of Doors* to concentrate his or her energies initially on this fourth movement. Bartók's writing here is complex and multilayered, and his ideal sound palette is difficult to translate. This is music that demands time and concentration; before the hands are ready to paint the picture, the brain must be able to decipher the language and understand its vocabulary.

In 1926, Bartók was also involved in editing the keyboard works of the seventeenth-century French composer Couperin. Perhaps Couperin's style of representing specific sounds influenced Bartók's choice of subjects for his *Out of Doors*. Both composers excel at imitating nature, and each is capable of expanding the color range of his instrument to achieve special effects. (Among Couperin's 240 pieces for harpsichord were compositions depicting two gondolas on the water, *Les Gondoles de Delos* and several about *La Musette*.)

In this fourth movement, Bartók achieves more than sheer imitative effects. As Beethoven did before him, Bartók asks the performer to transcend the instrument, to go beyond its limitations. Expert use of the pedal is imperative to mask the natural percussive quality of the instrument. The pianist must think orchestrally. The opening bars recall the difficult first measures of Ravel's "Ondine," from *Gaspard de la Nuit*. Their technical problems are similar. Regardless of technical considerations or instrumental limitations, from the first moment the pianist's fingers touch the keyboard a special soundscape must be created. These first measures set the tone and provide the backdrop for the entire movement. Both Bartók and Ravel do not make it easy; a new vocabulary must be learned, organized, mastered, and then translated into the right touch on the keyboard.

I live on a farm in the Allegheny Mountains of West Virginia. Sometimes I sit out on the porch and can hear the night. The buzzing sounds of the crickets and cicadas are constant. My ear quickly adjusts to these layers of sound; they are endemic to the landscape and become the backdrop for other voices that begin to emerge from the dark. It is quite amazing what one's ear can do. When concentrated, it can accept the background noise and is also capable of sorting out the other sounds that pop up from this ostinato sound stream, to hear their individual colors and textures: birds chirping at each other, most likely engaged in an important conversation, interrupted by the frequent basso interjections of the frogs in the creek, the bawling of cows out in the fields, the crickets buzzing . . . Bartók was trying to recreate a similar evening of haunting night music. Bartók's elder son, Béla, remembered that his father "would pay frequent visits to his younger sister who lived in Bekes County. His 'night music' took its origins from the same place; in it my father perpetuated the concert of the frogs and other evocative sounds heard in peaceful nights on the Great Plain."[2] Overlapping layers, each having its determined place within Bartók's structural mold, are woven in and out and form the complex texture of the night's polyphony.

It is preferable to understand initially the larger form into which Bartók pours these details to create his many layered effects; if this mold is not identified, there is a real danger of becoming completely overwhelmed and bogged down with minutiae. Basically, Bartók confines himself to a three-part structure, similar to the extended binary form of a Scarlatti sonata.

Opening section, m. 1–33
   A material (chirping birds, cicadas, frog sounds), m. 1–17

Example 6.17: *Out of Doors,* 4th mvt., p. 21, m. 9–11

B material: diatonic theme, m. 17–33

Example 6.18: *Out of Doors,* 4th mvt., p. 23, m. 16–21

Notice the similarity between this second theme and the slow movement material from the third *Piano Concerto.*

Example 6.19: Third *Piano Concerto,* 2nd mvt., Boosey & Hawkes (1947), m. 1–5, m. 48–54

Middle (developmental) section: m. 34–58

Example 6.20: *Out of Doors,* 4th mvt., p. 25, m. 37–40

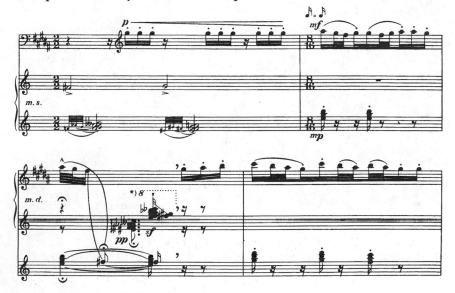

(The *sf* chord is played with the palm of the hand.)

Return: m. 58–71
  B material (combined with developmental material of middle section),
m. 58–66

Example 6.21: *Out of Doors,* 4th mvt., p. 27, m. 57–63

A material: m. 67–end

The real difficulty of this movement lies within its opening section. I spent many hours confined to that first measure, searching for the right color and touch. Bartók's writing here resembles a Chopin nocturne; the left hand provides the unity of a constant hypnotic rhythm, and above it the right hand freely and with its own rubato recreates distinctive sound effects. In other words, let not the left hand know what the right hand is doing. As with the cicadas' constant color, the ear accepts the sound plane that Bartók introduces and maintains throughout. Pedal is a necessity here, as no gaps or silences should be heard (even when going from A material to B material at m. 17, such as in example 6.18); flexible use of pedal vibrato will also help prevent the texture from thickening excessively.

I personally prefer the wet pedal/color approach, as opposed to a dry detailed landscape in which every individual note can be heard. What I want to hear is a slight overlap of colors, not the strongly etched outlines, but this is difficult to achieve and certainly only possible with an excellent color instrument. The dry approach usually sounds much too pedantic to my ears. It is an impression of sound that is wanted, not a firmly chiseled concretization.

From the very first opening measures, touch must be differentiated slightly with every chord. Even though Bartók uses the same five notes, these are rearranged with each beat; the top note of each chord, notated on the middle stave above each four-note cluster, must be audible, but just barely. I feel these opening measures organized not in three beats to a measure but in the following pattern of 4/5/4/2/3. This makes better musical sense to me and aids in the initial memorization of these complex variants.

Example 6.22: *Out of Doors,* 4th mvt., p. 20, m. 1–6

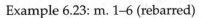

Example 6.23: m. 1–6 (rebarred)

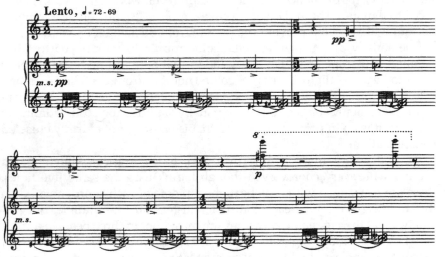

Compare these opening measures to the opening of Ravel's "Ondine."

Example 6.24: Ravel, "Ondine," Dover (1986), p. 89, m. 1

Each sound written on the upper stave imitates a different night sound and must possess a different color. It is helpful to organize this section, and to think of the first three measures as introduction, followed by an additional three-measure extended variant (notice the exact repetition of the left-hand chords of the first three measures).

At the end of m. 6 the bird chirpings begin to be heard, rather faintly at first. It helps to organize these bird sounds into three separate sequential phrases, all of irregular length, with each successive phrase being extended. The third phrase begins with a false start in m. 12 and then starts again in m. 13, building to the dynamic climax of all three phrases in m. 14, and then diminishing in preparation for the B material. Once the brain organizes and understands Bartók's phrasing, the shaping of each phrase becomes logical, facilitating the memorization of this complex material. When the vocabulary is translated and understood and has taken shape, then the entire section must be unified by its color and played as naturally and as effortlessly as possible, while maintaining a strict rhythm with the left hand. The best analogy to describe this sought-after unity would be to think of a loosely woven piece of material, characterized by varied nubby textures, little bumps randomly woven throughout the fabric. There is a shape of design that emerges, but more importantly, there is a unity and a consistency to the background of this tapestry, which is provided here by the overall color palette and by the left hand's unwavering rhythm.

Suggestions for Performance

The three successive bird-call phrases must be carefully paced, in relationship to what comes before and after. It is helpful to think of each phrase as having its own dynamic climax. The first phrase occurs in m. 7 to 9; the next variant at m. 9 to 12. The third phrase begins at m. 12, with the dynamic focus of the entire section occurring in m. 14 at the last sforzando of the measure. Notice the different accents used in m. 15:

Example 6.25: *Out of Doors*, 4th mvt., p. 22, m. 14–15

Notice the difference between the grupetti on the third beat of the second phrase at m. 9, and how it is written out in the last beat of the third phrase at m. 13:

Example 6.26: *Out of Doors*, 4th mvt., p. 21, m. 9; p. 22, m. 13

Not only is a slower metronome marking indicated at m. 13, but also the grupetti are notated to be played slower. With the use of two different accents on the first note of each group at m. 15 (example 6.25), a different touch and effect is desired in order to prepare the diminuendo and the new thematic material. Bartók gives the performer the freedom to stretch the tempo within reason and to play with rubato. (These grupetti motifs used throughout the movement will vary in accent indication, depending on their place and importance in the overall structural design.)

In m. 17 with the B diatonic material and the contrast in color, tempo, and motion, it is still important to maintain some of the background sound plane from the opening. (See example 6.18: At m. 19 the cicadas still continue their song.) Make sure to clear the pedal with pedal vibrato in m. 16. It might also be helpful at m. 17 to use the sostenuto middle pedal to hold onto the repeated G pedal, which continues for the entire section; try to put the pedal down on the last beat of m. 17. When this middle pedal is used, a different color will emerge. However, the advantage of not making use of the sostenuto pedal is in maintaining a color unity. Remember that in order to develop good pedal technique experimentation is necessary, but ultimately the ear remains the best judge of what is needed. In general, whichever pedal is used, pedal changes must not be perceptible.

For the più andante at m. 26, the pedal should be changed. A different color is desired here; Bartók's writing helps the change of color by extending the spread of the unisons in the two hands.

At m. 35, notice that the upper stave effects all begin on the offbeat, except the middle of m. 36 at the third beat. Actually, the grupetti do also occur on the fourth beat but are prepared by a crescendo before the beat. (These observations were helpful in my initial memorization, because they point out the differences in patterning.)

Example 6.27: *Out of Doors,* 4th mvt., p. 24–25, m. 34–36

Follow Bartók's instructions at m. 39: play the sforzato chord with the palm of the hand extended (see example 6.20). (The 8/16 material is a variant of the B material in example 6.18.)

At the return section (m. 58), try using the sostenuto pedal on the last beat of m. 60 to catch the D. It is important to create the impression of two distinct soundscapes coming together and moving horizontally. However, here the top stave definitely remains subsidiary to the diatonic melody. Make sure the sostenuto pedal is changed with each new pedal point (example 6.21). Another color possibility would be not to use the middle pedal, providing more flexibility to alter the pedaling as one goes along and also giving a completely different color sense to the passage. This is an individual decision of each pianist based on an imagined ideal sound. Try both of these techniques and then decide; I find myself going back and forth, depending on the hall and the instrument used.

At m. 67, notice that the left-hand cluster chords resemble the opening three-measure introduction; however the right hand is now varied with the return. (Memorization can be extremely difficult in this movement; whatever aids in remembering variants will prove useful.)

In the closing section from m. 67, think of m. 70 as if it were just an afterthought, a coda.

Example 6.28: *Out of Doors,* 4th mvt., p. 28, m. 70–71

Make sure to differentiate the touch of the last three sixteenth-note G-sharps (m. 71) from the previous three dotted-eighth-note G-sharps (example 6.28). (Changing fingers for the repeated eighth notes but playing the sixteenth notes with the same finger might help color the touch.)

The last note of the piece is the most difficult. Experiment with color: How far down can you go and still hear the sound? How long do you want the sound to linger before it disappears into the night?

Corrections from new edition:

- M. 13: In the right hand, at the second sixteenth note of the last beat of the measure, a flat sign before the E is necessary.
- M. 14: A flat sign before the E is again necessary in the right hand, but here it is on the third sixteenth note of the third beat of the measure.
- M. 48: The new edition deletes the previously printed quarter- and half-note rests in the tenor voice. (This affirms my opinion that Bartók wanted the colors to blend into each other; separations of sound should not be audible, as with the blurred visual outlines of an impressionistic canvas.)

This movement is more elusive than any of the other four pieces of the set and demands much more time to organize and learn. However, once it begins to take shape, the imaginative possibilities are infinite, and then the fun begins! The pianist can explore the sound possibilities of the instrument; with every performance, the piece will change, especially when playing on a different instrument or in a different hall. The pianist always must listen anew and ultimately learn to trust his ear. Unlike the painter, the pianist never completes the painting. As with the sounds of night, each night remains a separate memory.

"THE CHASE" [TRACK 21]

What a stunning contrast! Out of the silence of night emerges the fortissimo introduction to the chase. Begin this movement attacca, but be careful to pace your energy so that there will be enough saved for the last page. Remember, this is the exciting finish to the entire suite; after journeying so far, do not tire! This piece is most effective if tempo is maintained; then it will feel as if momentum gradually builds, cumulatively spiraling straight to the last note. (Bartók's pianistic writing aids in achieving this effect; even within Bartók's indicated tempo changes, a feeling of forward momentum is always maintained.)

The observation of accents is essential to the success of this movement and vital in creating its excitement. Notice that Bartók maintains the left-hand accents on each beat, two per measure until the middle/developmental section, when it shifts to one beat per measure (m. 91). Even though the tempo remains unchanged, the alteration of accents has the aural effect of increasing forward momentum during this complex, bravura development. It changes back to two accents per measure for four measures (m. 119), along with a decrease in dynamics, in preparation for the final return of material. After this, the pattern is not altered until three measures from the end, and then mainly in order to bring the movement to its firm conclusion by accenting the final Es of the bass figure. Accents are vital to this movement and contribute to the formal, harmonic, and dramatic logic of the finale.

This movement is the best answer to any criticism that might question constructing a composition with only repetitive material and ostinato effects. A good performance of this piece is never boring. However, to achieve the maximum excitement, it is necessary to analyze and understand the total design of the movement. After the four-measure introduction, which presents the rhythmic outline within a huge crescendo effectively made from *f* to *ff*, the next nine measures, starting from *p*, signal that the chase has begun. After the first statement (m. 14–39), followed by a six-measure bridge, the second statement is heard this time in octaves (m. 45–67), occasionally inverted, followed by a three-measure bridge. (Because of the octave piano writing and also for the benefit of the pianist, Bartók indicates a slightly slower tempo, which is barely noticeable because the pulse still remains constant.)

The middle/developmental section is pianistically the most difficult, especially the descending chordal scales beginning at m. 76 and m. 84. (The two-voice contrary motion in the right-hand writing is difficult and slightly awkward for the hand.)

Example 6.29: *Out of Doors,* 5th mvt., p. 34, m. 83–87

These chords must be prepared and played forte, staccato, and effort-lessly. The dynamic climax occurs at m. 89 with the fortissimo repeated chords; try throwing each chord for maximum effect and contrasting timbre. They should sound like bold exclamation points. Make sure that the bass as well as the right hand are both accented and that these offbeat syncopations are highlighted.

Example 6.30: *Out of Doors,* 5th mvt., p. 35, m. 88–93

Starting with m. 95, when the rhythmic accents appear only on the first beat of every measure, this section will prepare the gradual diminuendo until m. 123, when the crescendo toward the return begins again. Notice that another diminuendo occurs at m. 131, four measures before the final statement starts again from *mp*. Take full advantage of the dynamics and diminuendos Bartók indicates; these will not only help pianistically, but will also effectively and dramatically highlight the movement's structure.

(Erratum: In m. 108, a natural sign is missing before the G in the last beat chord of the right hand [corrected in the new edition].)

What is interesting here is Bartók's overall dynamic plan for his final movement. He does not need to end the movement fortissimo, mainly because rhythmic impact is a sufficient driving force. By having the dynamic climax occur in the development, where the sound is the thickest, dynamic contrast now becomes a formal device, aiding to prepare the return of the opening material. When this material makes its final return, an overall expansive effect, a stretching of its importance, is achieved. This is done by altering the bass variant and inserting the 9/8 measure.

Example 6.31: *Out of Doors*, 5th mvt., p. 38, m. 133–37

Even within the restrictive rules of ostinato bass, Bartók cleverly displays the genius of his craft. Pianistically speaking, Bartók is right to diminish the thickness of the movement toward the end; it is clarifying for the ear, as well as easier for the pianist, to bring the suite to its successful, exciting, and firm conclusion. Ultimately, it is the cumulative effect of the rhythm that will generate the movement's momentum and underscore its excitement.

Suggestions for Performance

Try to observe Bartók's metronome markings as guidelines. He goes back and forth between sections marked at 144 and at 160. Most of these are pragmatic indications in which choice of tempo depends on the difficulty of the passagework. Within the introduction, Bartók's metronomic changes indicate a gradual building of momentum to 160, when the theme is presented for the first time. When the octaves are added in its second statement, the 144 marking will be fast enough. The ear should not be able to hear a noticeable change if the pulse and forward energy are maintained.

Notice that in the final six measures, no accents are written in the right hand; here every note should be played forte with a big crescendo going to the final *f*.

Example 6.32: *Out of Doors,* 5th mvt., p. 39, m. 147–52

As I was learning this final movement, I realized that several passages, because of their irregular rhythmic stress, might benefit from rebarring during the initial memorization process.

Example 6.33: *Out of Doors,* 5th mvt., p. 32, m. 48–56 (rebarred)

Example 6.34: *Out of Doors*, 5th mvt., p. 36, m.103–5 (rebarred)

Example 6.35: *Out of Doors*, 5th mvt., p. 38–39, m. 133–43 (rebarred)

Under no circumstances should the sound be forced. If you feel that you are beginning to tire, stop and check that you are not doing something wrong, such as tensing your muscles. If you are not relaxed, you will not be able to play this movement and maximum excitement will not be achieved.

With a work of this complexity, there is the danger of concentrating too much on details and thus delivering a rather careful and pedantic performance that still correctly observes all of Bartók's markings. However, this is where your work should begin rather than end; go beyond the masses of details and risk that leap of faith in order to give the listener your own point of view. Be prepared to live with this work for a long time before even considering a public performance.

This composition demands much from the performer: stamina; complete concentration (memory is tricky!); a proper sense of pacing, combined with a flair for bravura; an ability to color and paint at the instrument; and, of course, that essential prerequisite, imagination. In depicting the sounds of the countryside, Bartók covers many different aspects of the keyboard within this challenging work. Seen as a whole, each movement concentrates on one aspect of the out-of-doors, but each has its unique place in relationship to its country neighbors.

Whether judged from the viewpoint of the pianist/performer, the composer/craftsman, or the listener/musician, the *Out of Doors* certainly deserves to be considered one of the masterworks of the twentieth century. This is music to be studied, to be performed, and to be enjoyed more with each successive hearing.

ADDITIONAL REPERTOIRE TO EXPLORE

Couperin	*Pièces*
Rameau	*Clavecin Pièces*
Scarlatti	*Sonatas*
Ravel	"Ondine" from *Gaspard de la Nuit*
	Miroirs
	Le Tombeau de Couperin
Debussy	*Preludes*
	"Pagodes" (from *Estampes*)

NOTES

1. Béla Bartók, "Harvard Lectures" (1943), in *Béla Bartók Essays*, ed. Benjamin Suchoff (Lincoln: University of Nebraska Press, 1976), 354–55.

2. Béla Bartók, Jr., "*Remembering My Father*," in *Bartók Studies*, ed. Todd Crow (Detroit: Detroit Reprints in Music, 1976), 151. [This article originally appeared in *The New Hungarian Quarterly* VII/22 (Summer 1966).]

7

+

Back to the Suite

In my opinion, all the progressive music of our day has in common two attributes which, however, are interlinked, so to speak, like cause and effect. The one attribute is a more or less radical turning away from the music of yesterday, particularly that of the Romanticists. The second attribute is the urge to approximate the musical styles of older periods. In this harking back to quite ancient musical styles . . . either there is a reversion to olden peasant music . . . or there is a reversion to the older art music—namely the art music of the seventeenth and eighteenth centuries.

—Béla Bartók[1]

The concise form of the ancient suite, with its short but contrasting movements, provided Bartók with a structural model of harmony, balance, and order. Two major works for solo piano, the *Suite* Op. 14 (1916) and the 1925 piano transcription of the orchestral *Dance Suite* of 1923, represent two separate approaches to the construction of this multimovement form and also reflect two significantly different pianistic styles: Op. 14 was born directly from simple peasant folk melodies; the 1925 piano work emerged from an earlier orchestral suite.

The *Dance Suite* with its ritornello motif looks back to the music of the seventeenth century and also recalls Liszt's motivic techniques. Most of its movements are linked together thematically by the recurring motif, and the finale functions as a summation of all previous material. It is heard more as a continuous work than the solo *Suite* Op. 14, which contains no thematic linkage between its individual movements. However, the contrasting and opposing forces of Op. 14 coexist and are unified within the

177

harmonious character of the total structure. Bartók's approach to the suite recalls Liszt's set of piano pieces, *Années de Pèlerinage,* and also resembles the contrasting character variations of Beethoven's *Diabelli Variations.*

Beethoven's influence on Bartók's compositional technique is evident. Both composers valued a musical motif, in its most concise form, to provide the material with which to demonstrate their craftsmanship. For example, Bartók's use of short motifs in the opening movement of Op. 14 resembles Beethoven's motivic development technique of the three-note motif in the opening movement of his *Sonata* ("Waldstein"), Op. 53. For both composers, the keyboard was their experimental field, and at their natural instrument they could be more adventurous. Just as Beethoven's thirty-two piano sonatas contain the seeds of what is perfectly crystallized in the string quartets, the experimental roots of Bartók's string quartets are revealed initially within his piano works. (The first *String Quartet* Op. 7 could not have been conceived without the freedom of line and melody introduced in the Op. 6 *Bagatelles.* The Arab folk influences in the slow final movement of the second *String Quartet* Op. 17 were first heard in Op. 14.)

SUITE OP. 14 (1916)

This four-movement *Suite* is not based on original folk melodies, but still possesses the strong folk flavor of Hungarian, Rumanian, and Arabic peasant music. In 1912, Bartók made a trip to North Africa to continue his study of the sources of Hungarian folk music and trace its relationship to Arabic music. It was during this visit to the Biskra region, southeast of Algeria, that he first encountered ancient string instruments, played with a bow or plucked, whose major seconds were divided into three tones instead of the usual two semitones. The fast third movement of the *Suite* imitates the whirling Bedouin dance rhythms, which Bartók experienced firsthand on this trip.

> When this work was composed I had in mind the refining of piano technique, the changing of piano technique into a more transparent style, more of bone and muscle, as opposed to the heavy chordal style of the late romantic period, that is, unessential ornaments like broken chords and other figures are omitted, and it is a more simple style.[2]

With the Op. 14, Bartók abandoned the style he had returned to briefly in his *Two Elegies,* Op. 8b and has softened and further refined the heavy percussive character of his *Allegro Barbaro,* Op. 11.

The *Suite* originally contained five movements, but Bartók removed the second-movement Andante, which had introduced the Scherzo movement. (The Andante remains unpublished but is included by pianist

György Sándor in his recent Sony recording, SK68277.) With the elimination of the Andante, three fast movements remain, making the slow Sostenuto conclusion even more dramatic. The Baroque practice of alternating slow/fast movements is here discarded by Bartók, but the customary terrace dynamics are preserved.

After listening to the Andante movement, which is written over a static F# pedal point, Bartók probably decided to exclude it because of its strong resemblance to the concluding slow movement. The *Suite* becomes a more coherent structure without the Andante. In contrast to the *Out of Doors* and the *Sonata,* Bartók does not conclude the composition with the fast, virtuosic perpetuum mobile movement. The final sostenuto movement with its veiled, ambiguous harmonies and elusive atmosphere provides a much more dramatic conclusion to the *Suite* Op. 14.

Allegretto

Suggestions for Performance

The first movement sets the character of the entire *Suite.* The spirit of the dance springs forth with lightness and flexibility. Bartók's tempo giusto is steady yet flexible, and capable of being stretched with rubatos as indicated in the score. The texture—melody and accompaniment—is now leaner, more transparent, even Mozartean. Voicing and articulation are essential. The light and bouncy dance rhythm, set within the opening four-measure staccato introduction, is constant and not altered significantly with the introduction of the melody. It is useful for the performer to remember that this is music meant for dancing. When performed well, this opening movement should bring a smile to the listener's face—its charm and humor must be communicated.

The first two notes of the melody must be light and staccato and should create the impression, without an accelerando, of forward motion toward the longer accented quarter notes at the midpoint and conclusion of the phrase. The tempo remains steady, although the harmonic change at the end of the phrase (m. 12) demands a little more time on the quarter notes. Bartók builds into his writing the slight breaths needed at the end of each vocal line.

Example 7.1: *Suite*, 1st mvt., Dover (1998), p. 52, m. 1–12

In the second *mf* repetition of the theme, notice the accent over the top G while the accompanying tenor voice remains staccato.

Example 7.2: *Suite,* 1st mvt., p. 52, m. 25–28

The sixteenth-note writing in the middle section provides an excellent exercise for independence of hands; the steady right-hand staccato accompaniment should not be inhibited by the sixteenth-note motion of the left, and all accents must be observed. The transition (m. 37–52) to this middle section recalls the "A Bit Tipsy" mood of the second *Burlesque.*

The transition from the meno mosso to the return must be natural and seamless. Instead of writing the expected crescendo, Bartók asks for a diminuendo back to Tempo I. He carefully indicates the terrace dynamics desired.

Example 7.3: *Suite*, 1st mvt., p. 54–55, m. 76–92

The dialogue exchange of the last page should sound witty and droll. Here, Bartók makes the most out of this simple three-note motif:

Example 7.4: *Suite*, 1st mvt., p. 55, m. 105–17

Scherzo

This effective movement is a study of touch, color, and contrasting sound planes. Broken augmented triads contrast with minor seconds and major ninths, and the tritone functions here as a consonance. This sarcastic, spicy movement sounds as if it could have been written by a young Prokofiev. The humor is dry, sharp, always witty, and very much to the point. Bartók provides the pianist with a funny, quirky, and rather likeable cast of characters.

Suggestions for Performance

Pay attention to articulation and to every rest indicated. These directions elucidate Bartók's phrasing and contribute to the humorous effect of this movement.

Example 7.5: *Suite*, 2nd mvt., p. 56, m. 1–8

Example 7.6: *Suite*, 2nd mvt., p. 56, m. 33–38

Make use of the C sostenuto pedal throughout the middle section: what a stunning color contrast to the pointed articulation of the opening section.

(Errata: The initial metronome marking makes more sense as 132.[3] Also, the tranquillo indication at m. 33 should be 92, the same tempo as indicated for its return.)

Allegro molto

This movement is not as difficult to play as the last movement of the *Out of Doors*. The writing here is much more pianistic, is less orchestrally conceived, and fits more easily under the fingers. Bartók indicates non legato, which is necessary in order to hear the right-hand melody articulated over the crescendos of the ostinato bass. The scherzo's sharp, etched-in-concrete directness is now replaced by a surging whirlwind dervish. The dramatic excitement of this movement is best achieved by strict control and maintenance of tempo. This three-part form, based on an ostinato figure that spans a tritone, is an excellent example of Bartók's variation technique; a figure never repeats itself in exactly the same way. As also heard in the previous scherzo, the tritone, with repetitive usage, functions as a consonance.

Suggestions for Performance

Make sure the sostenuto pedal is used on the second eighth-note bass in the last measure to prolong the D. This final D has to be caught with the middle pedal and held through the final measure. Bartók indicates attacca for the final movement, and the D continues to be heard as the pivotal note. It functions as an ending as well as a beginning.

Example 7.7: *Suite*, 3rd mvt., p. 67, m. 131–34

Use pedal sparingly in this movement. Pedal vibrato is recommended and will help the articulated eighth notes to be clearly heard.

Example 7.8: *Suite*, 3rd mvt., p. 63, m. 34–37

(I have indicated the fingering that works best for my hand, which is small and doesn't reach beyond a ninth.)

Exploit sharp color contrasts and the antiphonal character of the poco più mosso section. Think of brass or woodwinds. Carefully pace the dynamics with the return of the first theme, but be sure to save enough for the last page and its final measures.

(Note: For me, the allegro molto tempo works better at 144, not 124 as indicated in the score. Bartók plays this movement faster than 124 on his recordings.)

Sostenuto [Track 22]

The real drama of the *Suite* occurs not within the third virtuosic movement, but with the harmonic ambiguities and chromatically sliding rhythms of the *Suite*'s final sostenuto movement. Using the sound palette of French composers Debussy and Ravel, and recalling "Le Gibet" from *Gaspard de la Nuit,* swinging back and forth in the wind, Bartók creates a special atmosphere, an almost impressionistic canvas, awash with color and pedal effects. Veiled shadows from Dante's world seem to move in and out of focus. Beginning the movement on the dominant of the B-flat tonal center, the key center eventually appears as a pedal point in the right hand but is surrounded by harmonic ambiguity. From a simple three-part structure of minimal material, Bartók molds a poignant concluding statement.

Suggestions for Performance

Voicing and color possibilities are vast, and are essential to a good performance. Always be aware of the line, but distinguish what is foreground melody and what will remain background accompaniment. Within the chordal accompaniment, melodic voicing is essential.

The four-measure più sostenuto middle section with its chromatic harmonic changes should contrast the outer sections, which move horizontally over static pedal points. This episode, more vertical in its orientation with its faster harmonic changes, creates an underlying dramatic tension resolved only with the return section.

Experiment with pedal and color effects throughout, especially in the last six measures. How much pianissimo is possible while still retaining the general outline? The bold colors of the second and third movements have here dissolved into soft pastels.

Example 7.9: *Suite,* 4th mvt., p. 69, m. 29–35

Although not as outwardly virtuosic a composition as the *Sonata* or the *Out of Doors*, the difficulties of the *Suite* Op. 14 abide within its apparent simplicity. Similar to its Baroque models, this work is a study in economy and contrasts. Textures are lean, details exposed, filler eliminated. Playing the Op. 14 is like handling a fine piece of crystal; special care and attention are always required. As with a Mozart sonata, the music should emerge sounding fresh and spontaneous. However, for music to sound effortless requires a considerable effort! When performing the *Suite* Op. 14, the pianist must not interfere with or inhibit its natural rhythmic dance spirit and should concentrate on maintaining the harmonious balance of each movement while paying attention to its place within the larger design of the *Suite*.

DANCE SUITE (1925)

This is a piano transcription, made by the composer in 1925 from his 1923 orchestral suite commemorating the fiftieth anniversary of the unification of Pest and Buda. (Three prominent Hungarian composers were asked to write works for this special occasion; Kodály wrote *Psalmus Hungaricus* and Ernö Dohnányi contributed *Festival Overture*, Op. 31.) Bartók had composed two orchestral suites during the years 1905–1907 but had waited for fifteen years to write the *Dance Suite*. This work can be heard as Bartók's direct response to all accusations regarding ardent chauvinism and nationalism. Within one work, comprised of five dances, including ritornell and finale, Bartók has evoked and united folk material from Rumanians, Slovaks, Arabs, and Hungarians. The *Dance Suite* does not contain direct quotes of original folk tunes, but it mirrors with every detail the spirit of the national character of these peasant sources.

> No. 1 has partly, while No. 4 entirely an Oriental (Arabic) character. Ritornell and No. 2 have a Hungarian one; in No. 3 Hungarian, Rumanian, moreover Arabic influences alternate with each other; the theme of No. 5 is so primitive that one cannot speak of any kind of character but of a primitive peasant one, and must give up any classification according to nationality.[4]

(Originally, the third movement of the *Suite* was to be Slovak in character, but it was omitted from the orchestral version; the third movement became Hungarian and Walachian.)

All of these folk sources become united in the finale of the *Dance Suite*. It is right to assume, as Bartók himself observed: "This could not have been written by anyone but an Eastern European musician."[5] Surely it must be played as if an Eastern European, intimately acquainted with the dance steps of his native land, were performing the work in full native costume!

Bartók was very much influenced by Liszt's compositional craft. For him, the *Sonata* in B minor was revolutionary; its form, perfection. The ritornell used in the *Dance Suite* functions similarly to the opening motto theme of Liszt's B minor *Sonata*, appearing at the conclusion of the first, second, and fourth movements as well as in the finale.

Example 7.10: *Dance Suite*, 1st mvt., Boosey & Hawkes (1925), p. 6, m. 118–32

The *Suite* is linked together by this shared ritornell, which also provides the lyrical relief, and is then summarized in the finale by a recapitulation of thematic material. (Liszt also used the same technique in the finale of his first *Piano Concerto*.) Similar to the design of the Liszt *Sonata*, which can be organized into more than one formal mold, these six separate dance movements may also be viewed on two different planes. As a four-movement structure, the first three dances comprise the first movement; the fourth dance, the slow movement; the fifth, the scherzo movement; followed by the last movement finale. When interpreted within the context of a one-movement work, the *Suite* is organized by exposition (first, second, and third movements); middle section: minidevelopment (fourth and fifth movements); and recapitulation (finale). The continuous and cumulative nature of these six dance movements strongly suggests a one-movement, three-part outline.

The piano transcription, which remains completely faithful to its orchestral model, never achieved the popularity of the original *Dance Suite*. The work is extremely difficult, and for this reason most pianists do not choose to spend the necessary time required to master it. However challenging the writing may be, it is always pianistic, obviously written by a composer and performer who knew the instrument and understood how far virtuosity could be stretched. (Among Bartók's twentieth-century contemporaries,

Prokofiev also wrote for the instrument from a similar pianistic point of view, whereas both Shostakovich and Stravinsky seemed to have ignored the natural rules of piano technique with their generally awkward and unpianistic writing. Since Shostakovich was known to have been a very good pianist, his approach to the keyboard seems rather surprising.)

With this piano transcription Bartók reveals a significantly different orientation toward the piano. The leanness of texture of the Op. 14 is replaced here by a thicker and much more intricately woven fabric. The simple homophonic vocal model of melody plus accompaniment is still present, but its heavier texture indicates that Bartók started with a rich and varied orchestral sound palette already in his ears. From this sound plane, he then proceeds to extract a two-hand piano reduction, which accounts for the different approach to the piano writing. Passagework frequently is written as filler to prolong pedal sonorities. Had Bartók originally composed the *Dance Suite* for piano, its style would probably have been less repetitive, much simpler, and more similar to his Op. 14. The pianist must not only solve the increased pianistic difficulties of playing an orchestral transcription, but must also make its musical problems work using the restrictions of the instrument. Variation of color is possible in both versions, but the orchestral context can absorb repetitive material more effectively. (Bartók uses the same compositional approach with his difficult piano transcription of the orchestral work *Two Pictures*, Op. 10.)

Although the wide dynamic resources of the full orchestra are not available to the piano, Bartók's extremely virtuosic and naturally pianistic writing makes it easier for the pianist to explore the inherent orchestral sonorities and rich color possibilities of the instrument. Substituting the medium of the solo piano for the diverse but sometimes scattered timbres of the orchestra provides Bartók with a more unified sound, similar to the homogeneous fabric of stringed instruments within a string quartet. The ear naturally adjusts to these boundaries, and contrasts can be equally bold and dramatic. Thus, the solo and orchestral versions of the *Dance Suite* emerge as two separate and quite individual sound paintings, each possessing its own integral unity. (Liszt and Busoni achieved a similar result with their transcriptions of Bach's organ compositions, transcriptions that must qualify as separate works apart from their original source. Even though thematic content remains identical, the technical differences inherent in the two instruments alter the character and the musical style of the transcribed work. From a Baroque organ composition emerges a romantic hybrid piano work.)

It is recommended that this work first be studied at the keyboard. The pianist's imagination will have greater freedom to flower. Having reached a comfortable familiarity with the piano version, looking at Bartók's orchestration will then spark many more color possibilities. Bartók achieves wonderful orchestral effects: the opening bassoon melody and the trombone and brass of the second movement, the antiphonal string and brass writing in the third movement, the English horn solo and harp writing in the fourth movement, the trumpets of the finale, and the uniquely individual colors and voice clarity created with doubled brass and woodwinds. All are impossible to duplicate at the piano. However, the imaginative pianist, possessed with a good technical facility and knowledge of his instrument, will be able to deliver a different but totally satisfying performance of the *Dance Suite.*

As with most solo transcriptions of orchestral works, what formerly was divided among many instruments is now transferred to one soloist, who has only two hands to carry the entire load. Because of these orchestral roots and the piano's limitations, frequent use of the middle sostenuto pedal will be necessary throughout the *Suite* to faithfully observe all of Bartók's pedal points.

Example 7.11: *Dance Suite,* 1st mvt., p. 3, m. 21–35

Example 7.12: *Dance Suite,* 1st mvt., p. 4, m. 42–55

Example 7.13: *Dance Suite*, 1st mvt., p. 5, m. 76–81

Example 7.14: *Dance Suite*, 1st mvt., p. 5, m. 100–104

What the conductor can quickly evoke, with a simple hand gesture to various sections of the orchestra, the pianist must now deliver immediately and with the indicated subito color contrasts. The finale is probably the most difficult movement of the *Suite* because of these rapid sectional shifts.

(Note: A new edition of the *Dance Suite* with revisions by Peter Bartók was published by Boosey & Hawkes in 1991. The new edition includes markings for four optional cuts, suggested by Bartók to pianist György Sándor, who presented the world premiere of the work in February 1945.)

First Section: First, Second, and Third Movements

The opening melody of the *Dance Suite* is built on a four-note chromatic motif, unusual for Bartók's compositional style but probably influenced by the Arab music and microtonal folk instruments heard on his trip to

North Africa. Bartók was very much aware of the theorists who analyzed his work. Anticipating their pigeonholing his music into one category or another, Bartók directed his comments about the opening
theme to all of them.

Example 7.15: *Dance Suite*, 1st mvt., p. 3, m. 1–13

> My first "chromatic" melody I invented in 1923. I used it as the first theme of
> my *Dance Suite*. This music has some resemblance to an Arab melody. This
> kind of melodic invention was only an incidental digression on my part and
> had no special consequences.[6]

A great flexibility of rhythm is required in these first three movements.
The underlying pulse of these tempo giusto dance movements must be
maintained (usually by the left-hand bass accompaniment) while allowing for rhythmic shifts and occasional stretchings of tempo. Articulation
is essential and will help to make the rubatos indicated in the score sound
more like the natural continuation of the rhythmic pulse.

Example 7.16: *Dance Suite*, 1st mvt., p. 4, m. 48–75

The a tempo markings act as structural guideposts and frequently help to clarify the reasoning behind Bartók's detailed tempo indications. These metronomic indications are the checkpoints that will provide essential clues to the character of the dance. (When I am relearning a piece, I find it useful to pull out the metronome and check tempi; it's helpful for future performances to know if you're prone to exceeding the speed limit or if you can afford to go heavier with that gas pedal.)

After the larger formal design has been identified, the structural marking points should be noted, as they will help provide the basic outline and define the boundaries into which the short motif's irregular rhythmic patterns are developed. Despite all the irregular, rhythmic sequencing, a basic underlying pulse is always necessary to provide stability and the foundation for the dance. A proper balance of breathing spaces, combined with a constant rhythmic momentum, must be found, and this becomes the greatest difficulty in performing this work. What will tie together all the motifs and fragments is the underlying pulse. The fast, syncopated rhythms in the second dance are difficult. Its repetitions need to be analyzed; understanding its sequential patterns will aid with memorization.

Example 7.17: *Dance Suite*, 2nd mvt., p. 7–8, m. 26–50

I find it easier to organize this passage, after the initial eight-measure statement, into two similar three-measure units (2/4, 3/4), followed by two similar groups of two-plus-one measures in 3/4, followed by one measure before the subito piano. The more familiar and comfortable Bartók's piano writing and dance rhythms become, the more the overall logic and design of the work will be revealed.

The second and third movements abound in interesting fourth sonorities. A recurring and unifying structural theme in the second movement consists of fourths alternating with tritone chords, which create a wonderful coloristic effect. (In the original work, this is effectively played by the trombones.)

Example 7.18: *Dance Suite*, 2nd mvt., p. 10, m. 85–93

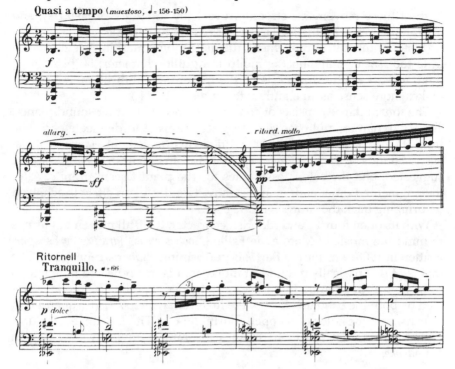

Bartók makes sure that the ritornell of the second movement is not repeated in exactly the same manner as stated in the first movement (example 7.10). He writes a melodic variant of the original simple but poignant melody.

In these first three dance movements, there are plenty of opportunities to experiment with orchestral sonorities and create effective color contrasts. Minimum use of pedal will be helpful, especially when carving out sudden sharp rhythmic outlines. Contrasts abound within the third dance. It begins as a seemingly innocent, light, and playful bagpipe dance but is interrupted by antiphonal brass effects, followed by a whirling-dervish-type dance and a brief return to its opening playful character before Bartók introduces a heavier stomping peasant dance. The sforzando chordal sonorities toward the end of this movement should imitate the doubled brass section.

After carefully working through the difficult details within these first three movements, all the pieces must be put back together, with the larger structural outlines predominant. Try to avoid too much fragmentation.

Second Section: Fourth and Fifth Movements [Tracks 23 & 24]

Both of these movements strongly reveal the influence of Debussy, and also allude to the Moorish character of Arabic folk music.

(Note: In the fourth movement, the metronome marking seems to be a little too fast to maintain the molto tranquillo character; 50 per dotted quarter works better for me. Also the metronome indication at a tempo makes more sense as an eighth note equals 132–144.)

The fourth dance consists of contrasting and alternating sound planes. Terrace dynamics and change of register are used to delineate each one from the other. Bartók might have titled this movement *Hommage à Debussy*. Sounds of *La Cathédrale engloutie* and his orchestral *Nocturnes* are suggested, and the color possibilities for the pianist seem infinite. After the augmented quiet ending, notice how wonderful an effect is achieved by bringing back the ritornell in the coda.

With its open fourths and Moorish character, the fifth movement brings to mind the music of Manuel de Falla. (*Noches en los Jardines de Espagne*, written in 1908, was part of Bartók's performing concerto repertoire.) The theme of this basically minimalist movement is one repeated note with a three-note appoggiatura motif over a static pedal point. The mood is created by both the ostinato effect of the material, which is also sequenced in fourths, and the color of its open fourth chords. The last three measures with their chordal fourth harmonies resemble Stravinsky's writing in *Petrouchka*.

Example 7.19: *Dance Suite*, 4th mvt., p. 19, m. 24–26

Third Section: Finale

The motif of the fourth spills over into the finale's introduction. Melodies are more difficult to extract here because of a thicker texture. Here the melodic line remains the most important, and once found, it must never be lost.

Example 7.20: *Dance Suite*, 5th mvt., p. 20, m. 1–10

With its rapid and dramatic sectional contrasts and variants of touch, articulation, sonorities, and texture, the finale qualifies as the most technically challenging movement of the entire *Suite*. When the pianistic problems are solved, the impression of ease, spontaneity, and joy will project the spirit, vitality, and true character of the work, which is all about rhythm and dance.

PETITE SUITE (1936, REVISED 1943)

For this work, Bartók transcribed Nos. 28, 38, 43, 16, 36, and 32 from his set of *Forty-Four Duos*, originally written in 1931 for two violins. The duos are Bartók's only set of teaching pieces for the violin and are comparable to his two sets of piano teaching pieces from 1908, *For Children* and *Ten Easy Pieces*. All are based on folk material (Hungarian, Slovak, Rumanian, Serbian, Ruthenian, and Arab melodies). The piano work generally remains faithful to the musical material of the original, with only minor changes made because of the instrumental differences between the piano and violin. This is why the piano writing appears awkward in places. Certainly, this suite is not as naturally pianistic as the music Bartók wrote originally for the piano. Here, and elsewhere in transcribing, it appears that Bartók the composer overrules Bartók the pianist-performer.

The key to a successful performance of this very effective work is maximum exploitation of contrast. The individual character of each movement must be captured by the pianist: the dirgelike heaviness of the "Slow Melody"; the joyfulness and abandon of the "Walachian Dance"; the cumulative dervish effect of the "Whirling Dance" (here, the MM seems to be in error; it is much slower than Bartók's interpretation and too slow to create any sense of wildness; try 144); the charm and coquettish quality of the "Quasi Pizzacato" (Bartók indicates a tempo of 116, much faster than the tempo heard on his recordings; the tempo of 104 is less pushed and allows for the rubato playing so necessary to make this piece effective); the naïve simplicity of the opening melody of the "Ukrainian Song" and the humor of its un poco più tranquillo theme; and finally the fun of playing the virtuosic "Bagpipe." Bartók has given the pianist a work that should appear more frequently on recital programs.

SUITE FOR TWO PIANOS OP. 4B (1941)

This work was transcribed for two pianos from the second orchestral *Suite* Op. 4, written between 1905 and 1907. Bartók returned to this work many times and each time made revisions. The fourth movement finale was written two years after composing the first three movements, and in 1941 Bartók transcribed the orchestral work for two pianos so that he and his wife Ditta would be able to perform it together. Bartók was particularly fond of this work, for it represented to him:

> . . . the freshening up of art music with elements of peasant art which had been untouched for many centuries . . . the fresh air that breaks into the closing movement preserved the experiences of my first folk song collecting tour.[7]

The *Suite* marked a turning point in Bartók's compositional style between the embracing of the old and the emergence of a new writing style. It also helped prepare the way for his Op. 6 *Bagatelles*, which would be the first significant piano work completely written in this new style. The second orchestral *Suite* represents a bridge between romantic stylized folk music, as represented in works of Liszt, Brahms, Smetana, and Dvořák, and that which is more directly folk-inspired. In this work, Bartók still vacillates between the two. His fourth movement, per finire, begins in his new style but then lapses back into a Wagnerian/Tristan digression that is charming but totally unexpected. The Op. 4 also represented a personal marking point for Bartók; beginning with its first performance, the composer noticed increased animosity and total rejection of all of his works by the Hungarian musical elite.

Bartók had originally called the entire composition *Serenade*; later he used this title only for the first movement. It sounds as if Brahms had written this serenade, with occasional bits tossed into the pot from Liszt's *Hungarian Rhapsodies*, Wagner's operas (especially *Tristan*), and also Richard Strauss. Bartók's working out of motifs recalls the motivic techniques of Beethoven and Strauss. In the second movement, "Allegro Diabolico," a fugue is substituted for the developmental middle section, a technique Bartók refined and later used in his 1926 *Sonata* and also in the *Sonata* for two pianos and percussion. Throughout the *Suite*, Bartók's color palette alludes to the music of Debussy and Ravel.

Listening to both versions of the *Suite* Op. 4, it is difficult to choose which medium works better overall. The playful and backbiting character of the fugue in the second movement seems to be enhanced by the uniformity of the two-piano color serving as a backdrop for its sharp barbs. Even the thick Brahmsian string writing of the opening movement sounds more dated and exaggerated than the later, simpler two-piano transcription. However, the third movement, "Scena della Puszta," with its bass clarinet opening and string and harp writing, proves to be much more effective in its original orchestral version. When two pianos play this movement, the sentimentality of the romantic melodies dominates, instead of its wonderfully rich and contrasting melodic colors. However, both versions are interesting and, unfortunately, too rarely heard in concert.

NOTES

1. Béla Bartók, "The Folk Songs of Hungary" (1928), in *Béla Bartók Essays*, ed. Benjamin Suchoff (Lincoln: University of Nebraska Press, 1976), 331.

2. Béla Bartók, "Béla Bartók's Last American Radio Interviews," in *Bartók Studies*, ed. Todd Crow (Detroit: Detroit Reprints in Music, 1976), 138. [This was originally published in *New Musical Review* VI/12 (December 1955).]

3. According to László Somfai, head of the Bartók Archives in Budapest, the original metronome markings for each movement in the first edition were 140/152/144/120–130. With the 1927 revised edition, Bartók changed these to 120/122/124/120–110.

4. Béla Bartók, "Hungarian Music" (1944), in *Béla Bartók Essays*, ed. Benjamin Suchoff, 396.

5. Bartók, "Hungarian Music" (1944), 396.

6. Béla Bartók, "Harvard Lectures" (1943), in *Béla Bartók Essays*, ed. Benjamin Suchoff, 379.

7. Béla Bartók, as quoted by Ernö Lendvai in the notes to the sound recording *Béla Bartók Complete Edition*: Hungaroton (LPX 11398).

8

+

Ten Plus Nine
Plus Two Plus . . .

Again and again I ask myself: Can one make a synthesis of these three
classics (that is Bach, Beethoven, and Debussy) and make it a living one
for the moderns?

—Béla Bartók speaking to Serge Moreux (1939)[1]

Artists have been known throughout history to "steal" from each other,
or, as expressed more politely, to gain inspiration from each other's
work. Perhaps T. S. Eliot said it best: "Immature poets imitate; mature poets steal; bad poets deface what they take, and good poets make it into
something better, or at least something different."[2] Picasso, Stravinsky, and
Bartók immediately come to mind as artists of the twentieth century who
were true synthesizers. They were capable of transforming what might be
a continuation of tradition by their contemporaries into something
uniquely personal; the traditional supplied the seeds from which the new
and the genuinely modern could blossom and flourish. What universal elements did they retain, and how were these absorbed and uniquely syn-
thesized within their creative work?

Bartók was strongly influenced in his youth by many late-nineteenth-
century composers: Brahms, Reger, Strauss, Liszt, Wagner. However, only
Liszt's influence managed to survive. Liszt passed on to Bartók a unique
pianistic legacy, both as a virtuoso performer and as a composer. Bartók's
compositional craft was developed initially by the study and performance
of Liszt's piano works. Liszt's music provided the foundation upon which
Bartók's natural pianism and pianistic technique could flourish, and
Liszt's work also served as basic models for formal and structural design.

Whereas Liszt gave Bartók the necessary tools with which to craft his trade, Bach, Beethoven, and Debussy provided him with the musical models. The classical elements of conciseness, economy, form, and structure—all the universals Bartók admired—were part of these composers' aesthetic and were characteristic of Bartók's mature work. The four principal works discussed in this chapter clearly demonstrate these composers' influences. The *Rondos* are classic not only in design, but also in the simplicity of their folk material; the *Burlesques,* which could be regarded as three twentieth-century versions of Beethoven's *Bagatelles,* demonstrate Bartók's craftsmanship in the use of Beethoven's motivic technique. The *Dirges* are pure Debussy, reflecting the French composer's unique approach to color and his individual concept of time and space; the *Nine Little Piano Pieces* of 1926 look back to the linear imitative writing of Bach and to his expressive and dramatic use of melody.

> When the restrictions of using the simplest means are put on the composer, the difficulty increases. For, generally, restrictions demand greater mastery of technique.[3]

Similar to the increased simplicity and childlike innocence found in Prokofiev's later piano works that followed his three massive "War" *Sonatas* (Nos. 6, 7, and 8), Bartók's new pianistic style eliminated everything that was nonessential to clarity of line and directness of statement. Both composers instinctively understood that profundity does not necessarily imply complexity; a simple unmannered melody can also provide the perfect foil needed to explore even the painful emotional depths hidden beneath the surface.

Listening to the opening measures of Bartók's first *Rondo* [Track 25], based on a child's nursery tune, evokes a melancholy sense of nostalgia linked, perhaps, to a memory of lost innocence (example 8.19). When transported from its roots and placed into Bartók's unique sound world, the emotional fabric of the peasant melody becomes transformed.

With the *Four Dirges*, Op. 9a, Bartók creates a series of mournful lamentations from simple fragments of folk song. (After hearing the sense of grief and heaviness of soul Bartók is able to convey in the third dirge [example 8.15], it is quite amusing to discover that the original words of the folk song describe the lament of a cowherd for his cows who have wandered off while he is fast asleep in the barn.)

The three *Burlesques,* Op. 8c, a series of character pieces, use motivic folk material to suggest three different soundscapes: a quarrel, a drunkard's stroll, and a humorous view of a series of sprightly antics. Even with the more sophisticated imitative piano writing (see the later *Nine Little Piano Pieces* of 1926), Bartók's simple folk melodies, heard within this complex texture, stand out in bold relief because of their very directness. The folk tune in Bartók's hands has been molded into a more complex statement possessing many emotional layers to be explored and peeled away in search of its core.

Bartók's music based on classical models could also bear the label *romantic* because of its wide expressive palette. Bartók equated the word *romantic* with a florid, excessive, hyperemotional nineteenth-century style; the composer's new language was a reaction against all that. However, in a more generalized sense, when applied to Bartók's folk material, the word *romantic* also can describe emotional expressivity. From Liszt, Bartók inherited a virtuosic romantic approach to the keyboard, as evidenced by some of his earlier piano works (e.g., the Op. 1 *Rhapsody, Four Early Pieces, Two Elegies,* Op. 8b). However, even though Bartók's new pianistic style did eliminate the excesses of Lisztian bravura, the basic elements of romantic nineteenth-century piano technique pervade all his works and serve as the strong foundation for a much leaner keyboard approach. Neither Bartók's piano music nor certainly his natural pianism would have existed without the legacy of Franz Liszt. Within the twentieth century, Ravel, Bartók, and the Russian school of composers, including Prokofiev, Scriabin, and Rachmaninoff, continued to build upon Liszt's romantic pianistic tradition.

THREE BURLESQUES, OP. 8C (1908–1911)

These three compositions not only expose Bartók's playful sense of humor but also reveal the pianistic roots of which he was not ashamed. The first piece is Bartók's equivalent of Chopin's B-flat minor *Sonata* finale, and also includes an allusion to Liszt's well-known *Mephisto Waltz.* In the final burlesque, the ghosts of Maurice Ravel and Richard Strauss are very much in evidence. These three pieces were not originally intended as a group; the first was initially written to be a companion piece for the first *Sketch* of Op. 9b ("Portrait of a Girl"). These compositions could be precursors to Prokofiev's *Five Sarcasms,* written a few years later (1912–1914), and all three are scherzos intended as musical jokes.

"Quarrel" (1908) [Track 26]

Bartók married Marta Ziegler, his sixteen-year-old piano student, in 1909; they were divorced in 1923. This piece was dedicated to Marta and perhaps served as a prediction of their future together. It is witty and droll and depicts the bickering of two parties. An unpublished title page reads: "Rage over an interrupted visit/ or/ Rondoletto à capriccio/ or/ Revenge is sweet/ or/ play it if you can/ or/ November 27/ Please choose from these titles!"[4]

In the first episode, his view is presented.

Example 8.1: *Burlesque*, 1st mvt., Dover Series II (1981), p. 83, m. 60–72

Followed by more back-and-forth quarreling, her view is heard. I find this passage reminiscent of Marguerite's sentimental melody from Liszt's *Mephisto Waltz.*

Example 8.2: *Burlesque*, 1st mvt., p. 84, m. 88–91

Judging by the closing sforzando Cs of the last four measures, a resolution is finally reached, but the composer has not revealed which party has emerged victorious.

Built on a four-note motif, resembling the finale of Chopin's B-flat minor sonata, this piece is difficult to play with the required evenness and lightness. Try using the fingering 1-2-1-2-1-4 in the left hand of the opening motive. This will enhance clarity and articulation.

Example 8.3: *Burlesque,* 1st mvt., p. 85, m. 115–24

Like Liszt, Bartók makes use of several varieties of accents. They fulfill different functions musically and structurally and contribute to the ongoing momentum.

Example 8.4: *Burlesque*, 1st mvt., p. 86, m. 130–44

"A Bit Tipsy" (1910) [Track 27]

This composition was a favorite performance piece of the composer. With his use of rhythm, long and short accents, and dissonant appoggiaturas, Bartók portrays a man who has had a little too much to drink, reeling from side to side as he tries to walk. Bartók used this piece as the fourth sketch in his 1931 orchestral work, *Hungarian Sketches*.

Example 8.5: *Burlesque,* 2nd mvt., p. 88, m. 3–6

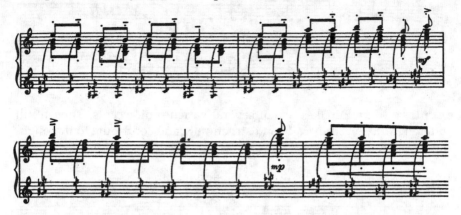

Bartók indicates molto rubato in the first measure. Think of the five beats in *mp* at m. 5 as a parenthetical insert, an echo effect to the previous measure. Bartók inverts the first section upon its return and even reverses some of the arpeggios.

Example 8.6: *Burlesque,* 2nd mvt., p. 91, m. 48–55

Try to make the most of this funny ending. The drunk is no longer staggering, but falls down to rest in the final measure. Finally, he's out cold.

"Capriccioso" (1910)

This is the only piece of the set without an official title. However, Bartók might have called it a homage to Ravel's "Scarbo" or to Strauss's *Til Eu-*

lenspiegel. The three-part episodic piece is a bit like a butterfly: light, fleeting, hard to catch, difficult to pinpoint, and always free to fly away. With a simple three-note motif, Bartók creates some wonderful color effects with his leggiero piano writing.

Example 8.7: *Burlesque*, 3rd mvt., p. 92, m. 1–10

The three separate voice lines should be maintained, always paying attention to the melody line, which must sound through.

This passage always reminds me of the writing in the second burlesque:

Example 8.8: *Burlesque*, 3d mvt., p. 95, m. 87–96

With the a tempo return, the texture becomes thicker; here, Bartók maintains two independent sound planes.

Example 8.9: *Burlesque*, 3rd mvt., p. 98, m. 144–53

Bartók gives the performer all the ingredients to make this music sound funny. Study it seriously; play it tongue-in-cheek.

FOUR DIRGES, OP. 9A (1909–1910)

These four compositions qualify as romantic because of their emotional roots. Dirges function as a necessary part of the mourning process within folk culture. (Bartók was not familiar with the Hungarian folk laments until 1915, when he and Kodály started collecting and recording them; he had heard only Rumanian laments in 1909, but these were sung in quite a different style and did not resemble the Hungarian lamentations. When Bartók composed these dirges in 1909, he intuitively captured the essence of the Hungarian lament without having heard it previously from the peasants.)

From the first chords of the opening dirge, evoking memories of "Clair de Lune," Debussy's presence is overwhelming. There is no doubt that the impressionist's canvas was the model for these soundscapes, and inspired the pianistic color and pedal effects required by the performer. Bartók's usual directness is replaced here by blurred boundaries and faint outlines, as evidenced by an overlapping wash of color and harmonies. Ever the master of the variant, Bartók molds minimal material into a three-part design built around one dynamic climax. He has written a seamless, through-composed composition, one carrying an extremely heavy emotional burden.

Four Dirges, No. 1 [Track 28]

This piece would serve as an excellent exercise in pedaling techniques and also could be used to enhance the art of concentrated listening. Bartók's pedaling directions in the first eight measures call for a seamless interpretation from the pianist.

Example 8.10: *Four Dirges* No. 1, Dover Series II (1981), p. 100, m. 1–8

Two separate sound planes are operating and must be distinguishable by color even though pedaled together. The pedal changes must not be noticeable. The depths of grief are captured here with few gestures: no animation, no heroics, just a dark heaviness deep within the soul.

Example 8.11: *Dirge* No. 1, p. 100, m. 9–14

The first dirge is constructed from a three-part dynamic plan. The *ff* represents the climax of the entire piece, which begins *pp*, builds to *ff*, and returns to *p*. (The coda, recalling the dynamic design and built over the tonic pedal point of B major, begins *p* and builds to *f* with a final return to *pp*.)

Four Dirges, No. 2

The dynamic design of the second dirge is based on a gradual increase in dynamics, building to a *ff* climax toward the end of the composition and only returning to *pp* within its last few measures. Bartók provides a kaleidoscope of color changes based on one simple folk melody. The second dirge was also used as the third sketch in Bartók's orchestral *Hungarian Sketches* (1931). This same folk melody was also used by Bartók in his fourth *Bagatelle*. However, here, the original seven-syllable line has been enlarged to thirteen. In the fourth bagatelle it appears as eight syllables.

Example 8.12: *Dirge* No. 2, p. 102, m. 1–7

Example 8.13: *Bagatelle* No. 4, Dover Series I (1981), p. 74, m. 1–2

Every statement of the melody differs slightly from the previous statement, and the melody climaxes with its final statement.

Example 8.14: *Dirge* No. 2, p. 103, m. 48–55

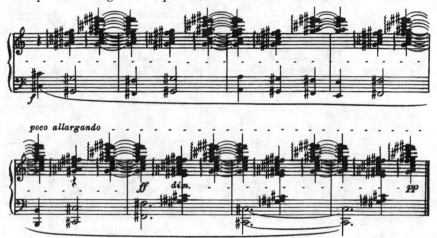

Four Dirges, No. 3

Even though the original folk melody tells of a farmer's lament for his runaway cows, because of its opening measures this dirge should bear the name *dies irae*.

Example 8.15: *Dirge* No. 3, p. 104, m. 1–4

The pianist must find the right touch, color, and feeling for each of the piece's two separate sound planes and concentrate on controlling the gradually increasing dynamic intensity. Similar in design to the first dirge, this piece builds to a dynamic climax of *ff* in the middle and descends back to *pp*.

Four Dirges, No. 4

The final dirge is the largest composition of the entire set and, technically, its most difficult. The dynamic design of the three-part form building from *p* and climaxing at *ff* is similar to that of the other dirges, but here the scale has become much more inflated.

Example 8.16: *Dirge* No. 4, p. 106, m. 39–49

The arpeggios in the left hand are difficult. Allow enough time and make sure the pedal catches the entire chord. When the arpeggios return *p*, make sure that the melody voice is heard and not lost.

Example 8.17: *Dirge* No. 4, p. 107, m. 56–65

Experiment with color and pedal in the coda. This is the ending to the entire set and therefore carries more weight. The sound of the last three octaves in the right hand should be suspended in space and allowed time to diminish gradually—to die a natural death.

Example 8.18: *Dirge* No. 4, p. 107, m. 66–70

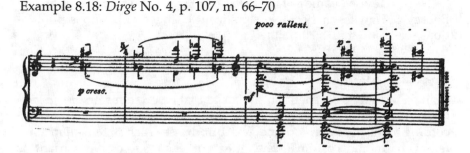

After studying these pieces, it also becomes apparent that Bartók was greatly influenced by Liszt's late piano compositions.

These four canvases, which describe different aspects of grieving, are analogous to the set of paintings of Rouen Cathedral by the Impressionist painter Claude Monet. He captured the cathedral at different times of the day, with different lighting, and by using a variety of color palettes. Each painting of the same subject altered the set of variables ever so slightly. The results were comparable, yet very different. Each of the four dirges functions in a similar manner. Bartók permits no exaggeration of sentiment; every word spoken has been chosen with great care. How emotionally profound the dirges become within their lean simplicity. How challenging and how difficult for the performer to go deep enough within himself to explore these emotions, to convey that mysterious, distant, and unfrequented world.

THREE RONDOS ON FOLK TUNES (1916–1927)

The *Three Rondos* demonstrate two different approaches used by Bartók when adapting the folk tune to the keyboard. The first rondo, written in 1916, resembles the transcriptions of folk songs found in Bartók's earlier compositions—*Rumanian Folk Dances, Three Hungarian Folk Songs, Fifteen Hungarian Peasant Songs, Sonatina*. The folk tune is transcribed with its melody basically unchanged but its harmonic language very much altered. The second and third rondos, written in 1927—in Bartók's mature, sophisticated, and sometimes contrapuntal style of the 1926 period—boast a dissonant vocabulary of cluster chords with increased emphasis on percussive martellato rhythms, and a fragmented, motivic, and more developmental sense. Whereas the first rondo presents a folk song in rondo form, the second and third rondos become compositions in rondo form that also include the folk song. In eleven years, Bartók's pianistic style had developed. Simplicity is still very much in evidence but is now veiled and surrounded by an increasingly dissonant harmonic vocabulary.

(Note: A revised edition of the *Rondos* by Peter Bartók was published by
Boosey & Hawkes in 1995. No significant changes to previous publications are found in this edition.)

Rondo No. 1 (1916) [Track 25]

Using a technique of repetition similar to that heard in his first *Improvisation* (1920), Bartók takes a simple folk tune and repeats it three times according to the lines of its original text, but dresses each statement in a different harmonic costume. The effect of each successive variant is
stunning; it is repetitive but not repetitious, always slightly different than
what was heard previously. Bartók combines the simplicity of melody
with harmonic interest but never interferes with the naïvely innocent feeling of the total statement.

Example 8.19: *Three Rondos* No. 1, Boosey & Hawkes (1957), p. 1, m. 1–23

Transparency of texture and clear four-part voice writing characterize
this opening rondo. At the end of the second line repetition, with the
overlapping of the third phrase, the voice leading toward the cadence
and the simultaneous beginning of the repeated melody should be delineated. This also applies to the two-measure transition to the allegro
giocoso section. Here Bartók asks for a large ritenuto (molto!). Enough

time must be taken to bring out the separate voice lines and prepare the next contrasting section with a large crescendo in the tenor voice, while still maintaining the feeling of a rhythmic pulse. Notice that the ritenuto is twice as slow as the tempo of the allegro giocoso. Thinking of this allegro giocoso section rhythmically in two, with emphasis on the squareness of the dance rhythm, will help create the jaunty, carefree feeling Bartók is looking for here.

(Note: There are several ossias (alternative versions) suggested by the composer. In several passages of the first and third rondos, Bartók suggests doubling the melody line with octaves. Even though these passages are technically more difficult, the octaves help achieve the appropriate increase in dynamic character.)

Based on a child's nursery tune, the first rondo is a particular favorite. I am attracted to its Mozartean, even Schubertian qualities. Bartók's key shifts from E major to A-flat major have a definite touch of Schubert about them, don't they? Perhaps Bartók was also thinking of Schumann's *Kinderscenen* when he wrote this rondo: both are about innocence and childhood, and the composers intended these compositions to be played not by children, but by adults sophisticated enough to believe in innocence.

Rondo No. 2 (1927)

It is immediately noticeable from the dissonant, droning seconds and sevenths in the opening measures of the second rondo that the writing eleven years later is not as transparent and is technically much more difficult. Some phrases hint at the piano writing that will come later in the third *Piano Concerto*'s second movement's adagio religioso.

Example 8.20: *Three Rondos* No. 2, p. 5, m. 22–36

Example 8.21: *Piano Concerto* No. 3, 2nd mvt, Boosey & Hawkes (1947), p. 44, m. 99–100

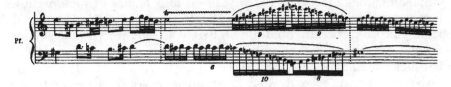

Bartók employs a greater and more extreme range of contrasts here than in the first rondo. In general, the piano writing has become more complex; dynamics cover a wider spectrum. The startling contrasts ensure that the simple folk tunes will sound even more naïve and innocent by comparison. Whereas Mozartean control is called for with the first rondo, this piece demands that the performer roll up his sleeves and pull out all the stops.

Rondo No. 3 (1927)

The third rondo is the most fragmented and sectional of the three, and Bartók's contrasts are more extreme. Its opening measures in the piano's lower register recall *Allegro Barbaro* and "With Drums and Pipes" from the *Out of Doors.*

Example 8.22: *Three Rondos* No. 3, p. 11, m. 1–5

Make sure that dynamics are well paced, especially when confined to the range of forte.

As with the repetition technique of the opening melody of the first rondo (example 8.19), Bartók at the molto tranquillo of m. 54 makes the most of repeating a simple tune by changing registers, transferring hands, and varying touch and articulation.

These three rondos sound deceptively simple, but, as is universally known, sometimes what is simple is also the most profound and, yes, also the most difficult to perform! The key ingredient necessary for a good performance of these rondos and also vital to their formal design is contrast: not only contrasts within each of the three rondos but also among each of them when performed as a set. The *Three Rondos* work extremely well on recital programs, especially when placed after the interval. They are the perfect length to introduce a larger work and, more importantly, are quite accessible for the public to hear and enjoy.

NINE LITTLE PIANO PIECES (1926)

This set of piano pieces was originally published as *Nine Little Pieces* in three separate volumes. The four dialogues, inspired by Bach's two-part inventions, comprise the first book. Four dances, including a "Menuetto" and three others in duple rhythm—"Air," "March of the Beasts," and "Tambourine"—make up the second book. Book III is devoted to the last piece of the set, "Preludio-All' Ungherese," written in two parts and by no means a "little" piano piece! (Note: Boosey & Hawkes has recently published a new edition that contains all nine pieces within one volume; this is the edition I have referenced.)

It is doubtful whether Bartók intended all nine pieces to be performed together as a complete set. The programming of one of these books or a selection of pieces is a much better concert solution for both performer and audience.

Book I: Four Dialogues [Track 29, No. 4]

> In recent years, I have considerably occupied myself with music before Bach and I believe that traces of this are to be noticed in the (lst) *Piano Concerto* and the *Nine Little Pieces*.[5]

Bartók's later, more sophisticated style is characterized by an increased use of contrapuntal techniques. This was demonstrated in the opening movement of his 1926 *Sonata,* especially in the fugal writing of its development, and certainly provides the inspiration for the first four pieces. These dialogues can be compared to Bach's two- and three-part inventions, and connections to earlier keyboard masters, such as Frescobaldi, Zipoli, and the French clavecinists Rameau and Couperin, are also appropriate. (During this 1926 period, Bartók was also occupied with editing the keyboard works of these early masters.)

A more polyphonic, linear texture is now evident with an increased use of canon, fugato, inversion, and freely imitative writing throughout. Unlike Schoenberg, Bartók never adheres to a rigid set of rules or a strict formula. Just look at the set of canons Bartók writes in his first dialogue.

As the three-part piece progresses, the rules begin to change. Bartók starts the canon a sixth below and one measure apart (example 8.23); then writes the canon a fifth apart (example 8.24); in the middle section he returns to the canon a sixth below, but now the time interval is shortened to one-half measure (example 8.25) and then continues with the canon a fifth below. Bartók concludes the piece with the canon a third below and with only one quarter-note beat between (example 8.26). Clearly, Bartók adjusted his own set of rules as the piece progressed.

Example 8.23: *Nine Little Piano Pieces* No. 1, Boosey & Hawkes (1954), p. 1, m. 1–5

Example 8.24: No. 1, p. 1, m. 6–10

Example 8.25: No. 1, p. 1, m. 15–18

Example 8.26: No. 1, p. 2, m. 34–41

(Erratum: The time signature at m. 34 should be 4/2, not 3/2.)

All four dialogues are cast in three-part form. The second dialogue is much freer in its imitation, with a canon making an appearance only in its return section. The third piece resembles Bartók's later piano writing in the slow movement of his third *Piano Concerto* (1945).

Example 8.27: *Nine Little Piano Pieces* No. 3, p. 6, m. 5–8

Example 8.28: *Piano Concerto* No. 3, 2nd mvt., Boosey & Hawkes (1947), p. 43, m. 91–95

This third dialogue also looks ahead to the opening fugal movement of Bartók's 1936 orchestral masterwork, *Music for Strings, Percussion, and Celeste,* and suggests as well the chromatic linear writing of his third and fourth string quartets. The fourth piece, clearly the most technically difficult of the four, is a wonderful example of freedom from the bar line and complete independence of hands. Once the rhythmic shifts become comfortable and second nature (so you don't have to think about them and count out loud!), this piece is great fun to play.

Suggestions for Performance

These first four pieces provide an excellent reminder of the importance of form in helping the performer shape a work. Dynamic indications are a useful aid in this sculpting process. Notice that the first piece journeys from *p* to *f*, then from *mf* to conclude *ff*. In both the first and fourth pieces, the pianist must differentiate between two different accents, > or ^, which are related to dynamic levels. The form of the fourth piece is shaped by these accents: The middle section lowers the dynamic level to *mf* and introduces the canon in the left hand; the return becomes a canon between two voices, with each voice retaining complete independence to insure that the syncopated accents of the theme will be clearly heard. Performed consecutively as a recital opener, these four pieces are extremely effective. (Erratum: The MM marking of the third piece should read dotted quarter [not quarter] equals 44.)

Book II

The four dances in Book II represent a twentieth-century vision of Schumann's nineteenth-century character piece. The texture is lean and transparent as well as imitative, but polyphony is not the central focus here as it was in the first book. These pieces are much sharper and more angular in style than the preceding linear dialogues. Bartók also reveals a sarcastic wit, combining playful humor with biting irony.

The "Menuetto" could be called a parody of a minuet. Its sparse material, leanness of texture, and basic simplicity contribute to an overall humorous effect. It needs to be played with a straight-faced, deadpan approach in strict tempo. If the low As are played seriously, then they will really be funny. (This passage is reminiscent of the drums from the first piece of the *Out of Doors,* written during the same period.) This is minimalism at its best; Bartók leaves the impression that he has not written one note too many.

Example 8.29: *Nine Little Piano Pieces* No. 5, p. 13, m. 42–51

The sixth piece, "Air," provides in its middle section an example of the simple, childlike innocence of the folk tune, surrounded in its outer sections by aggressive and angular sforzandos. Here Bartók allows the lyrical and the percussive elements to coexist, but contrasts must be exploited for maximum effect. This piece also recalls the expressive feeling of Bartók's first *Rondo* (example 8.19).

"Marcia delle Bestie" comes from the same family of folk dances as the second-movement "Bear Dance" of the *Sonatina* (1915) and the final "Bear Dance" from the earlier *Ten Easy Pieces* (1908). Cast in a larger, more extended three-part form, which includes an imitative motto/ritornello theme used as a structural marking point, this piece is the most technically difficult dance of the second book. Contrasts are rapid, and because of leanness of texture, any technical problems will be clearly exposed. Bartók makes effective use of the various registers of the keyboard. This dance demands more time and effort to digest than the other dances of this volume.

Written in a leaner percussive style than the 1911 *Allegro Barbaro*, "Tambourine" also looks back to the virtuosic keyboard writing of Domenico Scarlatti. "Tambourine" uses very minimal thematic material, and Bartók's shifting rhythms and sharp accents make repetition interesting and exciting. However, these rhythmic variants also make memory more difficult, as accents are irregularly dispersed and appear in unexpected places. An absolutely strict tempo is essential and spare use of the pedal required. Many later twentieth-century composers have been influenced by Bartók's martellato rhythms. Alberto Ginastera or Samuel Barber might have written this work; in fact, many years after 1926, they both did rewrite it! (Look at the "Danza Criolla" in the *American Preludes* of Alberto Ginastera, and also the final *Excursion* of Samuel Barber's set of piano pieces.) This piece would make a wonderful encore to a varied recital program.

Book III: *Preludio-All'Ungherese*

The final piece, based on one simple folk melody, embodies all the characteristics of Bartók's later piano style: leaner, more linear texture; increased use of imitation; basically not complex harmonies; sharp rhythmic shifts; a lyrical simplicity of melodic line; and a maximum exploitation of minimal motivic material. Written in two sections, the ninth piece makes use of one theme for both parts, only altered by rhythm and tempo.

Example 8.30: *Nine Little Piano Pieces* No. 9, p. 25, m. 5–9 molto moderato

Example 8.31: No. 9, p. 28, m. 52–60 allegro non troppo, molto ritmico

The piano writing in this final piece is not easy, especially in the second statement and coda of the second part, but it always is pianistic. (Bartók's suggested 2-1 alternation of fingers on the repeated left-hand figures is helpful.)

The *Nine Little Piano Pieces* (1926) are neither little nor easy, but all are worth exploring. The piano writing suggests and already looks toward Bartók's last major work for piano (without orchestra), the *Sonata for Two Pianos & Percussion* (1937).

TWO PICTURES (DEUX IMAGES), OP. 10 (1910–1911)

These transcriptions for the piano from the two orchestral pieces should not be confused with the *Two Portraits* for orchestra of Op. 5. (The second piece of the Op. 5 set is an orchestral transcription of the fourteenth *Bagatelle*, "Ma mie qui danse.") *The Two Pictures*, "In Full Bloom," and "The Village Dance" are interesting for the pianist, more musically than pianistically. Since the Op. 10 pieces are the most heavily orchestrated of Bartók's orchestral compositions, adding four trumpets and celeste, in addition to three players on every woodwind part, it is apparent that Bartók started from an orchestral color and sound palette. The first piece is strongly influenced by Claude Debussy's orchestral set of nocturnes, although Bartók's harmonies are not quite as static. "The Village Dance" is typical of Bartók's folk music writing, but this piano reduction is certainly not as pianistic as the solo *Improvisations* or *Fifteen Hungarian Peasant Songs* (discussed in chapter 4).

OTHER TRANSCRIPTIONS FOR SOLO PIANO

"Marcia Funèbre," sections 9 and 10 (1905) from *Kossuth* (for orchestra, 1903)

Bartók wrote this ten-part patriotic tone poem when he was only twenty-two. Halsey Stevens, Bartók's principal biographer, labeled *Kossuth* "a Hungarian's 'Hero's Life,'" and both Strauss and Liszt are heard as major influences. Liszt's *Hungarian Rhapsody* No. 2 is freely paraphrased in the "Marcia Funèbre." The seeds of Bartók's Op. 1 *Rhapsody* have already been planted.

The Wooden Prince, Op. 13 (one-act ballet, 1914–1916, transcribed for piano solo in 1921)

The orchestral score was transcribed for piano mainly for rehearsal purposes, to prepare the ballet before the full orchestra and conductor appeared. It is an excellent study guide for the student who wants to see and hear how Bartók has integrated the tale with what is happening in the music. However, it would not be suitable performed on its own as a solo piano transcription.

Sonata for solo violin (1944): *Tempo di Ciaccona* and *Fuga*, transcribed for solo piano by György Sándor (1977)

This is a faithful adaptation for keyboard of the first two movements of Bartók's last finished work, the four-movement *Sonata* for solo violin, commissioned by Yehudi Menuhin. This work is not pianistic; what is missing are the sounds of the bow crossing the strings to create thick chordal string sonorities. My preference would be to hear the work as Bartók wrote it—for the violin.

XVII and XVIII Century Italian Cembalo and Organ Music Transcribed for Piano (1926) (originally published in eleven volumes by Carl Fischer in 1930)

These piano transcriptions of Italian Baroque keyboard music that Bartók made during 1926 influenced his original works from this prolific period. Between 1925 and 1926, Bartók made five trips to Italy and purchased for his own library several reference books on early Italian keyboard music: Torchi's *L'arte musicale in Italia*, Volume III; *Antichi Maestri Italiani* ("Toccate" and "Fughe" volumes); and Pauer's *Alte Meister*: Volumes 3, 5, and 6.

Bartók made no apologies for utilizing all the resources of the modern-day piano when playing a work originally written for the clavecin or harpsichord.

> I think one ought not to assume the attitude of resurrecting the imperfections of the clavecin, the undeveloped ancestor of the piano, when dealing with old keyboard music for performance on the piano. It is highly probable that if, in some wonderful way, these old composers had suddenly become acquainted with the pianoforte, after a few short trials they would have recognized the advantages of the new instrument and would have altered accordingly the performance of their compositions. I think that any old clavecin music has to be performed in accordance with its character, utilizing all the perfections of the piano today.[6]

Bartók is not afraid of adding octave passages and pedal markings to enhance the color and texture of the original composition. However, these transcriptions are not the equivalent of Liszt and Busoni's nineteenth-century romantic, virtuosic transcriptions of Bach's original organ works.

In addition to transcriptions of compositions by Marcello, Rossi, della Ciaia, Frescobaldi, and Zipoli, Bartók also transcribed Bach's sixth *Organ Sonata* for piano (published by Rózsavölgyi in 1930) and five pieces by Purcell; several of these were published posthumously.

Bartók's transcriptions of his own music demonstrate how often he returned to his previous works in search of material for new compositions. Obviously, he approved of his earlier efforts. Coinciding with his serious folk music research, Bartók's personal language evolved in 1907, early in his composing career. After that, he never detoured from his set path, possessing the strength not only to know when to shed the youthful influences of Strauss, Reger, and Brahms, but also the good sense to decide what had to be retained in order to achieve complete balance and unity of musical style. How different a personality he was from Stravinsky, with his many stylistic periods and frequent twists and turns in the road.

Bartók's pianistic approach seems much more aligned with Prokofiev's piano writing. Both were terrific pianists who knew and respected the instrument and were at their most adventurous when writing for the piano. They built upon the grand romantic tradition of piano playing and used their pianistic tools to provide them with the foundation and freedom for an individual approach at the keyboard. However, Prokofiev, the "Russian Liszt," as he was nicknamed by Poulenc, possessed a brash, extroverted, and virtuosic pianism, well grounded within the Liszt tradition. Bartók's piano music, less obvious at first hearing and often needing to be translated and extracted from its many layers, is more akin to Beethoven's economic, motivic, and minimal compositional style. Prokofiev wrote in prose; Bartók composed poems.

What accounts most significantly for their different directions is Bartók's use of folk music, which remained at the core of his work after 1908. The basic simplicity of the folk tune allowed not only greater complexity within its surrounding harmonic language, but also provided the proper foil for the intricate compositional contrapuntal devices that Bartók was so fond of exploiting.

Both Bartók and Prokofiev were endowed with the gift of directness of musical statement, but often arrived there by taking totally different routes. Prokofiev allows the pianist to see behind his music much more readily; once the pianistic problems have been overcome, the directness of material and its sweeping pianism make the real impact. Bartók supplies many more layers, musical as well as emotional, that need to be sifted through before any understanding can begin to take place. The vocabulary is much harder and requires time to acquire fluency. Bartók thrives on these internal complexities, while Prokofiev demonstrates in a more outwardly bravura fashion pianistic difficulties that demand resolution. Whereas Prokofiev could be described as a ballet composer for the keyboard, with all the acrobatics and leaps in prominent view, Bartók always remained the anthropologist, trying in his music to capture the magical spirit he had experienced firsthand when he went out to search the Hungarian countryside for real peasant life.

Throughout his life, Bartók purposefully avoided theories and theorists to explain his work. As with Bach, Beethoven, and Debussy, no arbitrary turns existed, only a clear unwavering sense of direction and purpose.

I do not care to subscribe to any of the accepted contemporary musical tendencies . . . my idea is a measured balance of these elements.[7]

NOTES

1. Béla Bartók, "*Bartók, Schoenberg, Stravinsky*" by János Kárpáti," in *Bartók Studies*, ed. Todd Crow (Detroit: Detroit Reprints in Music, 1976), 93. [This article originally appeared in *The New Hungarian Quarterly* VII/24 (Winter 1966).]

2. T. S. Eliot, "Philip Massinger," *The Sacred Wood* (London: Methuen & Co. Ltd., 1928), 125.

3. Béla Bartók, "The Relationship Between Contemporary Hungarian Art Music and Folk Music" (1941), in *Béla Bartók Essays*, ed. Benjamin Suchoff (Lincoln: University of Nebraska Press, 1976), 352.

4. *Piano Music of Béla Bartók*, Series II, ed. Benjamin Suchoff (New York: Dover, 1981) xxi.

5. Béla Bartók, as quoted in Halsey Stevens, *The Life and Music of Béla Bartók*, 3rd ed., ed. Malcolm Gillies (New York: Oxford University Press, 1993), 231–32.

6. Béla Bartók, "The Performance of Works Written for the Clavecin" (1912), in *Béla Bartók Essays*, ed. Benjamin Suchoff, 285.

7. Bartók, as quoted in Stevens, *The Life and Music of Béla Bartók*, 307.

9

✛

The Composer as Teacher

The *Mikrokosmos* may be interpreted as a series of pieces in many different styles, representing a small world, or it may be interpreted as a world, a musical world for little ones, for children.

—Béla Bartók[1]

For Bartók, children represented hope for the future. "He had a great devotion to children," said his eldest son Béla in a 1966 interview. "He regarded them as the raw material from which a finer humanity could be shaped."[2] The enthusiasm, passion, and commitment Bartók brought to his folk music research were similarly channeled toward music education.

In 1907, four years after graduating from the Budapest Academy of Music, Bartók was offered the piano chair, succeeding his piano teacher, István Thomán. One year later, the Hungarian publisher Rozsnyai asked Bartók to edit some of Bach's keyboard music and to compose some easy pieces for the beginning student; the *Ten Easy Pieces* (discussed in chapter 2) were the result. Bartók edited and reorganized the forty-eight preludes and fugues from *The Well-Tempered Clavier* into two volumes in order of pianistic difficulty; the series begins with the G major *Prelude and Fugue* from Book II of the WTC and concludes with the B major *Prelude and Fugue* from the WTC, Book II. This was followed in 1909 by *For Children*, two volumes of short pieces based on Hungarian folk tunes, and two more volumes based on Slovak melodies, published in 1910.

In 1912, the Hungarian publisher Rózsavölgyi asked Bartók to construct a piano method that would take the pianist from the beginning to the most advanced level. Having had no previous experience teaching beginners, Bartók asked a colleague, Sándor Reschofsky, to collaborate with him on this project. In total, five volumes were produced, with Bartók contributing original pieces only for the first volume of the set; Reschofsky supplied the finger exercises and basic outline and was also responsible for Volumes 2 and 5. Volume 3 consisted of thirteen pieces from *Anna Magdalena Bach's Notebook*, edited by Bartók, and Volume 4 was written by Sándor Kovacs. Bartók's original pieces for Volume 1 were published in 1929 under the title *The First Term at the Piano*.

These early but brief pedagogical activities helped prepare Bartók for his monumental teaching work, the *Mikrokosmos*, which he began to write as early as 1926. According to Bartók, one *Mikrokosmos* piece had been originally intended to be the tenth piece for the set of the *Nine Little Piano Pieces*, composed during that year, but was somehow omitted from publication. Bartók subsequently made it part of his six-volume set of 153 pieces, completed in 1939.

> Already at the time I was thinking of writing very easy music for the teaching of beginners. It was only in the summer of 1932 that I really began working on it, and at that time I composed about forty pieces. In 1933–34, I wrote another forty pieces, and an additional twenty in the following years. Finally in 1938 I had 100-odd pieces together. But there were still some gaps. I filled these (1939) and completed the first half of Volume 1. I had an excellent opportunity to test these pieces in practice right at home. In 1933, my son Peter pleaded with us to teach him the piano. I had a daring idea and undertook this unaccustomed task myself. Besides vocal and technical practice, the child was given only pieces from *Mikrokosmos* to play. I hope they proved useful for him, but I must admit that this experiment taught me a great deal, too.[3]

Bartók's words confirm that with the continued writing and compiling of the pieces for *Mikrokosmos*, he was still directly involved with the piano even during the eleven years between 1926 and 1937, which was a lean period for piano composition. Between the prolific piano year of 1926, which produced the *Sonata, Out of Doors*, the *First Piano Concerto*, and the *Nine Little Pieces* and 1937, when Bartók wrote the *Sonata for Two Pianos and Percussion*, very little was published for solo piano. Only the *Second Piano Concerto* (1930), the *Petite Suite* of 1936 (transcriptions from the forty-four violin *Duos*), and the last two pieces of the *Three Rondos* (1927) date from this period, during which Bartók was writing his third, fourth, and fifth string quartets as well as his major orchestral work, *Music for Strings, Percussion, and Celeste*. However, at this time, he was composing simple pieces for his nine-year-old son Peter to learn at the piano.

MIKROKOSMOS

It was to Peter Bartók that Bartók dedicated the first two volumes of the six-volume *Mikrokosmos*: 153 pieces arranged in order of difficulty, with supplemental exercises included within the first four volumes and notes supplied by the composer. (The other four volumes Bartók dedicated to "children and their children," and the last six pieces of the set, *Dances in Bulgarian Rhythm*, were dedicated to the British pianist Harriet Cohen.)

> During the period when I knew him my father generally accepted only advanced piano students. Nevertheless, when I was about nine years old (1933), he agreed to start teaching me from the very beginning. His teaching program did not follow an accepted "piano school" technique. At first I was to sing only. Later, exercises were improvised, directed partly at the independent control of the fingers. In the course of our lessons he sometimes asked me to wait while he sat down at his desk, and I would hear only the scratching of his pen. In a few minutes he would bring to the piano an exercise, or a short piece, that I was to decipher right away and then learn for our next lesson. So were born some of the easier pieces of these volumes. However, he kept on producing others at a much faster rate than I could learn them. He wrote the little compositions as the ideas occurred to him. Soon there was a large collection to choose from, so I could learn those assigned to me from a fair copy of the manuscripts.[4]

Bartók wrote the first four volumes of the *Mikrokosmos* with the purpose of covering all the technical pianistic problems of the beginning student. The work is progressive, beginning with the most simple teaching pieces and advancing to the most difficult concert compositions of Volumes 5 and 6.

> The first four books of these piano pieces have been written for the purpose of giving material to beginners—young or old—which should embrace, as far as possible, all problems met with during the first steps. The first, second, and third books are designed for the first, or first and second year. These three books differ from a "Piano Method" in the traditional sense by the absence of any technical and theoretical description and instruction. Every teacher knows what is required in this respect and is able to give the earliest instruction without reference to a book or method. There are frequently several pieces dealing with the same problem, to give the teacher and pupil an opportunity of making a choice. It is not necessary to study all ninety-six pieces (Volumes 1–3).[5]

Bartók frequently included a group of pieces from the last two volumes of *Mikrokosmos* in his own piano recitals. Of the 153 pieces, 55 were part of his performing repertory. An excellent CD, recently reissued by Sony (MPK 47676), includes enchanting performances of Bartók playing selections from Volumes 3 through 6. He also arranged seven pieces from the set for two pianos so that he and Ditta could perform them together in concert: Nos. 69, 113, 123, 127, 135, 145, and 146.

Bartók recommended that pieces from *Mikrokosmos* be supplemented with singing and key transposition exercises and that Volume 4 be combined with a study of smaller pieces by J. S. Bach from Bach's *Anna Magdalena Bach Notebook*, and with technical studies by Czerny. He also noted in his introduction that some pieces would be suitable for harpsichord. Bartók saw these pieces as providing excellent sight-reading material for the advanced student.

In general, the six volumes of *Mikrokosmos* can be divided into three distinct groups: pieces for beginners (Volumes 1 and 2 and part of Volume 3); easy pieces for performance (part of Volume 3, Volume 4, and part of Volume 5); and difficult concert pieces suitable only for the advanced pianist (Volume 6 and part of Volume 5).

The titles included in the first four volumes are self-explanatory, with some of these pieces augmented by Bartók's notes explaining Bulgarian rhythms, contrapuntal techniques, the use of modes in folk tunes, etc. (Bartók did not include the notes about modes in the Hungarian edition, assuming that all Hungarian children knew the origins of their own folk music; these notes were printed only for the foreign-language editions.) Only three compositions from the entire set are based on actual folk material.

> My idea was to write piano pieces intended to lead the students from the very beginning and through the most important technical and musical problems of the first years, to a certain higher degree. This determined program involves a very strict proceeding: there must be no gaps in the succession of the technical problems, which have to follow each other in a very logical order. Of course, the realization of such a plan could hardly be based on folk music; it would have been quite impossible to find folk melodies for every technical or musical problem. So I decided to write pieces on entirely original themes. The whole collection, about 150 pieces, is entitled *Mikrokosmos*.[6]

Bartók also indicated that the metronome markings in the first three volumes should be flexible and varied, according to the individual student's level; however, all metronome indications in the fifth and sixth volume are to be followed as strictly as possible.

What Bartók gives to the beginning piano student is the material necessary to achieve complete independence and equalization of both hands at the keyboard. Rarely is the right hand favored over the left. Rhythmic restrictions of the bar-line are gradually removed, with the student required to play irregular rhythms and shifting meters as easily as if they had been notated squarely in 4/4. By learning Bartók's modal vocabulary, the ear is also freed from traditional major or minor expectations. This provides excellent material when dealing with the problematic beginner who refuses to read and relies on his ear instead; very often the culprit is the talented and gifted student who is blessed with perfect pitch.

Every piece of this set demands attention and discipline. These volumes read like a catalogue of twentieth-century compositional techniques: fourth chords, cluster chords, major and minor seconds, syncopation, inversion, mirror technique, free canon, etc. The music is concentrated; nothing is filler; nothing is given a literal repeat. Variation and contrast remain the vital ingredients of Bartók's style. These pieces are liberating not only for the fingers but also for the ears and for the mind.

For the more advanced beginner or the adult beginner, these short works from Bartók's later period provide insight and close observation into Bartók's compositional techniques. They reveal a further purification of his style. Their economy and brevity also contribute to their difficulty. Each is concerned with form, variation, and contrast achieved within a small, confined, generally three-part structure. No matter what the level of difficulty, these compositions should be approached similarly, with proper attention given to every detail. Bartók himself described these works as "a synthesis of all the musical and technical problems which were treated and in some cases only partially solved in my previous piano works."[7]

Volume 1 (1–36)

What is remarkable about the first book is that upon completion, the young beginner has learned to identify, define, and demonstrate at the piano a wide musical vocabulary including unison playing (1–6); parallel motion (11, 16); dotted quarter notes (7); syncopation (9, 27, 33); imitation (22, 23, 25, 29); inversion (23, 25); canon (28, 30, 31, 36); Dorian mode (32); Phrygian mode (34); and contrary motion (17). Bartók includes explanatory notes to help both the student and the teacher understand his language. He also demonstrates the concept of question-and-answer phrasing techniques by including a short children's piece (14) to be sung before it is played. He liberates the young pianist with his use of modal key signatures (10, 25), thus insuring that the student must learn to read without relying only on his ear. The chromatic exercises in the appendix also expand the conventional ear.

Most of the short two-voiced pieces are written in 2/4, 4/4, or 3/4, but Bartók also introduces the young student to 3/2, 2/2, and 6/4 rhythms, and the "Slow Dance" (33) provides some interesting and challenging cross-rhythms. Notice the use of nothing rhythmically smaller than quarter notes, which comfortably fit into the five-finger hand position. Dynamics are introduced by No. 22, and legato playing and expressiveness are called for in the "Pastorale" (24).

The student who is able to play through Volume 1 is on his way to achieving complete independence of the two hands. For the gifted student, transposition into other keys of some of the easier pieces would be beneficial.

Volume 2 (37–66)

Now the student begins to become musically much more sophisticated. The pieces are longer and more suitable as recital compositions, but still lie basically in the five-finger position. Bartók no longer confines himself to quarter-note writing. The pianist is introduced to the Lydian (37, 55) and Mixolydian modes (48); the difference between staccato and legato touch (38, 39); crescendo and diminuendo (49); accents (57); sforzato (47); pentatonic chords (61); major and minor juxtaposition (59); chromatics (54); minor sixths in parallel motion (34); triplets (55); augmentation and diminution (46); the minuet (50); and broken triads (42). Bartók now makes use of varied time signatures, including 5/4 (48) and even inserts a one-measure rhythmic change to 9/8 within a 6/8 composition (41). The rhythms are always varied and interesting and never seem imprisoned by the bar-line (41, 47).

Even when writing for the young student, Bartók is unpredictable and usually avoids squareness of phrasing. "Méditation" (45) consists of five asymmetrical phrases: three five-measure phrases followed by two six-measure phrases. In this volume, several pieces are included to be played with second piano accompaniment (43, 44, 55), and one composition (65) is written out for voice accompanied by a harmonically adventurous chordal piano part, but may be either transcribed by the student for solo piano or played as a duet with his teacher. Bartók felt that it was important to introduce young pianists to ensemble playing at an early age and also to expand their musical vision by occasionally giving them three staves of music to read.

The later pieces in this volume further challenge the imagination of the student rhythmically, harmonically, tonally, musically, and also technically. "Accents" (57) travels far harmonically, with changing key signatures inserted between six- and eight-measure phrases. This piece is modeled on the strophic folk song; Bartók introduces the student to varied accents and four-voice writing, and he inserts a breath (/) after every phrase. Both hands are treated equally and require complete rhythmic independence. "In Oriental Style" (58) leads to foreign and surprising cadences. "Major and Minor" (59) is a study of bimodality, with each hand juxtaposing different modes. Bartók resolves the conflict by ending on a single C, but forces the student to listen to how he arranges his twelve tones and expands his harmonic palette. "Canon with Sustained Notes" (60) is reminiscent of one of Bartók's earlier *Dirges*. "Buzzing" (63) seems to be a skeletal reduction of "From the Diary of a Fly" (142) in Book 6. "Pentatonic Melody" (61) and "Minor Sixths in Parallel Motion" (62) stretch the ear and move away from conventional tonality. "Line against Point" (64) is written in two parts, with the second part a chromatic compression of the original; here, Bartók allows the student to observe firsthand one of his sophisticated compositional techniques. The appendix includes a pedaling exercise and some studies in phrasing and chordal playing.

Volume 3 (67–96)

This volume expands the student's technique by focusing on chordal playing, thicker piano writing, more complex rhythms, increased dissonance, and the challenges of shaping a longer work. Book 3 also provides an excellent opportunity for the teacher to begin a discussion of the principles of form and structure. What is immediately noticeable is the variety of compositions the composer now offers the student. "Dragon's Dance" (72) is a character piece filled with tritones, written to challenge the imagination of the young performer. Two pieces are written out as a piano solo but also scored for voice with piano accompaniment (74, 95). "Hungarian Dance" (68) is arranged for two pianos. In No. 70, Bartók introduces the student to a piece that simultaneously uses two different key signatures. With "Hommage à J. S. B." (79), Bartók recalls one of Bach's two-part inventions. He plays with the major and minor third; the last two measures remind me of the clarinet and piano dialogue at the conclusion of the third *Piano Concerto*'s first movement.

Example 9.1: No. 79, Vol. 3, *Mikrokosmos*, Boosey & Hawkes (1987), p. 27, m. 14–17

Example 9.2: *Piano Concerto* No. 3, 1st mvt., Boosey & Hawkes (1947), p. 31, m. 183–87

A good warm-up for No. 79 is the "Little Study" (77), which will get the fingers moving. "Hommage à R. Sch." (80) quotes Robert Schumann's favorite rhythmic motif, the dotted eighth followed by the sixteenth note, and here Bartók seems to be paraphrasing the final movement of *Kreisleriana*—but the harmonies remain original Bartók. "Wandering" (81) also recalls Schumann's influence, but is a fine example of freedom from the restrictions of the bar-line. "Scherzo" (82) demonstrates its own rhythmic freedom by mixing 7/8 with 2/4, 3/8, and 3/4 rhythms.

"Melody with Interruptions" (83) reminds me of the writing in Stravinsky's *Petrouchka* suite. (Also look at No. 110 in Volume 4.) It is an excellent teaching piece, providing the student with the facility to move easily between different registers of the keyboard. This is one of the pieces the composer based on an authentic Hungarian folk song.

"Merriment" (84) calls for rhythmic contrast and asks the student to be able to project the mood. A more extended composition is encountered in "Broken Chords" (85); the challenge here is to analyze and shape this three-page work. "Two Major Pentachords" (86) also requires analysis, not only to explain the dissonance, but also to understand a compositional technique. The dissonance of the half-tone treated as a consonance and affirmed by its repetition makes "In Russian Style" (90) interesting. Bartók seems to be alluding to the Russian folk style and not the style of his Russian contemporaries.

Certainly among the more difficult pieces in this volume are the two "Chromatic Inventions" (91, 92). To master these two contrasting compositions, the student must acquire a freedom of line and be free from the expectations of traditional tonality. These pieces serve as excellent memorization exercises. By contrast, the simplicity of the "Variations" (87) could be a variant of the first *Rondo,* written in 1916. Also noteworthy in this volume is the set of expanded exercises in the appendix, which I strongly recommend.

Volume 4 (97–121)

Volume 4 confirms Bartók's description of these pieces as a "synthesis of the musical and technical problems which were treated and sometimes only partially solved in my previous works."[8] Each of these miniatures reflects Bartók's gift for succinct and direct purity of expression. All the filler has been removed, and this contributes to their difficulty. Every note matters and nothing is wasted when compressed in such a short time frame.

The *Mikrokosmos* not only looks to the future but also acknowledges various stylistic keyboard influences from the past: Bach, Couperin, Schumann, Chopin, Debussy, and Ravel, to name a few. The "Notturno" (97) is a simple and touching three-part nocturne in the style of Chopin and Scriabin, and provides an excellent example of Bartók's minimalism. Very subtle changes are capable of producing poignant contrasts. By changing the accompaniment figure of the left hand while repeating the melody an octave higher, Bartók achieves a lovely effect. Technical pianistic problems are dealt with in "Thumbs Under" (98)—augmented by the excellent exercise in the appendix that makes scale playing seem much more enjoyable—and "Hands Crossing" (99), an unusual little piece that highlights the independence of the two hands and the nonconformity of Bartók's key signatures.

Example 9.3: No. 99, Vol. 4, *Mikrokosmos* p. 13, m. 1–4

"In Folk Song Style" (100) underlines what Bartók can achieve within a forty-five-second time frame. In the first measure the interval of the seventh is presented as a consonance; when the interval of the sixth appears, it sounds less consonant than the seventh and creates a surprising effect on the ear, which Bartók exploits. Because of its lean texture, dissonance is heightened. "Diminished Fifth" (101) allows the student to see how the composer assembles his composition and the form to which he arrives. This is also a good demonstration of rhythmic augmentation.

Bartók cited Arnold Schoenberg as the first composer to make use of piano harmonics in his Op. 11 set of three pieces. However, Bartók was also acquainted with the works of American composer Henry Cowell (they had met in London in 1923), and Cowell could have put his own signature on "Harmonics" (102). This work is fun to play, and Bartók has completely mastered the technique of harmonics on the keyboard. The sound effects are wonderful and there are only four harmonic changes indicated for the entire composition. (Bartók instructs the student to play the harmonic chords by pressing down on the keys without sounding.)

Example 9.4: No. 102, Vol. 4, *Mikrokosmos* p. 16, m. 1–6

"Minor and Major" (103) introduces the student to the elements of Bulgarian rhythm. Bartók makes use of 9/8 (4&5), followed by 8/8 (2&3&3), and 3x2/8 (2&2&2), followed by 5/8 and 7/8 rhythms—surely a good exercise for those irregular rhythms that will be met later on in this volume and also in Volume 6. This piece also includes a device previously used in the second *Elegy* and the Musettes movement of *Out of Doors:* rep. ad libitum, giving the performer the freedom to decide how many times the measure should be repeated. Playing "Wandering Through the Keys" (104) is much more enjoyable than studying arpeggios in every key. This is also a wonderful exercise for reading quickly changing key signatures.

"Game (with Two Five-Tone Scales)" (105) and two different key signatures is reminiscent of the first *Bagatelle* and also recalls a theme from Stravinsky's *Le Sacre du Printemps*. Each hand is written in a different key, but ultimately it is the ear that decides the key center, not the eyes. The pure folk spirit is captured by the three stanzas of the "Children's Song" (106). The shades of Debussy and Ravel linger in "Melody in the Mist" (107), which is a good teaching piece for pedal and color effects.

Bartók describes the three-part "Wrestling" (108) as "a picturesque struggle between tones of a minor second."[9] The first section centers on the F-sharp pedal point; the middle section wanders through E-flat and G-sharp, and the return vacillates between F-natural and F-sharp, still wrestling with each other right up to the last-measure finish. And it's a draw! The piano imitates the droning seconds of the bagpipe sound, and some unusual and unnatural fingering is produced because of holding down the pedal points. With this challenging piece, Bartók conveys the feeling of physically wrestling with the instrument until the final chord resolution.

Example 9.5: No. 108, Vol. 4, *Mikrokosmos* p. 26, m. 25–33

"From the Island of Bali" (109) provides another excellent example of Bartók's minimalistic techniques. An impressionistic scene is created from a simple four-note harmony, which Bartók uses horizontally in the opening and reduces vertically in its last cadence. Observe Bartók's suggested pedal markings for using the middle sostenuto pedal.

Example 9.6: No. 109, Vol. 4, *Mikrokosmos* p. 28, m. 1–4

Example 9.7: No. 109, m. 36–43

"And the Sounds Clash and Clang" (110) reminds me of the piano writing in the final piano piece from Stravinsky's *Petrouchka*. "Intermezzo" (111) is a poignant study of imitation and inversion techniques, and an ideal teaching piece for demonstrating these compositional devices. "Variations on a Folk Tune" (112) is based on an original Hungarian folk tune. Bartók asks that the theme be played *ff*, with the first two fingers of each hand playing together for a special percussive effect. The melody used in the first "Bulgarian Rhythm" (113) is really Hungarian, but its rhythm qualifies as Bulgarian because of its 7/8 asymmetrical time signature (2&2&3). "Bulgarian rhythm refers to a rhythm where the beats within each bar are of unequal length, so that the subdivisions of each beat vary in number."[10]

The second "Bulgarian Rhythm" (115) is an original Bulgarian theme in 5/8 rhythm, alternating 3&2 with 2&3. Before tackling the extremely difficult set of six Bulgarian dances that conclude Volume 6, spend some time with these two pieces. The counterpoint techniques in "Theme and Inversion" (114), "Bourrée" (117), "Triplets in 9/8 Time" (118), and "Two-Part Study" (121) reflect Bach's influence, but the harmonies and the rhythms are pure Bartók. "Dance in 3/4 Time" recalls the style of Couperin. The percussive style of "Triads" (121) reminds me of the piano writing of the Argentine composer Alberto Ginastera, who was very much influenced by Bartók's music. "Song" (116) was inspired by the rhythms of the Hungarian folk song.

Volume 5 (122–139)

Looking at the piano writing in Volume 5, it is obvious that Bartók has now made the leap from piano pieces acceptable for a student recital to the more difficult solo repertoire of the advanced pianist. The key word to describe this volume is complexity. Just look at the difficult chordal clusters in the molto vivace "Chords Together and in Opposition" (122); the rhythmic writing of the two-voiced "Staccato and Legato" (123); the complex "Syncopations" (133) in 5/4 and 4/4, which resemble Prokofiev's writing;

the technical demands of "Staccato" (124), in which a dynamically varied staccato touch is a necessity to build its final cadence; or the pianistic difficulties of the "Studies in Double Notes" (134) and the "Perpetuum Mobile" (135). (These two works remind me of the technical problems encountered in the middle section of Ravel's *Scarbo*.) "Perpetuum Mobile" sounds as if it were inspired by Schumann's *Toccata*, which Bartók frequently performed. Notice his use once again of the marking repet. ad infinitum on the final measure, which in this case could be interpreted to mean, "Keep playing until the pianist gets tired!"

Even the piano accompaniment to the familiar "New Hungarian Folk Song" (127) gets progressively more difficult with each repeated phrase. (Bartók recommends performing this while singing, or playing it on two pianos or with solo violin.) In the final cadence of "Major Seconds Broken and Together" (132), a seventh chord is used as a consonance, but its linear chromatic writing underlines the harmonic complexities. Although the "Alternating Thirds" (129) is not as difficult as Debussy's étude by the same name, performing it up to Bartók's allegro molto metronome marking presents a challenge.

"Unison" (137) and "Whole-Tone Scales" (136), two of the longer pieces in the set, present formal problems. The harmonic wanderings in No. 136 must be contained within its three-part design, and the unison writing in No. 137 requires delineation and bold outlining of its three-part form. The main theme includes a two-measure motif followed by a one-measure interjection (the equivalent of an exclamation point!) and the return material utilizes rhythmic augmentation. The difficulty is to shape this three-part form and hold it together.

At first glance, "Fourths" (131) does not appear pianistically very difficult, but the awkward fingering presents a problem. Of lesser difficulty is the infectious "Stamping Dance" (128), which is a fine example of variation and motivic technique. The thematic material is embroidered upon its return, and the first four notes of the theme are motivically developed in the middle section.

Even with its alternating changes of rhythm, "Change of Time" (126) is not a difficult piece, although the syncopations in its final measures are good preparation for the difficulties of No. 133. (The metronome indication of 250 per eighth might have to be changed to 126 per quarter to adapt to today's metronome.)

"Boating" (125) might have been inspired by the Barcarolla movement from the *Out of Doors*, but this certainly is a purer, more distilled version. "Bagpipe Music" (138) is also simpler and much more naïve than the 1926 *Out of Doors* Musettes. Bartók described this piece: "Use of all three pipes: chanter, tonic, and dominant (that is, middle pipe), and drone. Interesting division of the pipes. Squeaky effects are typical."[11] Indeed, Bartók lets us hear all of them; we even hear when the pipes run out of air. The composer also makes use of interjection techniques as part of the return thematic material. This piece resembles the finale movement of the 1915 *Sonatina*. Humor is an important component in understanding Bartók's music, and "Village Joke" (130) and "Jack-in-the-Box" (139) are two excellent examples. Sudden accents and a cluster chord accompaniment help create the fun in No. 130, and it is amazing how the physical act of playing No. 139 resembles the up-and-down motion of the jack-in-the-box.

Volume 6 (140–153)

The last book of the *Mikrokosmos* finds Bartók at his most adventurous. These short, condensed statements read like a sketchbook of ideas, and Bartók allows us to observe close up his compositional style. It's as if we can hear him thinking aloud and are witnessing his working through and mastering a problem within a miniature format.

"Free Variation" (140), a theme with four variations, provides an outstanding example of Bartók's minimalistic motivic techniques. From a three-note motif (example 9.8), a three-part composition is constructed with the three notes repeated, inverted (example 9.9), and extended. Pianistic problems such as voicing, irregular rhythms, variations of touch, and phrase structure are also focused upon here. [Track 30]

Example 9.8: No. 140, Vol. 6, *Mikrokosmos*, p. 10, m. 1–4

Example 9.9: No. 140, p. 10, m. 13–18

Analyzing the sparse thematic material, Bartók relies on repetition but also supplies plenty of contrast within the repetitive figures. The same motif is used, inverted but altered by its place in the total structural design. Look at the eighth-note staccato figure of the transition to the middle section (example 9.10) and compare it to the extended first theme's accompaniment (example 9.11). The same motif is transformed rhythmically, and its character is changed by touch (leggiero), dynamics, and function.

Example 9.10: No. 140, p. 11, m. 33–37

Example 9.11: No. 140, p. 10, m. 9–12

Contrast is the essential ingredient needed both to underline the differences between such similar repetitive thematic material and to define the material's formal function within its three-part design. The character of the original three-note motif is dramatically transformed in the middle section by Bartók's "thematic extension of range."

Example 9.12: No. 140, p. 12, m. 51-58

This technique was described by Bartók in one of his Harvard Lectures of 1943:

> The extension of themes in their value is called augmentation, and their compression in value called diminution. These devices are very well known, especially from the art music of the seventeenth and eighteenth centuries. Now this new device could be called extension in range of a theme. For the extension we have the liberty to choose any diatonic scale or mode. We will choose one of them which will best suit our actual purposes. As you will see, such an extension will considerably change the character of the melody, sometimes to such a degree that its relation to the original, nonextended form will be scarcely recognizable. We will have mostly the impression that we are dealing with a new melody. And this circumstance is very good indeed, because we will get variety on the one hand, but the unity will remain undestroyed because of the hidden relation between the two forms. If, perhaps, you will object that this new device is somehow artificial, my only answer will be that it is no more artificial than those old devices of augmentation, diminution, inversion, and cancrizans of themes; in fact, cancrizans seem to be even much more artificial.[12]

Pianistically, this piece is difficult. The irregular rhythms and jabbing accents must become second nature, and the performer should be able to clarify for the listener what Bartók achieves with a minimal amount of material. The coda provides an excellent study in rhythmic momentum, direction, and pacing. Economy is achieved through the use of variation, contrast, and repetition, and everything occurs within the minimal time frame of one minute and forty seconds!

"Subject and Reflection" (141) is similarly concerned with variation and contrast. The right hand and left hand function here as mirror images of each other; the right-hand subject is reflected (mirrored) by the left hand. This piece demands total equality and separation of both hands.

Example 9.13: No. 141, Vol. 6, *Mikrokosmos,* p. 14, m. 1–3

"From the Diary of a Fly" (142) is a wonderful encore piece and reveals Bartók's very special sense of humor. It is a difficult work, as it must be played as evenly and lightly as possible, while highlighting its inner dramatic tensions. [Track 31]

I wanted to depict the desperate sound of a fly's buzz, when getting into a cobweb. He was buzzing about and didn't see the spider web. Then he is caught in the web (Agitato: "Woe, a cobweb!") but manages to get himself free before he is eaten, and he escapes. A happy (con gioia) ending.[13]

Example 9.14: No. 142, Vol. 6, *Mikrokosmos,* p. 17, m. 1–11

Using minor seconds and pedal points throughout, Bartók imitates the fly's buzzing. Repetition is always varied and Bartók is not restricted by the bar-line; patterns never repeat in exactly the same way, which might make memory a bit tricky. This is a gem, and so effective when played well!

The influence of Claude Debussy is present in "Divided Arpeggios" (143), as is Bartók's familiarity with his *Twelve Etudes* of 1915. This is a wonderful study for color and pedaling techniques.

Before tackling the fourth movement of the *Out of Doors* suite, "Minor Seconds, Major Sevenths" (144) should be studied. It is a more distilled version of the Night Music, operating within a much smaller framework. Debussy is again very much present; the parallel chords are reminiscent of his "Pagodes" of *Estampes.*

Example 9.15: No. 144, Vol. 6, *Mikrokosmos,* p. 24, m. 1–6

Example 9.16: *Out of Doors*, 4th mvt., Boosey & Hawkes (1954), p. 20, m. 3–6

"Chromatic Invention" (145) is one of the seven pieces that can be performed on two pianos. Here, Bartók shows his allegiance to Bach and his contrapuntal techniques. Each invention consists of a canon at the tritone.

"Ostinato" (146) is a distilled version of the 1911 *Allegro Barbaro*. Here, a new leanness of texture is apparent, but the barbaroso drive and excitement are still flourishing. Pacing is essential and contrast vital to the momentum of this effective piece. The second theme, according to Bartók, should imitate Bulgarian pipes. "Ostinato" also looks back to the finale of the 1926 *Sonata* and is reminiscent of some of the writing seen in the *Dance Suite* transcription. Pianistically difficult with its constant perpetuo mobile writing, this piece cries out for bravura playing. It also provides a shining example for thwarting any criticism of using ostinato, repetitive thematic material. This piece could never be boring! [Track 32]

Although pianistically much more difficult than the "Bear Dance" of the *Sonatina* and from the *Ten Easy Pieces*, "March" (147) belongs to the same genre.

Dedicated to the pianist Harriet Cohen, the difficult and effective "Six Dances in Bulgarian Rhythm" are an important part of the Bartók solo repertory. (A detailed discussion of the Bulgarian rhythm is included in chapter 4.) These six pieces are extremely pianistic and work well when performed as a complete set. The pianist must be able to sustain a beautiful melodic line in No. 1 (148), convey the rhythmic vitality of No. 2 (149), exploit the contrasts of No. 3 (150), feel the jazziness of No. 4 (151) (this is pure Americana jazz; how much of George Gershwin's music did Bartók hear?), have a wide range of touch and colors available for No. 5 (152), and pull out all the stops for the virtuosic finale (153). The Bulgarian rhythms must become as natural as one's mother tongue, and then the exuberant joyful spirit of these dances will spring forth and leap from the page.

The first dance (148) cries out for lyricism and rubato playing, which Bartók clearly writes out in the score. The problem spots are the transitions from section to section, where the rhythm is stretched but the seams should remain invisible. Here the momentum must always be sustained and the pulse never lost. Be careful that the Bulgarian rhythm of 4&2&3 is maintained. This is music to sing as well as dance, and its pianism is pure romanticism. [Track 16]

The rhythms of the second dance (149) remind me of Latin dance music: 1-2, 1-2, 1-2-3. Most of Alberto Ginastera's piano music is written using this pulse. Bartók asks for pedal and probably doesn't want a dry, hard percussive sound but rather the type of touch and color that a pedal vibrato would help produce. Proper pacing of color and dynamics is necessary for a good performance of this dance.

Contrast is the essential ingredient of the third dance (150). A problem spot is the transition before the return section. Make sure the rhythm is maintained and the four-voice writing is clear.

The fourth dance (151) represents a piece of Americana. Not only can the sassiness of George Gershwin be heard in these measures, but this dance also hints at the typically American harmonies of Copland and Barber. This is a set of rhythmic variations, and pacing is the key to an effective performance. As in all these dances, the rhythms have to feel "as natural (and spontaneous) as your mother tongue."

The fifth dance (152) in three parts demands a lightness of touch and variety of color. There are some awkward passages of crossed hands in the transition to the middle section. The final dance (153) is the most virtuosic of the set, and enough energy must be saved for the bravura finale. This dance always leaves me feeling that it should be declaimed from the highest mountain. It must sound joyful, and should be a joy to perform!

There is such wealth and variety within these pieces; there is something here for everyone! More importantly, these compositions are liberating for the young student; no longer are the previously existing rules in place. Melody has been liberated from the bar-line; the ear has been liberated by the melody and its harmonies. Rhythm, register, touch, range, dynamics—all reflect Bartók's independence of thought as well as absolute independence of hands!

FOR CHILDREN (1908–1909, revised 1944–1945)

> Already at the beginning of my career as a composer I had the idea of writing some easy works for piano students. The idea originated in my experience as a piano teacher; I had always the feeling that the available material, especially for beginners, has no real musical value, with the exception of very few works—for instance, Bach's easiest pieces and Schumann's *Jugendalbum*. I thought these works to be insufficient, and so, more than thirty years ago (1910), I myself tried to write some easy piano pieces. At that time the best thing to do would be to use folk tunes. Folk melodies, in general, have great musical value; so, at least the thematical value would be secured.[14]

These four volumes of eighty-five authentic folk songs of Hungarian and Slovak origin, even though specifically written for children, cover a wide emotional range and are proof that the use of folk material in no way inhibits inspiration. Composed before the folk-inspired *Fifteen Hungarian Peasant Songs*, the *Sonatina*, and the *Rumanian Folk Dances*, these were the first complete set of pieces to demonstrate the structural, harmonic, and emotional possibilities that could be derived from using only a simple folk melody. What Bartók has produced are poetic jewels, miniature gems tinged with the nostalgic melancholy of the countryside. *For Children* is Bartók's *Kinderscenen*. Although they are written for the child, it takes a great deal of sophistication and expertise for the pianist to communicate the innocence hidden within these little pieces.

It is important to remember that these compositions were originally composed twenty-five years prior to the *Mikrokosmos*. Unlike the six volumes of *Mikrokosmos*, there was no overall pedagogical plan. The only purpose was to provide nourishing, worthwhile material for the young student and, in Bartók's words "to acquaint children with the simple and nonromantic beauties of folk music."[15] Only minimal technical skills are required. In the original edition, the subtitle was "For beginners (without octaves)." The *Mikrokosmos* makes use of folk material only in three of its 153 pieces. What both works do share, however, is a spare and very concentrated language.

In 1909, Bartók's Hungarian publisher brought out Volume 1, consisting of twenty-one pieces based on Hungarian folklore. It was followed by the second volume, after which Bartók received a letter from the publisher requesting that the children's pieces be written in a more conservative manner. Of course, Bartók went his own way and delivered Volumes 3 and 4 based on Slovak melodies, which were even a bit more radical in their harmonic language.

In 1931, Bartók orchestrated the "Swineherd's Dance," listed in Volume 1 as No. 42 (early edition), the fifth and final piece of his *Hungarian Sketches*. A new version of *For Children* was published posthumously in 1947 by Boosey & Hawkes, Bartók's English publishers. The changes are few: The original edition did not have key signatures, metronome markings, or timings indicated at the end of the piece. These were added with the later edition. Titles have also been changed in the second edition, with occasional alterations in meter notations, mainly for clarification. This can be seen primarily in some of the slower pieces.

Example 9.17: No. 18, *For Children*, Dover (1909 edition), p. 16, m. 1–6

Example 9.18: No. 18, *For Children*, Boosey & Hawkes (1947), p. 17, m. 1–5

The number has also been reduced, from the original 85 pieces in four volumes to 79 in the two books of the Boosey & Hawkes edition. (Omitted were Nos. 25 and 29 based on Hungarian material and Nos. 23, 27, 33 and 34 from the Slovak album. It is interesting to note that Emma Gruber, Kodály's first wife, was the composer of Nos. 33 and 34.) Dover publishes only the original four-volume edition, which includes the words and complete translations of each folk tune, except where there is a note indicating that the "text is not suitable for publication." Was Bartók sometimes inspired by bawdy folk tunes for these children's pieces? The 1947 Boosey

& Hawkes edition does not provide any source material or additional textual information, and even the original folk song titles have been altered.

Most of the folk songs share a similar profile. The original folk melody is retained and repeated several times with varied accompaniment and usually episodic material in between. Harmonies remain simple but never conventional. In general, the simpler the melody, the more complex the harmonization. The seventh functions as a consonance, and melodies characterized by leaps of a fourth and chords constructed in fourths are a frequent occurrence.

From these pieces, the young student can learn phrasing, rubato techniques, and breathing and can also become comfortable and flexible with tempo changes. These pieces stretch the musicianship and imagination of a young pianist. Their harmonic language does not prejudice a young set of ears to conform to the aural expectations of major and minor tonality. What's more, they are fun and challenging for the student as well as the teacher, and are quite poignant in their simple beauty. For an adult to perform these works is probably much more difficult than for the uninhibited (Hungarian) child who has been given, from an early age, a steady diet of folk music.

FIRST TERM AT THE PIANO (1913, PUBLISHED IN 1929)

Eighteen of Bartók's original pieces, written for the Piano Method that he coauthored with Sándor Reschofsky, were collected in 1929 and published with the above title. The first nine pieces of the set resemble the easy pieces found in Volume 1 of *Mikrokosmos*, with the last nine being much more interesting for the young student to learn. They progress in order of difficulty and are based on folk material. No. 12, the "Swineherd's Dance," provides a good introduction to pedal points; No. 14 is written in the style of Bach. The folk tunes are catchy and fun to sing as well as play (No. 16); Bartók introduces the young beginner to his varied vocabulary of accents (^) and dance rhythms (minuet, waltz). If the teacher is not using the *Mikrokosmos* as a teaching tool, these pieces will be enjoyable for the very young beginner.

Perhaps Zoltán Kodály, Bartók's friend and colleague, said it best when speaking about the composer after his death: "Bartók was still sufficiently a child in spirit to be able to talk naturally to children."[16] Bartók believed that it was his responsibility to tap into the young listener's unprejudiced ears and natural instincts. The seriousness and passion with which Bartók collected folk music or wrote a string quartet were brought to composing an easy piece for his young son Peter. With the innocence and curiosity of the child, Bartók is able to explore, and invites all children to join him.

NOTES

1. Béla Bartók, from a WNYC Radio interview, "Ask the Composer" (1945), foreword to the *Definitive Edition of Mikrokosmos* (London: Boosey & Hawkes, 1987), 4.

2. Béla Bartók, Jr., "*Remembering my Father*," in *Bartók Studies*, ed. Todd Crow (Detroit: Detroit Reprints in Music, 1976), 150.

3. *Complete Bartók Recordings*, Hungaroton (LPX 11405–07).

4. Peter Bartók, in the foreword to the *Definitive Edition of Mikrokosmos*, 4.

5. Béla Bartók, "Preface to *Mikrokosmos*" (1939), in *Béla Bartók Essays*, ed. Benjamin Suchoff (Lincoln: University of Nebraska Press, 1976), 424.

6. Béla Bartók, "Contemporary Music in Piano Teaching" (1940), in *Béla Bartók Essays*, ed. Benjamin Suchoff, 427–28.

7. Béla Bartók, "Introduction to *Béla Bartók: Masterpieces for Piano*" (1945), in *Béla Bartók Essays*, ed. Benjamin Suchoff, 432.

8. Bartók, "Introduction to *Béla Bartók: Masterpieces for Piano*" (1945), 432.

9. Béla Bartók in *The Bartók Companion*, ed. Malcolm Gillies (Portland, Oreg.: Amadeus Press, 1994), 201.

10. Notes from the *Definitive Edition of Mikrokosmos*, Volume 4 (London: Boosey & Hawkes, 1987) 56.

11. Bartók in *The Bartók Companion*, ed. Malcolm Gillies, 205.

12. Béla Bartók, "Harvard Lectures" (1943), in *Béla Bartók Essays*, ed. Benjamin Suchoff, 381.

13. Bartók in *The Bartók Companion*, 207.

14. Béla Bartók, "Contemporary Music in Piano Teaching" (1940), in *Béla Bartók Essays*, ed. Benjamin Suchoff, 426.

15. Bartók, "Contemporary Music in Piano Teaching" (1940), 427.

16. Zoltán Kodály as quoted in Notes to the *Béla Bartók Complete Edition*, Hungaroton (LPX 11394-95).

10

+

The Three Piano
Concertos and the Piano
Chamber Repertory

I wrote my first *Concerto* for piano and orchestra in 1926. I consider it a
successful work, although its writing is a bit difficult—one might even
say very difficult!—as much for orchestra as for audience.

—Béla Bartók[1]

T he three concertos for piano and orchestra reveal the special path
Bartók traveled during his last twenty years. By studying these works,
all cast in a similar three-movement formal design, we can better understand Bartók's journey. Because he was a performer with a thorough
knowledge of the instrument and no limitations whatsoever on technical
skills, his unique evolving relationship with the piano concerto, written
primarily for performance by himself or his wife Ditta, is significant. Gen-
eralizations can be dangerous, but the clear differences in stylistic purposes of these three major compositions are telling. We can say that he
started from a point of complexity in 1926 with the first *Concerto*, then, in
reaction to this composition, aimed for a simpler, more melodic style in the
neo-Baroque second one (1931), and finally, with his last work, the more
classical *Piano Concerto* No. 3—completed, except for the orchestration of
its final seventeen bars, just prior to his death in 1945—ultimately achieved
a sense of peace and lyrical simplicity.

When viewed separately, the middle movements of these works, all cast
in three-part form, summarize the path Bartók generally followed with
each concerto. In the first, the piano functions not as a soloist but as an
equal member of the percussion, and in the middle section even assumes
full responsibility for the rhythmic accompaniment to the predominantly

woodwind melody. The hammerlike aspects of the instrument far outweigh its lyrical qualities, and melodic content is limited to brief, imitative, four-voice fragments; the piano writing is angular, although occasionally interspersed with cadenzalike arpeggios functioning as sound
filler.

With the second *Concerto,* Bartók moves out of the primitive depths
explored in the first and sets out to alter the texture, allowing much
more light and air to shine through. The muted strings with their parallel fourth chords set the tone for this Adagio movement. Layers of complexity are peeled away to reveal more of a melodic line, and the piano
is now returned to a more prominent role, although still strongly inter-
acting with the percussion: The middle section Scherzo becomes the central focus, and the rich, percussive, and varied color effects of the instrument are exploited. Bartók is unrestrained and is no longer the
minimalist repeating one three-note motif; the piano is now featured as
a true virtuoso instrument. Bartók uses every pianistic tool to create
marvelous sound effects within a perpetuo mobile driving rhythm. The
middle section becomes a mini-étude in the use of clusters, arpeggios,
staccato, and leggiero playing and qualifies as one of the most difficult
and extraordinary movements in the entire piano concerto literature.
The Scherzo occupies the central position not only within the second
movement but also within the formal design of the entire work, representing the apex of a mirror form. More importantly, what sets this
movement apart from the Andante of the first *Concerto* is its emotional
tone. Helped by an increased clarity of texture and the colors of the
muted strings of its opening measures, the piano seems better able to
communicate and directly touch the emotions, without having to sift
through so many layers.

With the andante religioso of the third *Concerto,* Bartók continues
down this path, further whittling away at all that might be considered
superfluous in order to hone a more direct statement, generating a feeling of arrival at some ultimate destination when the chorale theme returns. The word religioso is exceptional and unique for Bartók, but
seems to explain the impression conveyed of being present while the
soul gradually begins its ascent toward heaven. With his last concerto,
Bartók sheds most of the intricate Baroque devices used in the second
(fugue and canon beget fugato) to achieve a true classical simplicity. All
the battles fought in the earlier two concertos seem to have resolved
themselves, and harmony and balance are restored. The middle section
now becomes a much purer distillation of the "Night Sounds" fourth
movement from the 1926 *Out of Doors.* Harmonic language has been
simplified and reduced to diatonic proportions; unisons are the norm,

and even the return section of the opening chorale reveals a spare counterpoint, occasionally punctuated by the extended embellishments of the piano's cadenzas. Here, it is obvious that less equals more, and at the end of his life, Bartók's personal relationship with the piano has come to a resting place where the essence of lyricism and simplicity has been revealed.

PIANO CONCERTO NO. 1 (1926)

It had been at least twenty years since Bartók had written a work for piano and orchestra, and the first *Piano Concerto* was born from necessity. Having evolved into a new and certainly different piano style from that in his earlier romantic and virtuosic Op. 1 *Rhapsody* or the Op. 2 *Scherzo* for piano and orchestra (1904–1905), Bartók now needed another vehicle, one written in his current musical language, to play as soloist with orchestras on tour.

Coming out of the rich piano year of 1926, a time that also produced the *Out of Doors,* the *Piano Sonata,* and the *Nine Little Piano Pieces,* the first *Piano Concerto* is an obvious sibling of the piano *Sonata.* They strongly resemble each other in their percussive/martellato approach to the keyboard and contrapuntal emphasis, and both certainly qualify as very difficult and complex pianistic works. In both compositions, Bartók is concerned mainly with rhythmic repetition; from a single repeated note, a theme is constructed. The following repetitive themes also reaffirm the point Bartók returned to so often in his writings: The important issue is not the quality of the composer's thematic material but into what shape and form the material will be molded.

Example 10.1: *Piano Concerto* No. 1, 1st mvt.; Universal (1927), Boosey & Hawkes (1954); m. 38–49

Example 10.2: No. 1, 2nd mvt., m. 1–8

Example 10.3: No. 1, 3rd mvt., m. 5–7, 11–14

Example 10.4: *Sonata,* 1st mvt., Boosey & Hawkes (1927, 1955), p. 3, m. 1–6

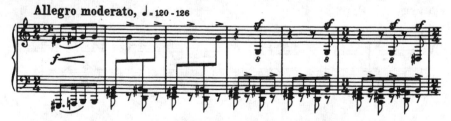

Example 10.5: *Sonata,* 2nd mvt., p. 14, m. 1–5

The piano is here treated by Bartók primarily as a percussion instrument. The martellato-barbaroso style first seen in 1911 with his *Allegro Barbaro* is now carried to the extreme while at the same time adding the necessary bite needed to compete with and cut through a thick orchestral sound. Occasionally, Bartók does allow influences from Debussy's coloristic palette to creep in, but modified by percussive, rhythmic effects.

Example 10.6: *Piano Concerto* No. 1, 1st mvt., m. 190–92

Example 10.7: No. 1, 1st mvt., m. 181–89

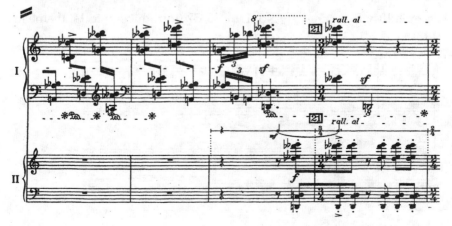

(This passage [example 10.7] from the beginning of the development section is always interpreted with such seriousness. I find a bit of humor in the way it is written, especially the sudden *sf* in the solo piano, answered by the orchestra's *mf*. The rhythmic outline should be strictly observed, but the passage should be made to sound like pure slapstick.)

In an interview given in 1927, shortly after composing the first *Concerto*, Bartók spoke of his preoccupation with exploiting the piano's hammering repetitive rhythms:

> The neutral character of the piano tone has long been recognized. Yet it seems to me that its inherent nature becomes really expressive only by means of the present tendency to use the piano as a percussion instrument. Indeed, the piano always plays the part of universal instrument. It has not lost its importance for concert performances.[2]

How drastically Bartók has altered the role of the solo pianist since writing his Op. 1 *Rhapsody*. No longer the featured soloist, carrying most of the burden while primarily being accompanied by the orchestra, the piano functions here as an equal member of a tight, coherent ensemble passing imitative material back and forth, usually at very short intervals. Only occasionally is the piano pitted directly against the entire orchestra.

> It should also be noted that neither of my (first) two concertos was written for piano followed or accompanied by orchestra, but that they have been concerted for piano and orchestra—soloist and ensemble have been assigned equally important parts.[3]

(Bartók returns to a more classical relationship between piano and orchestra in his third concerto.)

Throughout the *Concerto*, Bartók demands that piano and percussion work together and share their material. From the opening measures of the introduction, these roles are defined and the back-and-forth give and take built into thematic content. This observation becomes vital to understanding and solving the many performance problems inherent in this concerto.

Example 10.8: *Piano Concerto* No. 1, m. 30–37 (introduction to 1st theme in 1st movement)

The dialogue at the opening of the second movement (example 10.2) reaffirms this relationship and shows the piano to be not only an equal member of the percussion but also capable of supplying the rhythmic backbone for the middle section and the repetitive material for its dramatic climax. Repeating the same three-note rhythmic motive for a total of fifty-eight measures while building in dramatic intensity and increasing sonority creates a hypnotic, rather primitive effect. Bartók gradually adds notes to these cluster chords as the repetition continues. What a fine example of minimalism!

Example 10.9: *Piano Concerto* No. 1, 2nd mvt., (a) m. 87–89, (b) m. 101–102, (c) m. 122, (d) m. 126–27

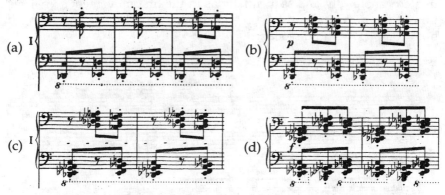

Accepting the democratic principle of the equal partnership of the piano soloist in this concerto, a careful analysis of the score to distinguish between what is sound filler and what is primary material is essential for the performer. Many ensemble-performance problem spots within this work are clarified by the realization that the piano part was not meant always to be prominent; occasionally it must follow the orchestra and remain in the background. Because of the extremely percussive and complex nature of this work, the formal and structural pillars must be firmly in place; this will help define the interpretation and also aid in the evaluation of each participant's thematic material.

Pianistically, Bartók exploits all his nineteenth-century Lisztian tools to produce a percussive, bravura, and very exciting concerto. Octaves are in abundance, as well as big chordal-block sonorities and even some virtuosic cadenzalike improvisatory runs in the middle movement. Bartók also explores sudden shifts of registers covering a wide distance and exploits the use of primitive, motoric, driving toccata rhythms throughout. The final movement is built on an ostinato, but the repetition is never boring, always being dramatically and musically inspired. Bartók also makes use of rhythmic blocks, similar to his use of sound planes, varying the rhythmic profile by slight tempo changes yet always maintaining the momentum in between structural marking points. Not only is a bravura technique and a big sound required here, but also the necessary stamina and energy to see the work through to its last bars and negotiate all changes of rhythmic pulse, without running out of steam or losing the conductor.

Bartók's constant use of imitation and contrapuntal techniques between the piano and various sections of the orchestra produces a complex overlapping and thickening of texture that makes listening to this work for the first time rather difficult. The abundance of dissonance—seconds, ninths, and cluster chords—also increases the challenge, but these are primarily used as spice for the movement's repetitive rhythms. However, these dissonances become heightened by Bartók's use of imitative devices. When treated canonically, and sequentially as in the first movement's final section of the development, the textural layers are piled up, increasing in both complexity and dissonance.

Example 10.10: *Piano Concerto* No. 1, 1st mvt., m. 352–59

When the theme returns in the recapitulation, it is stated directly, in stark relief to what has appeared before. Despite occasional moments of tonal ambiguity, Bartók, like Chopin before him, still nicknamed his first *Piano Concerto* "Concerto in E minor."

Bartók's use of contrast within the context of such repetitive and complex material is crucial. Contrast is built into classical sonata form with its second theme, and the lighter and more playful quality of this material should be fully exploited.

Example 10.11: *Piano Concerto* No. 1, 1st mvt., m. 105–19

In the recapitulation, Bartók combines the playfulness of the second theme with a sharp barbaroso/martellato quality, alternating back and forth for maximum effect (see example 10.16). A wonderful contrast is also achieved in the development of the first movement by creating a respite from the imitative dialogue between the orchestra and the piano. Within this extensive section, which consists of big building blocks of sonorities and constant propelling rhythms, Bartók momentarily lapses into a playful bit of imitation, recalling writing from one of his *Nine Little Piano Pieces*.

Example 10.12: *Piano Concerto* No. 1, 1st mvt., m. 249–54

This passage must be played with the necessary lightness. Bartók also does something similar in the complex last movement at the end of the development, just prior to the return of material. It's as if he calls a time-out before surging ahead yet again. Both the pianist and the listener appreciate this change of pace.

Example 10.13: *Piano Concerto* No. 1, 3rd mvt., m. 318–27

It is necessary to point out that the first *Concerto* contains its share of publishing errors, mainly some of the metronome markings in the older Universal edition. Often Bartók will cite a return to an a tempo and indicate a metronome marking that seems to makes no sense within the context of the movement. The Allegro of the first movement is originally listed as a quarter note equals 116; along the way the a tempo has become 130 without any explanation. The meno vivo indication at 120, which follows the original Allegro of 116, also seems to make no sense within its context. Also confusing is the mosso before the second theme in the first movement at m. 100, without a metronome indication. Here Bartók implies a change of character without any tempo alteration. The second theme is more effective when played in the same tempo as the opening, which will allow for more playfulness and freedom of rubato.

(Note: In the newly revised edition by Peter Bartók, published in 1992 by Universal, these discrepancies in tempo markings have been noted. What the new edition suggests is to change the original Allegro metronome marking to 120, thus altering the meno vivo marking at m. 27 to less than 120 in order to follow, at one bar after rehearsal number 21, the sostenuto's original metronome marking of 100. The revised edition agrees that the composer wanted all the allegro sections to be played at approximately the same tempo.)

The first *Piano Concerto* is a three-movement work. The Allegro begins with an introduction, containing the seeds of the material to be used and developed in the first movement. A case could easily be made that the first and second theme already appear before the sonata-form Allegro begins; Bartók's compositional device of "thematic extension" is observed throughout this work, with every theme somehow related and germinating from one another. Bartók clouds the introduction on the dominant B by highlighting second and seventh dissonances (example 10.8). In general, the Allegro is characterized by a thickness of texture. Starting as soon as the sixth measure, Bartók begins the overlapping of layers to produce a complex imitative weaving of line. Fugal, canonic writing abounds, adding to the aural complexity and also increasing rhythmic momentum.

Example 10.14: *Piano Concerto* No. 1, 1st mvt., m. 55–57

Example 10.15: No. 1, 1st mvt., m. 129–32

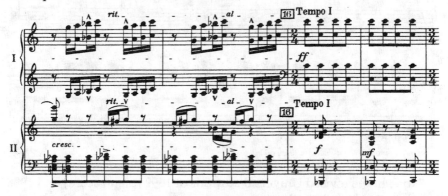

This two-measure ritardando before Tempo I is always a problem spot for piano and orchestra; the Tempo I first theme return functions here as a needed structural marking point.

The extensive development section is the central focus and the real problem of the first movement. Divided into three big sections, each possessing its own rhythmic profile, the first two sections are divided by a contrasting transition/bridge passage (example 10.12) before the propelling rhythms start up again. The third section is delineated by the return of the opening theme, but this is not the recapitulation. Bartók makes uses of this opening theme as a motto to set off the various sections. Notice that the motto also returns after the second theme appears in the exposition. It functions as a signpost, a point of punctuation, letting us know where we are and where Bartók is headed. Since this movement is so percussive and driving in its character, be sure to exploit as much as possible any opportunities for contrast. This section does allow a certain elasticity of tempo within its motoric rhythmic profile. In fact, the freedom, as well as the discipline, needed to stretch the tempo is vital to a good perform-ance of this work.

The second theme will be a good vehicle for use of rubato. Bartók has written a funny and playful theme in these eight measures. Try to make the most of the theme's humor whenever it returns in the recapitulation, and also in the coda (also see example 10.7 from the beginning of the de-velopment section). A smile between these driving rhythms would cer-tainly be welcome.

Example 10.16: *Piano Concerto* No. 1, 1st mvt., m. 415–21

(Note: In the revised Universal editions of 1992 [piano score] and 1998 [orchestral score], the following corrections have been made: At the end of m. 117 in the two-piano reduction, the second sixteenth-note motif in the second piano part should begin on the fifth beat and be contained within this measure; it should not start on the sixth beat and go over the bar-line as notated in the older edition. One measure before rehearsal No. 49, a # sign needs to be added to the D on the last beat of the right hand.)

The second movement, Andante, written in three parts with the middle section providing the dramatic climax of the movement, is built primarily on rhythmic repetition with stunning effect. An extended coda, played by the brass, continues the use of a repeated rhythm and also functions as an exciting transition and introduction to the finale ostinato movement. This movement shares many similarities with the first movement of the *Out of Doors,* "With Drums and Pipes," written during the same time period.

The Allegro molto is a very large and extended movement cast in sonata form, which must hold together despite all its shifts in tempo and thematic transformations. But, because of its driving energy and rhythmic momentum, this movement seems to play by itself, once its structure is clarified, and it is less problematic musically than the first movement. Ideally, the impression should be given that the finale is shorter than actually written, and this will occur only if there is unity of pacing within its shifting tempos. In other words, the pianist needs to map out a route and destination. Its initial repetitive thematic material (example 10.3) recalls the thematic material of the first movement (example 10.1). Repeated driving rhythmic patterns, ever-increasing sonority, create its excitement and also its problems. This is not a work for just solo piano; when the tempo shifts, the pianist, the conductor, and all the members of the orchestra must suddenly change gears and react as one. These ensemble problems of changing, propelling rhythms and exchanging material certainly outweigh the individual pianistic problems of performing the work. However, pianistically, this final movement is certainly not easy. In addition to all the blocks of octaves, this movement also contains several fleet sixteenth-note finger work passages, made even more complex by their irregular rhythmic profile and independent voices.

Just as Bartók built up the layers of texture in the first movement, the effect of thinning out the layers is stunning at the beginning of the development section. This is a problematic section to hold together; the piano part consists of much sixteenth-note passage filler, and the performer must remember that the orchestra has the more important role here. The recapitulation and its successive canonic building up of textural layers must also be carefully paced, right up until the meno mosso coda. The stops and starts in between these rhythmic blocks are the problem and must be meticulously prepared with conductor and orchestra. The choice of the right tempo is crucial; there is always a danger of playing this movement too fast, thus making it even harder for the listener to understand. Excitement can be achieved only by strict control—and remember that this requires a team effort. Have fun with the meno mosso, and take full advantage of one last chance to be coy and playful and funny before the conclusion of the percussive, driving first *Concerto*.

(Note: In the revised edition, in the penultimate measure of the third movement, the second beat of the left hand should be G-sharp. [In the early edition, it is notated as G-natural.])

The first *Piano Concerto* is perhaps the most difficult of all of the three concertos, not because of technical pianistic problems but because of the demands of the orchestral ensemble. Here the piano must become an equal member of the orchestra. Imitative dialogue, usually using very short motifs, becomes a vital ingredient, and the piano sound needs to be large enough to cut through such a thickly layered imitative orchestration.

Bartók is writing difficult chamber music here for a very large ensemble. The *Concerto* abounds in dissonance, containing lots of seconds, ninths, and tone cluster chords, but real excitement is achieved by rhythmic momentum. This is an example of Bartók's barbaroso style, taken right to the edge of the precipice; Bartók himself admitted that it probably was too difficult for the audience.

Technically, Bartók uses Liszt's pianistic tools to create bravura octave passages; big chordal-block sonorities require the pianist to travel large distances, and martellato and percussive rhythms of the instrument are exploited to produce a demanding, virtuosic, and extremely exciting work. It needs a bravura technique, stamina, energy, and total concentration from the pianist.

What also contributes to the difficulty of achieving a good performance of the first *Piano Concerto* are the ensemble problems, which, unfortunately, will not be aided by today's usual lack of sufficient rehearsal time. Two rehearsals will not be enough unless everyone involved—conductor, pianist, and orchestra—has performed this work more than once. Therefore, this concerto is not as practical a program choice as the lighter and more melodic second or the more accessible and poignant third. However a good performance of this work by orchestra and pianist, complete with its driving motoric rhythms, visceral energy, and ever-increasing blocks of sonorities is certainly an exciting event.

Bartók used the first *Concerto* to experiment with various ideas that would be developed in his later works for piano and orchestra. The middle movement's use of percussion with piano certainly foreshadows the later 1937 *Sonata/Concerto for Two Pianos and Percussion,* and the outline of this movement also paves the way for the Adagio and Scherzo of the second *Concerto,* which in turn prepares for the Andante Religioso of the last *Concerto.* Bartók's orchestration in this middle movement of piano, percussion, and winds also looks ahead to the second *Concerto*'s opening movement, in which strings are eliminated entirely. Bartók's frequent use of trombones and trumpets in the outer movements, as well as at the end of the second movement, strongly suggests the brass fanfare themes of his second and third *Concertos.* The first and final movements share thematic material, and this practice will be exploited in a more sophisticated fashion in the second *Concerto,* where Bartók's transformation of previously used material becomes an intrinsic part of the formal, mirrored structure.

Bartók realized that the complexity of his first *Concerto* was much too difficult to be aurally understood by his audience—and even by some of the conductors with whom he himself performed this work. (For Bartók's scheduled American debut as soloist, No. 1 had to be replaced at the last moment by his Op. 1 *Rhapsody* because the conductor, Willem

Mengelberg, had not spent enough time with the complicated score prior to rehearsal.) However, it remains the job of the performer to peel away the many layers of this complex composition and to create as much lucidity as possible between its rhythmic and thematic material. An understanding of the larger formal design and an analysis of its structural marking points will give shape to complexity and is the prerequisite for arrival at any interpretive viewpoint. The intricate weave of this *Piano Concerto* No. 1 certainly influenced Bartók to go toward a much more homophonic, melodic, and lighter texture in his *Concerto* No. 2 although, pianistically speaking, the second *Concerto* certainly qualifies as the more difficult work.

PIANO CONCERTO NO. 2 (1931)

That is why some years later (1930–1931), while writing my second *Concerto*, I wanted to produce a piece which would contrast with the first; a work which would be less bristling with difficulties for the orchestra and whose thematic material would be more pleasing. This intention explains the rather light and popular character of most of the themes of my latest concerto: a lightness that sometimes also reminds me of one of my youthful works, the first *Suite* for orchestra, Op. 3.[4]

Bartók's early orchestral *Suite*, Op. 3, written in 1905, sounds as if it could have been written by a young Elgar or a youthful Richard Strauss. Listening to these courtly dances helps to understand the mood and sentiment Bartók tried to convey with his *Piano Concerto* No. 2 and also underlines how contrasting in conception were Bartók's first two *Piano Concertos*. How far Bartók has traveled from the extremely driven and aggressive, barbaroso-martellato style of his first *Concerto*. With the second, Bartók wants the pianist to behave in a far more "gentlemanly" manner and to imitate the lilting, rhythmic, and tuneful dance melodies of the seventeenth-century dance suite. This is Bartók's version of Stravinsky's *Suite Italienne* whereas his first *Concerto*, with its visceral approach, more resembles *Le Sacre du Printemps*. Based on the Baroque concerto model, the second with its lighter, generally homophonic texture is much less complicated for the ensemble than the first; however, pianistically, it is much more difficult, and certainly does qualify as the better-crafted composition. Although imitation and contrapuntal techniques abound in both concertos, in the first, Bartók exploits smaller motifs that are imitated successively within a shorter time frame and passed back and forth, thus creating a much more complex and overlapping texture. In the second, the contrapuntal techniques become thoroughly integrated within the work's formal structure.

Studying this second *Concerto*, it is obvious that only a first-class pianist with a large technique and thorough knowledge of the instrument
could have written this piano part. Thick chordal passages must be ne-
gotiated without heaviness and with a light staccato touch, in order to
bring out the lilting rhythm of the melody. The problem for the performer is how to convey a rhythmic lightness while at the same time
giving the impression that the work is easy to play, despite its technical
hurdles. Most performances of this work suffer from heaviness and too
much martellato technique.

Example 10.17: *Piano Concerto* No. 2, 1st mvt.; Universal (1932), Boosey &
Hawkes (1941); m. 1–7

This example from the opening measures of the first movement is certainly more tuneful than most of the first *Concerto*'s short percussive
motifs. However, Bartók makes the pianist struggle with the thickness
of the chords, which must be played allegro and properly voiced so the
melody comes through. There are also occasional chordal passages
throughout the first movement that might prove awkward for a small
hand.

Example 10.18: *Piano Concerto* No. 2, 1st mvt., m. 74–79

With the second theme, Bartók returns to writing reverse arpeggios, first used in his 1908 second *Elegy*, Op. 8b. A grazioso effect is called for here, with the left hand being an inversion of the right.

Example 10.19: *Piano Concerto* No. 2, 1st mvt., m. 80–86

Bartók makes use of all the nineteenth-century bravura pianistic tools, even including a virtuosic, improvisatory cadenza in the opening movement that could qualify as a mini-étude for the study of double thirds.

Example 10.20: *Piano Concerto* No. 2, 1st mvt., m. 222–28

Bartók combines a Lisztian pianism and virtuosity within the glossary of Baroque imitative and contrapuntal devices; themes are turned around and inverted, written in cancrizans (retrograde), in augmentation, in canon. Bach's shadow is evident throughout, along with Debussy's coloristic influence. Bartók also manages successfully to merge elements of the Baroque with primitive folk rhythms. The piano is still a prominent member of the percussion section, and repetition of one rhythmic idea using one tone is exploited, reminiscent of the opening movement, "With Drums and Pipes," from the *Out of Doors*.

Example 10.21: *Piano Concerto* No. 2, 1st mvt., m. 136–40

The codas of the outer movements and the middle Scherzo of the Adagio must also be mentioned as excellent studies for fleet leggiero finger work.

In the second *Concerto*, complex Baroque compositional devices are used within a clear classical structural design.

> The orchestra for the first movement is comprised of wind and percussion instruments; for the Adagio, the strings (muted) and the timpani; strings and a group of wind and percussion instruments for the Scherzo; only the third movement employs the full orchestra.[5]

Allegro

> As far as its form is concerned, my *Piano Concerto* No. 2 by and large corresponds to the classical sonata form. First movement: exposition, development, recapitulation. Here are some observations on form: (1) the thematic unity of the first and third movements . . . [6]

To understand Bartók's craft, the thematic material shared by the first and last movements should be analyzed.

Example 10.22: *Piano Concerto* No. 2, 1st mvt., m. 1–3; opening (a) motif

This has been nicknamed the Stravinsky *Firebird* fanfare theme.

Example 10.23: *Piano Concerto* No. 2, 1st mvt., m. 3–5; (b) motif/main theme

Example 10.24: No. 2, 1st mvt., m. 5–8; (c) motif/counterpoint to the main theme

". . . (2) In the so-called recapitulation section of the first movement and in the corresponding place in the third movement, the [above] themes appear as inversions. . . . [7]

Example 10.25: *Piano Concerto* No. 2, 1st mvt., m. 173–75; inversion of the fanfare (a) motif that introduces the recapitulation

Example 10.26: *Piano Concerto* No. 2, 1st mvt., m. 180–81; inversion of the first theme/(b) motif in the recapitulation

Example 10.27: No. 2, 1st mvt., m. 192–93; inversion of (c) motif in recapitulation

Example 10.28: No. 2, 1st mvt., m. 32–33; counterpoint theme from transition

Example 10.29: No. 2, 1st mvt., m. 200–201; its inversion in recapitulation

". . . (3) In the 'codas' of these two movements, the first theme (in inversion) is employed in so-called 'cancrizans' form, that is, in retrograde motion."[8]

Example 10.30: *Piano Concerto* No. 2, 1st mvt., m. 211–17

Example 10.31: No. 2, 3rd mvt., m. 306–10

Adagio

Movement II is a scherzo within the frame of an adagio, or if you prefer, an adagio containing a scherzo as its nucleus. The adagio itself is subdivided into several corresponding and contrasting sections, the first section—the introductory one—consists of superimposed fifths played by the strings . . .[9]

Example 10.32: *Piano Concerto* No. 2, 2nd mvt., m. 1–5

". . . the other one is a unison melody played by the piano with an accompaniment of glissandi on the timpani."[10]

Example 10.33: *Piano Concerto* No. 2, 2nd mvt., m. 23–26

"Thus the entire work shows symmetrical form: Movement I, adagio, scherzo (as nucleus), variation of the adagio, variation of Movement I. A similar construction was used in my *String Quartets* Nos. 4 and 5 also."[11]

Structurally supported by the pillars of the difficult outer movements, the central focus of the second *Concerto* becomes the scherzo-presto section of the middle movement. Bartók's mirror design of the entire work also confirms this view. With the final movement's shared thematic material looking back toward the first movement, the scherzo, surrounded by its two adagios, is highlighted. It also qualifies as the work's most demanding section. Overflowing with sixteenth-note passages and cluster chords, it must be played leggiero and as rhythmically as possible.

Example 10.34: *Piano Concerto* No. 2, 2nd mvt., m. 164–73

Example 10.35: No. 2, 2nd mvt., m. 98–102

Bartók admitted that the tone-cluster technique was not his own invention. According to Henry Cowell, Bartók met the young American composer quite accidentally in 1923 in London, and overheard him playing some of his music, in which he made use of tone-clusters. "Bartók was extremely interested in this new technique, and later wrote asking if he might be permitted to use similar tone-clusters in his own compositions."[12]

Allegro molto

> The third movement is a masterwork of thematic transformation. Third movement: rondo; I must note here that only the exposition in the third movement has the character of a rondo . . . The third movement is actually a free variation of the first, with the exception of one new theme, which serves as a "frame" (holding together the various sections of the third movement which are constructed out of the transformed subjects from the first movement).[13]

Example 10.36: *Piano Concerto* No. 2, 3rd mvt., m. 4–18; "new" theme

Example 10.37: *Piano Concerto* No. 2, 3rd mvt., m. 144–51

This rondo theme appears a total of four times, with the third variant (example 10.37) being an inversion of the original. The tympani becomes an important participant in this thematic material.

The first episode transforms rhythmically the first theme of the first movement (example 10.23).

Example 10.38: *Piano Concerto* No. 2, 3rd mvt., m. 45–47

The second digression uses the (c) motif from the first movement exposition (example 10.24) and later inverts it.

Example 10.39: *Piano Concerto* No. 2, 3rd mvt., m. 94–95; m. 101–3

The third episode uses the second theme from the first movement (example 10.19) altered dramatically in character and develops the tail of the inverted theme in sequential octaves.

Example 10.40: *Piano Concerto* No. 2, 3rd mvt., m. 162–65

The development section of this movement begins with the third statement of the Rondo theme.

The orchestral tutti announcing the recapitulation is similar to the first movement's orchestral transition to the recapitulation (example 10.25) and the tutti announcement of the piano cadenza (example 10.30).

Example 10.41: *Piano Concerto* No. 2, 3rd mvt., m. 203–6

The difficult coda mirrors the coda of the first movement with its melody derived from the second theme of the first movement (example 10.19).

Bartók creates an intricate and well-crafted puzzle for the pianist, and different relationships reappear every time the score is studied. At the conclusion of this movement, the linkage is complete with the opening *Firebird* theme (example 10.22) presented in augmentation by the piano, and inverted in the orchestra. A perfectly balanced formal structure has been achieved.

The second *Concerto* ranks as one of the more difficult works of the pianist's concerto repertory, but is well worth the effort. Once understanding the way the work is constructed, the pianist must conquer its technical hurdles. It needs to be played with a light rhythmic lilt, but the piano sound must be large enough to cut through the orchestration. This works suffers too often from an overly aggressive interpretation, which was certainly not Bartók's intention, as he himself stated when writing this work. (Bartók's own recording [Hungaroton HCD 12334–37] of some fragments from this concerto is a revelation of his conception of the work, inspired by the lilting dance movements of a Baroque suite.) The ensemble problems are less than those of the first *Concerto*. Coming out of the complexity of the first, Bartók has used the intricacy of Baroque devices within a more homophonic texture, to create clarity and unity of structure. The balance between the classical and the Baroque will be further crystallized in his classical third *Concerto*.

PIANO CONCERTO NO. 3 (1945)

> I should like to write a piano concerto for Mother. This plan has long been in the air. If she could play it in three or four places, then it would bring in about as much money as the one commission I refused.[14]

In this 1945 letter to his son Peter, Bartók was speaking about his refusal to write a two-piano concerto. His wife Ditta Pásztory, for whom this last work was written, never played the *Concerto*, nor did Bartók ever completely finish the composition, dying on September 26th, 1945. The first draft had been made, and Tibor Serly, a close friend of Bartók's, deciphered Bartók's markings after his death in order to orchestrate the last seventeen measures of the work.

With this *Concerto*, Bartók leaves the world of the Baroque to venture into the classical realm. There is harmony and balance here, and much less use of dissonance; in fact, the concerto is clearly in E major! The piano has regained its featured role as a soloist accompanied by orchestra. The canons and fugues have been made simpler, now reduced to fugatos; texture has become leaner, and unison writing is frequent. The form is direct, more concise and strictly classical, even in its key relationships. The interval of the third becomes a unifying element throughout the work. As the second *Concerto* was modeled on a Bach concerto, the third conjures up the ghost of Beethoven.

The simplicity of writing in the *Piano Concerto* No. 3 represents a major shift in Bartók's style, and it is the only work that is truly representative of Bartók's newfound classical clarity. Many have advanced the theory that because Bartók was writing this work as a birthday gift for his wife, and not for himself, it had to be written in a leaner and much easier style. Certainly, it is acknowledged that Ditta did not possess the pianistic gifts of her husband and could not master the piano writing in Bartók's physically and technically demanding second *Concerto* or the complexities of the first. For this reason she never publicly performed these works. However, Bartók did write for Ditta the "Night Sounds" movement from the *Out of Doors*, which certainly qualifies as one of his more complex and difficult compositions; he dedicated his 1926 *Sonata* to her; and the *Sonata* for two pianos and percussion, written specifically to be played by Mr. and Mrs. Bartók, could not be labeled an easy work. It is possible that Bartók's evaluation of his former pupil's pianistic skills did have some influence on his piano writing, but certainly, it would have been completely out of character for Bartók ever to have consciously altered his stylistic direction or compromised himself musically. He was never a man to adapt his beliefs in order to fit the elements of circumstance. Rather, it is my opinion that Bartók, like Prokofiev, had the need at the end of his life to purify, distill, and to make even more direct that which he needed to say. (After the huge proportions of the "War" *Sonatas* Nos. 6, 7, and 8, Prokofiev returned to the simple, innocent, and much more melodic style of his C major ninth *Sonata*.) Bartók was headed in this direction with his later works. He had already experienced his love affair with complexity in all forms in the twenties and thirties, and was stylistically ready to shed everything superfluous. This view certainly was in harmony with Bartók's musical values and can explain the special relationship he experienced with folk music, being attracted primarily to its simplicity as a direct reaction to all romantic excesses. Always, his objective remained to search and to arrive at the musical "truth." To reveal the essence of an idea meant exposing its innate simplicity.

The *Piano Concerto* No. 3 is in three movements, with the central focus of the work being the middle movement adagio, which contains some of the most poignant writing of the entire concerto.

Allegretto

Most performances of this movement fail to capture Bartók's playfulness and mischievous sense of humor and usually suffer from an overly serious, much too earnest approach. The mood is set in its opening measures, and Bartók carefully writes out in the score the rhythmic rubatos to be included. Rests are introduced as breaths, and the choice of sixteenth- or thirty-second-note upbeats clearly differentiated. Within the strict tempo maintained by the ostinato accompaniment, the pianist must create the impression of flexibility in his declamation, while at the same time following Bartók's precise markings and capturing the playful irony of Bartók's sharp wit.

Example 10.42: *Piano Concerto* No. 3, 1st mvt., Boosey & Hawkes (1947), m. 2–9

Example 10.43: No. 3, 1st mvt., m. 117–27

When the return occurs (example 10.43), Bartók replaces the unisons with open fourth chords, creating some difficult passagework for the pianist. (I have indicated the fingering I use to help articulate the melody. On the first beats of m. 126 and 127, it might be easier to divide the chord so that three notes are played with the right hand.)

Throughout Bartók's piano music, the improvisatory quality desired is usually meticulously indicated.

Example 10.44: *Piano Concerto* No. 3, 1st mvt., m. 13–19

This is a wonderful example of Bartók's writing-out technique. He makes us see and hear exactly what he is doing to help the pianist give the impression of pure improvisation.

Comparing the piano writing in all three concertos, it is clear that Bartók has utilized the same pianistic tools but now achieves a leaner, but no less effective, approach with his use of octaves, chordal blocks, and finger passagework. The transitional passages to the second theme

in the first movement of the second concerto and in the third concerto illustrate this marked difference. Bartók functions like a good editor with
the third; everything excessive has been cut out and honed down to the
basics.

Example 10.45: *Piano Concerto* No. 3, 1st mvt., m. 40–42

Example 10.46: *Piano Concerto* No. 2, 1st mvt., m. 32–33

The second theme is marked grazioso. Bartók's orchestration captures the
humorous mood and, with its leaner texture, allows the pianist the freedom to be light and graceful.

Example 10.47: *Piano Concerto* No. 3, 1st mvt., m. 44–46

When a motive from the second theme returns as a closing theme before
m. 54, also in the development before m. 99, and at m. 162, I insert a brief
comma—the equivalent of a tiny breath. This helps to delineate contrast
and highlights the playful character of the writing.

The editor has suggested the metronome marking of 88 per quarter for
the opening movement. Bartók writes only allegretto and wants a comfortable tempo—not too pushed or frantic—a tempo giusto to capture the
lilting dance rhythms and playfulness of the score. Try the metronome
marking of 84; this works better for me.

Bartók has structured a very concise first movement, with classical Beethoven proportions. The development is short, direct, and to the point; how far he has traveled from the long, extended, complex sectional developments within the first *Piano Concerto*. This is the brass's moment; the piano provides only sound filler and accompaniment. Use of the middle sostenuto pedal as Bartók indicates will lessen the thickness of the lower register and still create the sonority needed. The pianist only briefly expounds on the first theme's transformation before the return. In this concerto, it is noticeable that Bartók has shed all the accoutrements of sheer virtuosity, but the piano writing still remains effective. Bartók ends the movement as it began, and the interval of a third takes on a unifying significance. This concerto is generally not problematic for the ensemble, and this last page of the first movement qualifies as its most difficult interchange between piano and orchestra. Bartók leaves us basking in the sunlight of E major.

Adagio religioso

Bartók has chosen C major as the key of this poignant movement that seems to evoke Beethoven's presence, especially in its outer sections. (Listen to the adagio of Beethoven's Op. 132 string quartet.) The descriptive title of religioso is significant, and it becomes the performer's responsibility to reveal the emotional depths hidden beneath the notes of this simple chorale. Recalling the use of the virtuosic cadenza in the second *Concerto*'s first movement, Bartók now makes use of the cadenza when the chorale returns played by the orchestra, and the piano embellishes the theme at the conclusion of each line with a vocal cadenza (à la Rossini) that has dramatic significance as well as serving to prolong the sound.

Example 10.48: *Piano Concerto* No. 3, 2nd mvt., m. 100–104

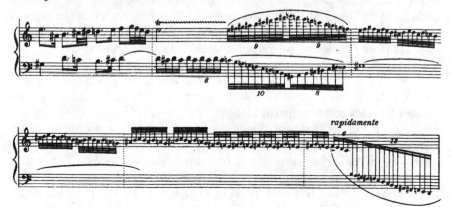

The innocence of the chorale return is especially stunning after the night sounds developmental middle section. Bartók said that he based the trio upon actual birdcalls he had heard while convalescing in Asheville, North Carolina, in 1944.[15] Natives of North Carolina will recognize the songs of the tufted titmouse (also heard at the end of the first movement and before the development) and the wood thrush, among others. The trio recalls the "Night Sounds" movement from the *Out of Doors*.

When the piano takes over the chorale theme from the orchestra in the coda, coinciding with the appearance of the tam-tam, the emotional intensity of this dramatic moment must be conveyed and its descent to the final and magical E major chord properly prepared. Surely, this qualifies as one of the movement's most religious and revelatory moments.

(Note: In the revised full orchestral score, the tempo of the slow movement has been changed from 76 per quarter in previous solo editions to 69. I agree that the 76 tempo for the opening chorale sounds a bit pushed and should be saved for the middle section poco più mosso night sounds.)

Allegro vivace

More than any other movement included in the three piano concertos, this third movement captures the infectious ebullient spirit of the folk song. Complexity has been replaced here by simplicity. The same pianistic tools are used but with the thinness of the orchestration, the piano writing now is much more accessible.

Contrapuntal techniques are still in evidence, but fugues are reduced to the leaner texture of fugatos in predominantly two-voice writing; imitation and inversion are also present, but not as integrated and vital to thematic and formal design as found in the second concerto. The virtuosic coda with its wonderful leggiero writing recalls the codas of the second, but the language here is completely diatonic, with some humorous play (à la Schubert) back and forth with major and minor thirds.

Economy is the essence of Bartók's final work. All has been removed except what is truly important and essential. With this *Concerto*, Bartók certainly achieved his musical ideal.

(Note: In the most recent Boosey & Hawkes full score edition of the *Concerto*, published and revised in 1994, an error in a tempo indication at m. 392 in the third movement has now been corrected. The tempo change in previous editions of più tranquillo had not been in the original score, as Bartók left no tempo indications at all for the last movement. Musically, this sudden slowing down of tempo alters the rhythmic pulse and interferes with the folk spirit of the final movement. Without this change, more sense can be made of the 2/4 section at m. 427, followed by the 3/8 return at m. 473 of the material from m. 392, all to be played at the same tempo. Even though this tempo change is currently observed by most performers of this work, it is totally out of character with the dance movement. The only tempo change should be at the presto coda, where the pulse is maintained but the note value shifts from dotted quarter to dotted half notes.)

Another important change is a clarification of the figures at m. 154, 155, and 157. Observe how these are notated in the older edition; the rhythm has now been clarified by the corrected notation.

Example 10.49: *Piano Concerto* No. 3, 1st mvt., (a) m. 155; (b) m. 155, revised edition Boosey & Hawkes (1994)

(a)

(b)

Other significant changes, corrected in the revised 1994 edition:

Example 10.50: *Piano Concerto* No. 3, 2nd mvt., m. 16–20 (whole note changed to two half notes in right hand of m. 19)

Example 10.51: No. 3, 2nd mvt., m. 81 (change of first and last notes in l.h.)

Example 10.52: No. 3, 2nd mvt., m. 86 (change of D to D-sharp in second beat in both hands; next-to-last sixteenth note in l.h. is F, not D)

Example 10.53: No. 3, 2nd mvt., m. 127

Example 10.54: No. 3, 2nd mvt., m. 133

Example 10.55: No. 3, 3rd mvt., m. 309–12 (E changed to E-sharp in m. 310)

Example 10.56: No. 3, 3rd mvt., m. 388–96 (B changed to B-flat in m. 394)

Example 10.57: No. 3, 3rd mvt., m. 761–68 (octaves added to left hand in m. 764–65 two measures earlier than in original score; this change was suggested by several performers)

Another interesting revelation from the notes to the revised edition indicates that in the composer's manuscript the third movement began at m. 141, which means that the soloist's opening three measures were included in the second movement and treated as a transitional link. Therefore, observation of the attacca indicated at the end of the Adagio is musically necessary. (In the new edition the measures of the second and third movements are numbered consecutively.) The metronome marking for the finale has been slightly changed, down a notch to 92 from the 96 indicated in previous editions. Also the metronome marking to the finale's presto coda has been altered from 96 in previous editions to 69. Certainly the slower tempo works better technically both for the pianist and helps facilitate the difficult writing in the strings. However the suggested tempo of 69 is extreme and stops the momentum that should be building towards the final note of the composition. A good compromise would be to start the presto at 84. At this tempo the eighth-note orchestral accompaniment is not impossible to play, and forward energy has not been sacrificed. Gradually, increase the tempo to 88 for the eighth-note passage-work (m. 673), going forward to return to the opening tempo of 92 by m. 705. Arrive at 96 for Tempo I; this is the metronome marking suggested in previous editions. Notice that at m. 730 in the coda, the low G notated in the piano part does not exist on the Steinway; Bartók was writing with his Bösendorfer in mind. Start the glissando on the keyboard's lowest note.

A truly successful performance of this final concerto is rare. Most pianists want to make more out of the work than is necessary and tend to treat it a bit too seriously. They fail to capture its playful, unpretentious qualities and try to substitute inflated virtuosity for Bartók's infectious simplicity.

THE PIANO/CHAMBER REPERTOIRE

Sonata No. 1 for violin and piano (1921)
Sonata No. 2 for violin and piano (1922)
Rhapsody No. 1 for violin and piano (1928, revised in 1929)
Rhapsody No. 2 for violin and piano (1928, revised in 1944)

Aside from some very youthful works that include a violin sonata written in 1903 when he was twenty-two, Bartók had completely avoided writing for the solo violin until the 1920s, concentrating instead on the instrument he knew best, the piano. Within the string family, he was much more at home writing for the string quartet medium, with its homogeneous sound, than for the challenging tonal combination of violin and piano. However, in 1921, Jelly Arányi, a fine violinist and an old friend of

Bartók's, asked him to write a sonata for her, and two sonatas for violin and piano were composed during the period 1921–1922. It is interesting to note that at the Paris premiere of the *Sonata* No. 1, given by Bartók and Arányi in 1922, new as well as established composers were present, including Stravinsky, Poulenc, Milhaud, Ravel, and Szymanowski.

Both of the sonatas are difficult works for the violinist and the pianist, who function as equal but totally independent partners; Bartók provides each performer with different material. Overflowing with dissonant sevenths, ninths, major and minor seconds, and the piling up of fourths, the writing shows not only Debussy's influence but also reflects Bartók's increasing familiarity with Schoenberg's music. Even though Bartók clearly states that these works are firmly in C-sharp and C tonality, they are the closest that Bartók will get to Schoenberg's language, short of a twelve-tone row. However, the folk idiom is not abandoned, and Bartók manages to combine successfully a "sophisticated" modernism with primitive peasant melodies. Both of the sonata's final movements make use of folk-related material. The first *Sonata*'s first movement also evokes some of the thematic material that will be later heard in the third *Piano Concerto* as well as the *Sonata* for two pianos and percussion.

Bartók was much more partial to the second *Sonata*, written in two movements, preferring it to his three-movement first *Sonata*. The second was, in his opinion, the more concise work of the two, with the main theme of the first movement returning in the final movement. The first movement of the first *Sonata* is indeed large and problematic, and it was once suggested by Bartók that perhaps only the second and third movements of this *Sonata* should be performed together. Both violin sonatas are large and challenging works too rarely heard in concert, mainly because of the technical and musical difficulties for both instruments.

The two rhapsodies are much more popular and more accessible, especially the first *Rhapsody*, which exists in many versions: for violin and piano, for violin and orchestra, for cello and piano, and also with two different endings. The first *Rhapsody* is dedicated to Josef Szigeti and the second to Zoltán Székely, another old friend of Bartók's. (The definitive recording of the *Rhapsody* No. 1—and also the *Sonata* No. 2—is the 1940 Library of Congress recital with Bartók and Szigeti on Vanguard VCD 72025. This recording includes the second ending to the *Rhapsody*.) In these two works, the pianist no longer functions as an equal partner, but acts more as the accompanist for the featured violin soloist. Both compositions are in two movements: lassu, friss (slow, fast) and are based on authentic folk material, using dances originally written to be played by the violin. (From 1912 to 1914, Bartók and Kodály went to the countryside and heard and recorded the music of the Rumanian village gypsies.)

It is this style of performance that Bartók imitates, especially apparent in the ornamented, wild style of the second *Rhapsody*. Usually, the gypsy violinist was accompanied by a second instrument: a guitar providing the rhythm on the open D and A strings, or a second violin specifically tuned to provide the simple chordal accompaniment. The *Rhapsody* No. 1 uses six folk dances of Rumanian and Hungarian origin; No. 2 makes use of nine from Rumanian, Hungarian, and Ruthenian sources. The second *Rhapsody* was revised in 1944 and also exists in two versions (with piano and with orchestra, as well as in its original edition and its later condensed and revised version.) The cello version of the first *Rhapsody* is a faithful transcription of the original. In 1930, Bartók wrote in a letter to his mother: "Casals is playing my *Rhapsody* all over Europe!"[16]

Contrasts for Violin, Clarinet, and Piano (1938)

> I can assure you that whatever a clarinetist is physically able to do at all, Benny can get out of the instrument and wonderfully (in much higher regions than the high note of the *Eulenspiegel*).[17]

Bartók accepted this commission from the jazz clarinetist Benny Goodman and was paid three hundred dollars for Goodman's performing rights to *Contrasts* for three years. Originally the work was supposed to be only two movements, which would be long enough to fill up two sides of a 78 recording, but ended up as a three-movement work, with the "Night Music" movement placed in between its faster outer movements. Josef Szigeti sent Bartók all of Benny Goodman's jazz recordings, and according to Goodman, "Bartók derived his inspiration to write *Contrasts* from listening to a number of records by my old jazz trio: Teddy Wilson, Gene Krupa, and myself."[18] The jazz influence is definitely here, and there are moments when even George Gershwin's clarinet has crept into Bartók's writing.

This is a work written primarily to feature and show off the clarinet and the violin. Both instruments are given difficult, virtuosic cadenzas, and the piano functions mainly in a supporting role. In the last movement, Bartók writes not only for the normal violin but also asks for a special violin to be tuned to G-sharp/D/A/E-flat, creating a wonderful country fiddler effect. In this last movement, the clarinet uses both the B-flat and A clarinet.

This unique instrumental combination is exploited to its best advantage. The definitive recording—which should be a part of every basic record collection—is the performance of this work with Szigeti, Goodman, and Bartók, reissued on CD by Sony (MPK 47676). Impossible to imagine this work played any better!

NOTES

1. Béla Bartók, "Analysis of the Second Concerto for Piano and Orchestra" (1939), in *Béla Bartók Essays*, ed. Benjamin Suchoff (Lincoln: University of Nebraska Press, 1976), 419.

2. Béla Bartók, "About the Piano Problem" (1927), in *Béla Bartók Essays*, ed. Benjamin Suchoff, 288.

3. Béla Bartók, "Analysis of the Second Concerto for Piano and Orchestra " (1939), in *Béla Bartók Essays*, ed. Benjamin Suchoff, 423.

4. Bartók, "Analysis of the Second Concerto for Piano and Orchestra " (1939), 419.

5. "Analysis of Second Concerto," 423.

6. "Analysis of Second Concerto," 419.

7. "Analysis of Second Concerto," 420.

8. "Analysis of Second Concerto," 421.

9. "Analysis of Second Concerto," 422.

10. "Analysis of Second Concerto," 422.

11. "Analysis of Second Concerto," 423.

12. Henry Cowell in *Bartók Remembered*, ed. Malcolm Gillies (New York: W. W. Norton, 1991), 118.

13. "Analysis of Second Concerto", 419–20.

14. Béla Bartók in *The Bartók Companion*, ed. Malcolm Gillies (Portland, Oreg.: Amadeus Press, 1994), 538.

15. The Albemarle Inn in Asheville, North Carolina, where Bartók lived from December 1943 through April 1944, is still open to guests. It is possible to visit Bartók's room on the third floor.

16. *Complete Bartók Recordings*, Hungaroton (LPX 11357).

17. From a letter sent to Bartók by Szigeti (August 11th, 1938): Josef Szigeti, "Letters to Béla Bartók," in *Bartók Studies*, ed. Todd Crow (Detroit: Detroit Reprints in Music, 1976), 131. [This letter first appeared in *The New Hungarian Quarterly* XI/40 (Winter 1970).]

18. Benny Goodman, "Contrasts," *Listen* (November 1940).

11

✛

Clarity and Rubato: Bartók as Pianist

Instinctive and conscious elements must be in equilibrium within the
creative imagination.

—Béla Bartók[1]

Béla Bartók was an original at the keyboard. Thanks to excellent modern technology, it is now much easier to hear what he was able to
achieve at the piano. When one listens to recent remasterings of his old
recordings, the piano playing leaps out and demands attention. It is playing that has character more than personality, and this is not limited to interpretations of his own music. Bartók combines structural clarity with
the freedom of natural speech. When joined and molded together, these
two essential ingredients give special definition to Bartók's unique rubato
style. He possessed an extraordinary facility for the instrument, combined
with a remarkable and varied touch. In our present age, when sameness
appears to be the norm and the lack of distinctive pianistic personalities
among our young pianists is so often lamented, such personal and convincing piano playing imbued with true strength of character makes us
want to shout, "Yes, but of course, this is the way music should be
played!"

The numerous recent CD reissues provide excellent teaching guides for
the performer and serious student of Bartók's music and capture the
essence of the composer as teacher. Bartók's discography forms an important part of his original source material. He personifies in the best
sense the composer as performer of his own music, always illuminating
what is written in the score. A former piano student of Bartók, Lajos

Hernádi, said, "It was beautiful because it was true."[2] Even when performing works by other composers such as Liszt, Debussy, Mozart, Beethoven, Brahms, and even Chopin, Bartók makes us aware of what initially attracted him to their music and helps us to understand and evaluate how his own music fits within the historic continuum.

Unfortunately, too often the predominant view of Bartók's piano writing has focused only on the distorted allegro barbaroso image and has categorized Bartók as a percussive, hard, brittle, unbending, and inflexible pianist, totally lacking in color, charm, and spontaneity. His playfulness, humor and wit, and vitality of spirit usually get overlooked. However, these ingredients are in abundance in his recordings, always accompanied by a direct, unmannered, no-nonsense approach to the music. The serious performer of Bartók's piano works has the obligation to explore all of the music's coloristic riches and subtleties and not perpetuate the distorted image of Bartók's piano writing.

Bartók, a strong and uncompromising personality, had a very personal style and a unique physical approach to the instrument. According to people familiar with his piano playing, including former students and colleagues, he was rather rigid and angular-looking when seated at the piano. His technique was formidable but not usually noted for its subtle coloristic palette. Contemporaries observed that he was much more comfortable playing Beethoven or Bach than Chopin, even though Chopin's music remained an essential part of Bartók's teaching repertoire. "Bartók interpreted and played Chopin as if it were Mozart. And he taught it like that, too. To him a melody of Chopin had to be unaffected, strict, like a chorale, never sentimental, not something to start sobbing about," according to Júlia Székely, a former student.[3]

Lajos Hernádi observed: "Bartók was not a colorist when he played the piano. Probably this was the only deficiency in his playing, and it appeared when—very rarely—he played works by composers like Chopin, whose colors and specific instrumental sounds are inseparable from the fullness of aesthetic effect. These pieces sounded somewhat strange, as if they had been carved in granite—but they were granite masterpieces all the same. . . . His wrists and arm were all fixed. That is why he sounded, as I said, as if he had carved each piece in stone. No one with a personality different from Bartók could make use of this sound convincingly—it was too specific, too unique to create a school."[4]

Obviously, a pianist's interpretation will be directly influenced by the predominance of his pianistic strengths over his weaknesses. Because of the extraordinary level of Bartók's piano playing on these recordings, it would be difficult to fully agree with the observations of these former students. What is apparent is that Bartók possessed a phenomenally natural technique at the keyboard. However, he never discussed piano technique with his students; when asked about a technical problem, his advice was to go home and practice! What is obvious from listening is Bartók's un-mannered approach, his complete lack of sentimentality, and the elimina-tion of all exaggerated effects. Contrasts and colors abound. However, the coloristic palette that might have been proper for the playing of a Chopin nocturne in Budapest at the beginning of the century certainly would not be appropriate when applied to Bartók's melodies. (Listening to the only Chopin excerpt contained in these recordings, a four-minute incomplete performance of Chopin's C-sharp minor nocturne [Hungaroton 12334-37], the realization that Bartók can create his own sound-world and suspend all sense of time with extraordinary effect, poignancy, and absolutely no sen-timentality is a revelation!) This is very personal playing; it seems to emerge from the heart of the performer and go directly to the listener. It jumps out and communicates!

Bartók's music is too universal to be restricted to interpretation only by someone with a fluent knowledge of Hungarian language and folklore. However, any serious interpreter of Bartók's music should certainly try to acquaint himself with the native folk song tradition. Several recordings of the original folk music that Bartók recorded on his field trips were issued in the 1930s on the Hungaroton label. *Hungarian Folk Music Collected by Bartók* (LPX 18069) allows the listener to hear the folk tunes as Bartók heard the peasants sing them in 1908. Also on the same label are the fol-lowing recordings, which unfortunately are no longer available except in secondhand shops: *Anthology of Hungarian Folk Music,* Volume I (LPX 18112-16), Volume II (LPX 18124-28), and Volume IV (LPX 18159-63); *Hun-garian Instrumental Folk Music* (LPX 18050-53); *Hungarian Folk Music* (LPX 18045-47); *Hungarian Folk Music,* Volume 1 (LPX 10095-98), Volume 2 (LPX 18001-04), and Volume 3 (LPX 18050-53); and *Hungarian Folk Music from Rumania* (LPX 18107-18111). The only folk recording currently available on CD is Bartók's *Turkish Folk Music Collection* (HCD 18218-19) issued by Hungaroton. The Bartók Archives, located in Budapest, house the bulk of Bartók's original folk material and manuscripts.

Much of the piano music Bartók wrote was intended as repertory for himself and Ditta Pásztory to perform on their concert tours. Bartók and, to a lesser extent, his wife were the only genuine advocates of his piano music. Any real performance tradition would probably rest with Bartók himself and be represented by his writings, manuscripts, and piano recordings.

But Bartók acknowledged the difficulty of finding a definitive interpre-tation, even if it came directly from the composer himself. This applied to his folk music research as well as the realm of performance. Unlike his col-league Stravinsky, who believed that the ideal performance existed in the composer's ears at the moment of creation, Bartók believed in the talent of the individual artist. He was flexible enough to trust a gifted performer's ideas and to allow for other interpretations, in addition to his own. So many of the ad libitum performance practices indicated in his scores underscore his faith in the performer's judgment. For the composer Bartók, certainly there was not only one way to play his compositions; similarly, he acknowledged that there was never only one correct version of the folk tunes he had collected. Perhaps every composer would be inclined to agree with the words Bartók used to describe the young Yehudi Menuhin's performance of his solo violin *Sonata:* "When there is a real great artist, then the composer's advice and help are not necessary; the performer finds his way quite well, alone!!!"[5]

These piano recordings will aid the exploration and immersion into this wonderful and difficult repertoire. They are a treasure chest, with many surprises in store for those who listen.

> I have composed music and will compose music as long as I am alive; this music then is to hold its own and speak for itself . . . in this it does not need my help.[6]

DISCOGRAPHY OF BARTÓK PIANO RECORDINGS

> Even if one succeeded in perfectly preserving a composer's work according to his own idea at a given moment, it would not be advisable always to listen to these compositions in this manner. This would bury the composition in boredom. It is conceivable that the composer himself would have performed his works better or less well at some other time—but, in any case, differently. This applies equally to any performing artist of a stature equivalent to the composer in question.[7]

A series of complete recordings entitled *Bartók at the Piano* is now available on six CDs produced by Hungaroton. Several other companies (Sony, EMI, Pearl, Vanguard) have also reissued certain parts of the same Hungarian collection, which had originally been recorded for HMV, Columbia, Continental, and Patria Records. In general, the Hungaroton sound is much more strident than these other remasterings, which seem to soften the hard edges and produce a much more pleasing piano sound. The real advantage of the Hungaroton collection lies in its completeness. What will not be found on any of the other reissues are the piano roll recordings of 1920; Bartók's wonderful performances of Scarlatti sonatas; a not-so-wonderful ensemble performance (due to lack of sufficient rehearsal time with the percussionists) of his *Sonata* for two pianos and percussion; Bartók acting as accompanist for several Hungarian singers in Kodály's songs; and a tape of a radio broadcast recorded in New Jersey near the end of his life in 1945.

Recordings of Bartók from private collections have also been assembled on four CDs by Hungaroton. All together, these two collections, which fill ten CDs, cover nearly everything that Bartók had ever taped or recorded, including interviews given by him about his music for American, Belgian, and Hungarian radio. The sound quality of the recordings from private collections is generally poor; however, the musical insights heard in his excerpts from the second *Piano Concerto* and the Op. 1 *Rhapsody* are well worth the static noise and expensive purchase price for both sets of recordings.

Complete Collections

Bartók at the Piano (studio, broadcast, and piano roll recordings by Bartók ca. 1920–1945) 6 CDs; Hungaroton (HCD 12326/31):

1. Welte Mignon piano rolls (1920?): *Ten Easy Pieces: Evening in Transylvania; Fifteen Hungarian Peasant Songs* (Nos. 6–10, 12, 14, 15); *Sonatina; Rumanian Folk Dances*
2. HMV recording (1929, Budapest); these recordings are included on EMI Composers Series (72435-5503121) and also on Pearl (GEMM CD 9166): *Ten Easy Pieces* (Nos. 5, 10); *Rumanian Dances* Op. 8a (No. 1); *Fourteen Bagatelles* (No. 2); *Three Burlesques* (No. 2); *Allegro Barbaro; Suite* Op. 14 (a second version, the test recording, is offered only on Hungaroton)
3. Scarlatti sonatas: L. 286, L. 135, L. 293, L. 50, originally released on Bartók Records by Bartók's son Peter, and now only available on Hungaroton
4. Patria recordings (1936, Budapest); this material is also included in the Pearl recording (GEMM CD 9166): *Années de Pèlerinage* No. 7 (Liszt); *Fifteen Hungarian Peasant Songs* (Nos. 7–10, 12, 14, 15); *Three Rondos* (No. 1); *Nine Little Piano Pieces* (Nos. 6, 8); *Petite Suite* ("Bagpipes")
5. HMV recordings (1928, Budapest) with Hungarian singers Mária Basilides, Vilma Madgyaszay and Ferenc Székelyhídy singing songs of Kodály and Bartók (performances by these singers of the Bartók songs are also included in the EMI recording 72435-5503121)
6. Columbia recordings with violinist Josef Szigeti playing his arrangement of *Hungarian Folk Tunes* and Z. Székely's arrangement of *Rumanian Folk Dances* from 1930, recorded in London (the EMI recording also includes these two compositions but claims they were recorded on the same date, July 1, 1930, in Budapest); the *Rhapsody*, No. 1, recorded in 1940 in New York; and *Contrasts* with Benny Goodman, also from 1940 (the *Contrasts* are included in the Sony recording MPK 47676)

7. Columbia recordings of Bartók playing pieces from *Mikrokosmos*: No. 124 *Staccato* and No. 146 *Ostinato*, both recorded in 1937; and the following pieces, all recorded in 1940: No. 113 *Bulgarian Rhythm*; 129 *Alternating Thirds*; 131 *Fourths*; 128 *Peasant Dance*; 120 *Fifth Chords*; 109 *From the Island of Bali*; 138 *Bagpipe*; 100 *In the Style of a Folk Song*; 142 *From the Diary of a Fly*; 140 *Free Variations*; 133 *Syncopation*; 149 *Six Dances in Bulgarian Rhythms*; 108 *Wrestling*; 94 *Tale*; 126 *Change of Time*; 116 *Melody*; 130 *Village Joke*; 139 *Merry Andrew*; 143 *Divided Arpeggios*; 147 *March*; 144 *Minor Seconds, Major Sevenths*; 97 *Notturno*; 118 *Triplets in 9/8 Time*; 141 *Subject and Reflection*; 136 *Whole-Tone Scale*; 125 *Boating*; and 114 *Theme and Inversion*. The two pieces recorded in 1937 in London, *Staccato* and *Ostinato*, are available as part of the EMI and Pearl recordings. The rest of the *Mikrokosmos*, recorded in 1940, has been reissued by Sony (MPK 47676) except for No. 143, *Divided Arpeggios*, which is not included.

8. The Washington/Library of Congress 1940 recital with Josef Szigeti: This recording was originally released by Vanguard (OVC 8008) and is currently available on CD (a must-have for any collection!); Beethoven: *Sonata* No. 9 ("Kreutzer"); Debussy: *Sonata*; Bartók: *Sonata* No. 2, *Rhapsody* No. 1

9. CBS Radio broadcast of 1940, originally released by Vox: *Sonata* for two pianos and percussion, with Bartók, Ditta Pásztory, and percussionists Henry Baker and Edward Rubsam

10. Continental recording made in 1942, also available on Pearl (GEMM CD 9166): *Petite Suite*; *Bagatelle* No. 2; *Rondo* No. 1; *Improvisations* Nos. 1, 2, 6, 7, 8; *Nine Little Piano Pieces* No. 9; *Three Hungarian Folk Tunes*; seven pieces from *Mikrokosmos* for two pianos (Nos. 2, 5, 6), with Ditta Pásztory

11. From a radio broadcast given in 1945 in New Jersey and originally released by Vox: *Ten Easy Pieces* Nos. 5, 10; *For Children* Nos. 3, 4, 6, 10, 12, 13, 15, 18, 19, 21, 26, 34, 35, 31, 30

Bartók's piano playing always makes sense out of the music. What is immediately obvious from the opening measures of these recordings is his strong feeling for the lyrical line, combined with a wonderful touch and genuine rubato playing. Bartók makes us aware of how much the piano can become an imitative instrument of color and how frequently folk instruments are depicted in his keyboard writing. He is capable of making the piano sound like a bagpipe, and his own playing always captures the true spirit of the work. Bartók is not afraid to improvise and take liberties with the ornamental line. Occasionally, when repeating a folk melody, he will double it in octaves or go an octave higher or lower, as he does in his performance of the *Rumanian Folk Dances* and in some of his pieces from *For Children*.

Joy is transmitted in his playing, as well as a sense of humor and surprise. The rubato principles of playing a Chopin nocturne can be applied for the most part to much of Bartók's folk material: An ongoing rhythm is maintained, while the other voice freely declaims in the manner of parlando speech, including breaths and commas; the accents Bartók indicates and observes in the score underline the voice's natural punctuation.

Quite surprising to hear is Bartók's romantic interpretation of *Allegro Barbaro,* with its color variations, antiphonal effects, and rubato. Both performances of the *Suite* Op. 14 show great flexibility of tempo without sacrificing its dance qualities. The two different versions show that he never played a piece in exactly the same way. (Bartók takes more liberties in the fourth movement of the second version.) He also lets us know how difficult the third movement is to play.

However, it is in Bartók's performances of other composers' music that his excellent pianism is revealed. He is not afraid of taking risks at the keyboard. His recordings of Scarlatti sonatas are not note-perfect but convey a sense of freedom and rhythmic vitality. Even in his editing of these sonatas, he explains his musical flexibility. It's as if he edits musically; he has the freedom to indicate breaths in between phrases and tempo changes and is not governed by any strict rules of early performance practice. Like his playing, his editing is musical, direct, and unmannered. In his performance of the Liszt piece, it is obvious that he knew very well the full range of the piano's sonorities. These are performances with character, with all traces of sentimentality removed. Bartók was also a superb accompanist, and it is a pity that we don't have any recordings of his playing Schubert lieder. His wonderfully colored piano playing inspires the singers to capture the spirit of the song.

Above all, Bartók's performances are musical clarifications. Listening to his interpretations, we can better understand what the composer is saying. Bartók is able to make convincing sense out of the musical language.

Bartók: Recordings from Private Collections (Hungaroton: HCD 12334-37)

1. Cylinder recordings (1910–1915): *For Children* Vol. 3, No. 22; *Seven Sketches* No. 3; *Ten Easy Pieces* No. 10 *Bear Dance*; *Seven Sketches* No. 6; *Fourteen Bagatelles* Nos. 10, 11; *For Children* Vol. 1, No. 10; *Rumanian Folk Dances*
2. HMV recording 1929: *Rumanian Dance* No. 1
3. Broadcast recordings 1932–1935: from Frankfurt Radio (1932): *Improvisations* Nos. 4, 5; From Hilversum, Dutch Radio (1935): *Allegro Barbaro; Ten Easy Pieces,* No. 5 *Evening in Transylvania* and No. 10 *Bear Dance; Rumanian Dance* No. 1

4. The Babits/Makal Collection (1936–1939): Bach: *Partita* in G
   (*Praeambulum, Passepied*); Kodály: *Seven Piano Pieces*, Op. 11, Nos. 2,
   4, 6; Bach: the A major *Concerto (Allegro)* (orchestra conducted by
   Dohnányi); Mozart: *Concert Rondo* in A major (fragment, orchestra
   conducted by Dohnányi); Liszt: *Variations* on Bach's theme
   "Weinen, Klagen"; Bartók: *Piano Concerto* No. 2 (five fragments from
   three movements, orchestra conducted by Ernst Ansermet);
   Beethoven: *Six Variations* Op. 34 (fragment); Brahms: *Capriccio* in B
   minor Op. 76, No. 2; Chopin: *Nocturne* in C# minor (fragment);
   Bartók: *Mikrokosmos:* No. 138 *Bagpipe* (fragment); No. 109 *From the Island of Bali* (fragment); No. 148 *Six Dances in Bulgarian Rhythm,* No.
   1 (fragment); Mozart: *Sonata* in D for two pianos (six fragments from
   three movements with Ditta Pásztory); Debussy: *En Blanc et Noir*
   (five fragments from three movements with Ditta Pásztory); Bartók:
   Rhapsody Op. 1 for piano and orchestra (five fragments, orchestra
   conducted by Dohnányi); Brahms: *Sonata* in F minor for two pianos
   with Ditta Pásztory; Bartók: *Rhapsody* No. 1 for violin; *Hungarian
   Folk Songs* Part 1, arranged by Országh, played by violinist Ede Za-
   thureczky; Liszt-Bülow: *Concerto Pathetique* for two pianos with
   Dohnányi

5. Spoken material: words to *Cantata Profana*, read by Bartók in Hungarian; lecture on the collecting tour in Anatolya in Hungarian (three
   fragments); interview with Brussels Radio (in French); interview
   from "Ask the Composer" series (WNYC, 1944); recordings of family talks (three fragments including Bartók's singing of a Hungarian
   folk song)

In general, the sound on these recordings is of very poor quality, but they
do provide important supplementary material to the basic Bartók piano
recordings that will certainly be of interest to the serious musician. In
spite of the extraneous background noise, these recordings still manage to
capture the freedom of Bartók's Mozart playing, the classical proportions
of his Beethoven, and the poignant lyricism of Chopin. It is regrettable
that the entire *Piano Concerto* No. 2 performance has not been preserved,
but the fragments are revealing and give us Bartók's clear intentions regarding tempo, touch, and overall atmosphere. Five fragments are heard
but unfortunately do not include the Presto section from the second Adagio movement. There is also an excellent fragment of the Op. 1 *Rhapsody*,
followed by a Brahms performance. Heard back to back, it's startling how
much they resemble each other! If only for the excerpts from the Op. 1
Rhapsody and the second *Concerto*, this collection is well worth having. It
is a unique set of unusual recordings.

Individual Recordings

1. *Bartók Plays Bartók: Bartók at the Piano (1929–1941)*, Pearl (GEMM CD 9166): *Suite*, Op. 14 (complete); *Rumanian Dances* Op. 8a, No. 1; *Ten Easy Pieces* Nos. 5, 10; *Allegro Barbaro*; *14 Bagatelles*, Op. 6, No. 2 (two versions: 1929, 1941–1942); *Burlesque* No. 2; *Nine Little Piano Pieces* Nos. 6, 8 from 1936, No. 9 from 1941–1942; *Petite Suite* (complete 1941–1942) (two versions of No. 5: 1936 & 1941–1942); *Rondo* No. 1 (two versions: 1936, 1941–1942); *Fifteen Hungarian Peasant Songs* Nos. 7, 10, 12, 14, 15; *Mikrokosmos* Nos. 124 *Staccato*, 146 *Ostinato*); *Improvisations* Nos. 1, 2, 6, 7, 8; *Three Hungarian Folk Tunes* (complete); from seven pieces arranged for two pianos from *Mikrokosmos* Nos. 1, 2, 3 with Ditta Pásztory; also included is Liszt: *Sursum Corda* from *Années de Pèlerinage*.

   Bartók's recording of his *Suite* Op. 14 demonstrates just what must be emphasized by the pianist in performance. The line remains prominent and the pulse is always maintained. The *Suite* abounds in contrast, with the underlining of its larger structural outlines. Bartók's performance makes the listener aware of structure and content but never in a pedantic fashion. This is superb and effortless piano playing—an inspiration for all pianists and a model of performance for all repertory, not only Bartók's. His playing of the first *Rondo* is touching, with the melody declaimed in the manner of rubato speech. The quality of the sound transfer is excellent, without sacrificing articulation and color. This CD should be part of any basic piano collection. All of Bartók's performances are quite special and wonderfully personal, but "Tambourine" from *Nine Little Pieces*, "quasi Pizzacato" from *Petite Suite*, "A Bit Tipsy" from *Three Burlesques*, "Staccato" and "Ostinato" from *Mikrokosmos*, and the three two-piano pieces with Ditta Pásztory are extraordinary. I cannot imagine any other performances that would be comparable.

2. *Contrasts with Benny Goodman and Joseph Szigeti, (rec. 1940) and 31 Selections from Mikrokosmos:* Sony MPK 47676

   This is the definitive recording of *Contrasts* with its original interpreters and is a must for the serious listener's record library. As a bonus, you will also receive thirty-one pieces from *Mikrokosmos*. Excellent sound.

3. *Library of Congress Concert (rec. 1940) with Joseph Szigeti*: Second *Violin Sonata; Rhapsody* No. 1; Beethoven's "Kreutzer;" Debussy's *Sonata*: Vanguard OVC 8008

   This recording should be part of everyone's basic collection. This is music-making at its best, and reveals Bartók to be a supreme colorist.

4. *Bartók: Solo piano music, chamber music with Szigeti and Songs (Dohnányi plays Variations on Nursery Tune)*: EMI Classics CDC55031

This recording is part of EMI's ongoing series *Composers in Person,* and is devoted to music by Bartók and Dohnányi. Bartók's music comes from recordings made in 1928–1937. Recommended if not purchasing the complete collection on Hungaroton.

COMPLETED PIANO WORKS

- *Sonata* in four movements (1898), unpublished (part of the Robert Owen Lehman collection on deposit at the Morgan Library in New York City)
- *Four Piano Pieces* (1903)
- *Piano Quintet* in four movements (1903–1904)
- *Rhapsody* Op. 1 in two movements (1904) for solo piano
- *Rhapsody* Op. 1 for piano and orchestra (1904–1905), revised with added introduction from original solo work
- *Scherzo,* Op. 2 for piano and orchestra (*Burlesque*) (1904)
- "Marcia Funèbre" from *Kossuth* (1905), sections 9 & 10, transcribed from symphonic poem, *Kossuth,* of 1903
- *Three Folk Songs from the Csík District* (1907)
- *14 Bagatelles,* Op. 6 (1908)
- *Ten Easy Pieces* (1908)
- *For Children* (1908–1909), 85 pieces arranged in four volumes
- *Two Elegies,* Op. 8b (1908–1909)
- *Two Rumanian Dances* Op. 8a (1910)
- *Seven Sketches,* Op. 9b (1908–1910)
- *Four Dirges,* Op. 9a (1910)
- *Three Burlesques,* Op. 8c (1908–1911)
- *Two Pictures,* Op. 10 (1910–1911), transcription for solo piano from original orchestral work written in 1910
- *Allegro Barbaro* (1911)
- *Sonatina* (1915)
- *Rumanian Folk Dances* (from Hungary) (1915)
- *Rumanian Christmas Carols* (*Colinde*) (1915), two series of ten pieces each
- *Suite,* Op. 14 (1916)
- *Three Hungarian Folk Songs* (1914–1918)
- *Fifteen Hungarian Peasant Songs* (1914–1918)
- *Three Studies,* Op. 18 (1918)
- *Improvisations on Hungarian Peasant Songs,* Op. 20 (1920)
- *Sonata* No. 1 for violin and piano (1921)
- *Sonata* No. 2 for violin and piano (1922)

- *Dance Suite* (1923–1925), original work written for orchestra in 1923; transcribed for solo piano in 1925
- *Sonata* (1926)
- *Out of Doors* (1926)
- *Nine Little Piano Pieces* (1926)
- *Concerto* No. 1 for piano and orchestra (1926)
- *Three Rondos on Folk Tunes* (1916–1927)
- *Rhapsody* No. 1 for violin and piano (1928–1929)
- *Rhapsody* No. 2 for violin and piano (1928), revised 1944
- *Concerto* No. 2 for piano and orchestra (1930–1931)
- *Petite Suite* (1936, revised 1943), transcription of six pieces from *44 Duos* for solo violin
- *Sonata* for two pianos and percussion (1937)
- *Contrasts* for violin, clarinet and piano (1938)
- *Mikrokosmos*, six books (1926, 1932–1939), 153 progressive piano pieces arranged in order of difficulty
- *Seven Pieces from Mikrokosmos*, arranged for two pianos (1939–1940)
- *Concerto* for two pianos and percussion and orchestra (1940), transcription of *Sonata* for two pianos and percussion (1937)
- *Suite* for two pianos, Op. 4b (1941), transcribed from orchestral *Suite* Op. 4 (1905–1907)
- *Concerto* No. 3 for piano and orchestra (1945), last seventeen measures completed by Tibor Serly after Bartók's death

OTHER MAJOR WORKS IN CHRONOLOGICAL
RELATION TO PIANO REPERTORY

- *Violin Concerto* No. 1 (1907–1908) Op. Posth.
- *Two Portraits* for orchestra, Op. 5 (1907–1908)
- *14 Bagatelles*, Op. 6 (1908)
- *Ten Easy Pieces* (1908)
- *For Children* (1908–1909)
- *Two Elegies*, Op. 8b (1908–1909)
- *String Quartet* No. 1, Op. 7 (1909)
- *Two Rumanian Dances* Op. 8a (1910)
- *Seven Sketches*, Op. 9b (1908–1910)
- *Four Dirges*, Op. 9a (1910)
- *Two Pictures* for orchestra, Op. 10 (1910)
- *Three Burlesques*, Op. 8c (1908–1911)
- *Two Pictures*, Op. 10 (piano transcription, 1910–1911)
- *Duke Bluebeard's Castle*, Op. 11 (one-act opera, 1911)
- *Allegro Barbaro* (1911)

- *Sonatina* (1915)
- *Rumanian Folk Dances* (from Hungary) (1915)
- *Rumanian Christmas Carols (Colinde)* (1915)
- *The Wooden Prince,* Op. 13 (one-act ballet, 1914–1916)
- *Suite* Op. 14 (1916)
- *String Quartet* No. 2, Op. 17 (1915–1917)
- *Three Hungarian Folk Songs* (1914–1918)
- *Fifteen Hungarian Peasant Songs* (1914–1918)
- *Three Studies,* Op. 18 (1918)
- *Miraculous Mandarin,* Op. 19 (one-act pantomime, 1918–1919)
- *Improvisations on Hungarian Peasant Songs,* Op. 20 (1920)
- *Sonata* No. 1 for violin and piano (1921)
- *Sonata* No. 2 for violin and piano (1922)
- *Dance Suite* for orchestra (1923)
- *Dance Suite* (transcribed for solo piano, 1925)
- *Sonata* (1926)
- *Out of Doors* (1926)
- *Nine Little Piano Pieces* (1926)
- *Concerto* No. 1 for piano and orchestra (1926)
- *Three Rondos on Folk Tunes* (1916–1927)
- *String Quartet* No. 3 (1927)
- *Rhapsody* No. 1 for violin and piano (1928–1929)
- *Rhapsody* No. 2 for violin and piano (1928, revised 1944)
- *String Quartet* No. 4 (1928)
- *Cantata Profana* for double mixed chorus, tenor, baritone, and orchestra (1930)
- *Concerto* No. 2 for piano and orchestra (1930–1931)
- *44 Duos* for violins (1931)
- *String Quartet* No. 5 (1934)
- *Petite Suite* (1936, revised 1943)
- *Music for Strings, Percussion, and Celeste* (1936)
- *Sonata* for two pianos and percussion (1937)
- *Contrasts* for violin, clarinet, and piano (1938)
- *Violin Concerto* No. 2 (1937–1938)
- *Divertimento* for string orchestra (1939)
- *Mikrokosmos,* six books (1926, 1932–1939)
- *String Quartet* No. 6 (1939)
- *Concerto* for two pianos, percussion, and orchestra (1940)
- *Suite* for two pianos, Op. 4b (1941)
- *Concerto for Orchestra* (1943)
- *Sonata* for solo violin (1944)
- *Concerto* No. 3 for piano and orchestra (1945)
- *Viola Concerto* (1945, incomplete)

NOTES

1. Béla Bartók, "*A 1932 Interview with Bartók* by Magda Vámos," in *Bartók Studies*, ed. Todd Crow (Detroit: Detroit Reprints in Music, 1976), 189. [This interview originally appeared in *The New Hungarian Quarterly* XIV/50 (Summer 1973).]

2. Lajos Hernádi, "Bartók—Pianist and Teacher," in *Bartók Studies*, ed. Todd Crow, 156.

3. Júlia Székely in *The Bartók Companion*, ed. Malcolm Gillies (Portland, Oreg.: Amadeus Press, 1994), 87.

4. Hernádi, "Bartók—Pianist and Teacher," 156.

5. Belá Bartók, as quoted by Halsey Stevens in *The Life and Music of Béla Bartók*, 3rd ed., ed. Malcolm Gillies (New York: Oxford University Press, 1993), 99.

6. Béla Bartók, as quoted by Denijs Dille in *Béla Bartók: His Life in Pictures and Documents*, ed. Bertha Gaster and Ferenc Bónis, trans. Lili Hálapy (Budapest: Corvino Kiadó Press, 1980), 25.

7. Béla Bartók, "Mechanical Music" (1937), in *Béla Bartók Essays*, ed. Benjamin Suchoff (Lincoln: University of Nebraska Press, 1976), 298.

Afterword

Living in rural West Virginia, I frequently have the chance to watch some of the old-timers in town patiently whittling away at a piece of wood. Very slowly, a form emerges and, depending on the craft of the artisan, becomes more refined with each knife stroke. The process of studying Bartók's piano music is quite similar to what a West Virginia farmer does with a chunk of wood in his hand. As one digs and chips away, the soul of this music slowly begins to emerge, and the work starts to take on its own shape. As Bartók himself said, every piece finds its own form.

The many indications and directions Bartók left for the performer also need to find their proper place within the form. These details must be deciphered and shaped within Bartók's formal hierarchy. Bartók's markings, never arbitrary, leave sufficient clues for the performer to realize the meaning behind every accent and tempo indication. This music demands to be read between the lines (and spaces) and challenges the pianist to go beyond the limited notational process.

I found that by studying these works my musical reasoning became sharpened. Bartók's music requires, in addition to accurate observation of all of his directions, musical intelligence and a refined intuitive sense. The interpreter must become familiar enough with Bartók's language to be able to detect a possible mistaken metronome marking or a misprint in the printed score. However detailed, the manuscript can provide only a general idea of the composer's intentions. The performer always has to go beyond the notes, behind them and under them, to understand the spirit with which they were written. Fortunately, Bartók as pianist and performer of his own music has left to future generations of pianists good instructions

301

and pianistic insights, which will bring them closer to a just interpretation of his music.

The more I live with this music, the greater awe I have for its complexity and craftsmanship. Every time I restudy one of Bartók's piano works, I feel as if I am confronted with a new challenge and realize that I have only just begun to peel away its many layers—technical and musical, as well as emotional—to get to the core, to arrive at the soul that holds the true unaffected spirit of this music. Bartók wrote in his diary that his happiest days were spent living among the peasants. Naturalness of expression, spontaneity, the pure simplicity of the folk tradition he loved—these need to be communicated with every performance.

The genuine test of any great composition is whether it will wear well; will it continue to challenge the interpreter's mind and his heart? As I have learned by writing this book, there are no simple rules or concrete formulas to follow with Bartók's piano works. Each piece embodies different sets of problems. The performer must constantly search to create clarity from complexity, to demonstrate a clear logic that can then be communicated to the listener. This is not easy; any insight to this composer will rest within his music.

Bartók was a serious scholar concerned with accuracy and precision and innumerable details, but it is important to remember that this scholarship was always combined with a higher intuition and musical inspiration. He composed without set prescribed theories, to allow his music the freedom to go the way it needed to go. He also had faith that interpreters could be trusted to find their own way within the music. At the beginning of the new century we have only just begun to explore his vast pianistic legacy. It is ripe for discovery, and a welcome challenge for all pianists.

Annotated Bibliography

Antokoletz, Elliott. *The Music of Béla Bartók: A Study of Tonality and Progression in Twentieth-Century Music.* Berkeley: University of California Press, 1984.

This in-depth study of Bartók's harmonic language is recommended only for the very advanced student of Bartók's music. A sample of Antokoletz's detailed analysis can be found in his essay on the *Bagatelles*, published in *The Bartók Companion*.

Bayley, Amanda, ed. *The Cambridge Companion to Bartók.* Cambridge: Cambridge University Press, 2001.

This recently published compendium offers excellent individual essays, written by prominent Bartók specialists, focusing not only on a wide range of repertoire but also on broader political, social, and cultural issues. A good supplement for the serious Bartók student, this book should serve as a catalyst for further reading and discussion. An in-depth historical chronology is also included.

Bartók, Béla. *Black Pocket-Book: Sketches 1907–1922* (facsimile edition of the manuscript with a commentary by László Somfai). Budapest: Editio Musica, 1987.

Bartók's piano music is represented by four of the *Bagatelles*, one of the *Burlesques*, two of the *Dirges*, one *Elegy*, and several pages from the two violin and piano sonatas. Sketches from the first two quartets and excerpts from *Bluebeard*, *Wooden Prince*, and *Miraculous Mandarin* are also included.

Bartók's Workshop: Documents of the Compositional Process. Exhibition of the Budapest Bartók Archives in the Museum of Music History of the Institute for Musicology of the Hungarian Academy of Sciences, Exhibition and Text by László Somfai. Budapest: MTA Zenetudományi Intézet, 1995.

This exhibit was one of the highlights of my 1995 visit to Budapest, inspiring me to go more deeply into Bartók's music. To be able to see firsthand the original drafts and numerous changes that Bartók made to his 1926 *Sonata*, as well as the manuscripts of his *Violin Concerto*, second violin *Sonata*, second violin *Rhapsody*, and third *String Quartet*, among others, was well worth the trip. László

Somfai has produced an excellent catalogue of what was an exceptional and memorable exhibit.

Bónis, Ferenc, and Bertha Gaster, eds.; Lili Hálapy, trans. *Béla Bartók: His Life in Pictures and Documents.* Budapest: Corvino Kiadó Press, 1980.

　　Originally published in Hungary for the Bartók Centenary, this handsome picture book includes an excellent and concise biography of the composer, followed by a large and fascinating collection of personal photographs.

Chalmers, Kenneth. *Béla Bartók.* London: Phaidon Press, 1995.

　　This is a fine biography of the composer but contains neither musical examples nor detailed technical analysis. However, it provides a good overview of Bartók's complete repertory as seen within the progression of his life. The illustrations are wonderful, and the book is extremely enjoyable to read but written mainly for the general reader.

Crow, Todd, ed. *Bartók Studies.* Detroit: Detroit Reprints in Music, 1976.

　　Most of the authors of these essays, originally published in the *New Hungarian Quarterly*, are Hungarian musicologists and theorists. Also included here is an essay by Lëndvai, the theorist who applies his "golden section" theory to Bartók's later works. This is a valuable source book. I was especially drawn to Bartók's essays about Liszt's music and about that composer's influence on Bartók's own work. The book also includes articles by former piano students, offering an evaluation of their professor's teaching and piano playing. Also included here is an interview with Bartók by Magda Vámos from 1932, which is worth reading.

Demény, János, ed. *Béla Bartók: Letters.* New York: St. Martin's Press, 1971; London: Faber & Faber, 1971.

　　These annotated letters are an invaluable reference tool for the student of Bartók's music. This collection allows the reader a glimpse into Bartók's short but productive life. Although currently out of print, the book is worth the effort to find.

Fassett, Agatha. *The Naked Face of Genius: Béla Bartók's American Years.* New York: Houghton Mifflin Company, Riverside Press, 1958.

　　Unfortunately, this book is no longer in print, but if you can find a copy, you will be rewarded. Written by a personal friend of the Bartóks, this moving book describes the composer and his wife's difficult years in America (1940–1945). The author allows the reader to share her experiences befriending the Bartóks, and each page reveals both Bartók's humanity and his pain. His wife Ditta is quoted as saying, "All you have to know about Béla is that he loves everything that's real." After reading this book, we begin to understand this truth.

Frigyesi, Judit. *Béla Bartók and Turn-of-the-Century Budapest.* Berkeley: University of California Press, 1998.

　　This book provides a cultural history of Bartók's milieu as well as a discussion of his contemporary, the poet Endre Ady. These two "radicals" form the core of Frigyesi's excellent study. Only two of Bartók's works are explored in depth: *Bluebeard's Castle* and the first *Piano Concerto*. For me, this book filled in the spaces and was a valuable aid in understanding Bartók's music within its proper cultural context.

Gillies, Malcolm, ed. *Bartók Remembered.* New York: W. W. Norton, 1991.

　　The editor has compiled nearly 100 recollections of Bartók, arranged to chronicle the composer's life. Even Stravinsky is represented. This book is a wonderful addition to Halsey Stevens's definitive biography. The chronology given in the front of the book is extremely useful and also includes a chronology of contemporary personalities and events.

Gillies, Malcolm, ed. *The Bartók Companion*. Portland, Oreg.: Amadeus Press, 1994. (Reprinted by arrangement with Faber & Faber, London.)

Arranged by musical genre, this book provides a series of essays written by respected musicologists and theorists on both sides of the Atlantic Ocean. Most of Bartók's major works are discussed, but the book need not be read in its entirety. An excellent supplementary resource for the serious student.

Griffiths, Paul. *Bartók*. Master Musician Series. London: J. M. Dent, 1984.

A thorough biography offering musical analysis of Bartók's major works, but this book cannot compete with nor replace the Halsey Stevens biography.

Kenneson, Claude. *Székely and Bartók: The Story of a Friendship*. Portland, Oreg.: Amadeus Press, 1994.

Zoltán Székely, the first violinist of the Hungarian Quartet and the dedicatee of Bartók's *Violin Concerto* and *Second Rhapsody*, was a dear friend and frequent sonata partner of the composer. This is a chronicle of their friendship and provides a general overview of musical life in mid-twentieth-century Europe. Also included is a set of letters between the two men not found in the published volume of Bartók's letters.

Kroó, György. *A Guide to Bartók*. Budapest: Corvina Press, 1974.

Although not readily available in the English edition, this book is an excellent handbook to Bartók's complete works, providing general background information plus specifics about instrumentation, timings, first performances, and publishers.

Laki, Peter, ed. *Bartók and His World*. Princeton, N.J.: Princeton University Press, 1995.

This book functions as an excellent supplement to the Stevens biography. A set of essays by outstanding scholars about the cultural milieu surrounding Bartók comprises Part 1 and includes an excellent article about the relationship between Bartók and Stravinsky. Parts 2 and 3 contain letters and interviews with the composer and writings about Bartók by his contemporaries. "Recollections of Béla Bartók" are the real highlight; these profiles enhance the musical portrait to reveal the "hidden" composer, as seen only by the people who knew him.

Lendvai, Ernő. *Béla Bartók: An Analysis of His Music*. London: Kahn & Averill, 1991.

The author of the "golden section" theory of proportions applies his work to a study of Bartók compositions, including a detailed analysis of the *Sonata* for two pianos and percussion. This highly technical study is recommended only to advanced students. However, the important questions to be asked are these: Did Bartók compose instinctively and without formulas? Can the "golden section" theory be applied to all of Bartók's compositions, or does the theory reaffirm Bartók's view that most of the theorists or the "experts" who write about music make use of the music to provide proof for their own theories? However, Lendvai makes a convincing argument using the two-piano *Sonata* and the *Contrasts* as good examples of his thesis.

Somfai, László. *Béla Bartók: Composition, Concepts, and Autograph Sources*. Berkeley: University of California Press, 1996.

This invaluable sourcebook, written by the director of the Bartók Archives in Budapest, provides an extensive listing of Bartók's manuscripts, sketches, and drafts. In his detailed musical analysis, Somfai understands and respects Bartók's "instinct and intuition," and the composer as pianist and performer is always relevant to his musicological reasoning. He believes (as I do) that Bartók's oeuvre "rests on a Romantic foundation." This book provides an in-depth analysis of Bartók's musical choices. For the serious Bartok scholar, this book is a valuable reference tool.

Somfai, László, ed. *Béla Bartók: Eighteenth- and Nineteenth-Century Italian Cembalo and Organ Music Transcribed for Piano.* New York: Carl Fischer, 1990.

This is a valuable addition to the pianist's library and includes an excellent introduction to these early music transcriptions by László Somfai.

Stevens, Halsey. *The Life and Music of Béla Bartók,* 3rd ed., prepared by Malcolm Gillies. New York: Clarendon Press/Oxford University Press, 1993.

This book, originally written in 1953, still remains the definitive work on the life and music of Bartók. Composer Stevens has the remarkable gift of being able to explain with directness and lucidity Bartók's most complex work. This is the one book to which I always return. There is an excellent chronological listing of Bartók's complete works included at the end of the book.

Suchoff, Benjamin, ed. *Béla Bartók Essays.* Lincoln: University of Nebraska Press, 1976. (Reprinted by arrangement with Faber & Faber, London.)

Most of Bartók's quotes cited in this book have been taken from his *Essays.* Suchoff has included for the reader not only a sampling of Bartók's extensive writings on folk music but also his *Autobiography* from 1921, as well as the composer's musical analyses of several of his major works. This book is a treasure and a valuable reference tool for the serious Bartók student.

Suchoff, Benjamin, ed. *Piano Music of Béla Bartók, Series I & II.* Archive Ed. New York: Dover, 1981.

The former director of the New York Bartók Archives is responsible for this edition. I do not recommend using this edition for all of the earlier piano pieces (here, the Op. 8a *Rumanian Dances* are published in their earlier and less satisfying version). However, the introductions to these two volumes provide a wealth of information including all the folk song texts of *For Children.*

Yeomans, David. *Bartók for Piano.* Bloomington: Indiana University Press, 1988.

This is a valuable sourcebook for Bartók's piano music. Yeomans provides the piano student with lots of relevant information, arranged chronologically, including translations of the texts of folk song material that Bartók used. The book also includes a listing of all Bartók editions available as of 1988.

The American Exile of Béla Bartók: After the Storm. A Public Media, Inc. release; BBC/MTC Hungary co-production in association with Portobello Productions, R. M. Arts, and La Sept.; Copyright: BBC, 1989. (Distributed in USA by Home Vision Videos.)

This video focuses on the last five years of Bartók's life (1940–1945) and includes excerpts of performances of his works dating from this period: the solo violin *Sonata,* the *Viola Concerto,* the *Concerto for Orchestra,* and the third *Piano Concerto.* Reminiscences by his son Peter, conductor Georg Solti, pianist György Sándor, and Yehudi Menuhin make this a poignant, personal memoir.

Bartók Béla: Complete Edition. Sound recording issued by Hungaroton on LP. (LPX 1299-1300, LPX 1405-1407, LPX 11335-11338, LPX 11394-11395, LPX 11479-11480, LPX 11517-18).

These old LP recordings of Bartók's complete oeuvre are an invaluable reference tool and include in-depth program notes written by noted Hungarian musicologists. The performances by Hungarian artists are consistently on the highest level. Although some individual records have been reissued on CD by Hungaroton Classic, the complete collection is not yet available. However, Japan Polygram has plans to reissue the complete set on CD and will also include some additional material not yet recorded.

CD Track List

Chapter 1
Sonata (1898)
    1. Adagio (second movement)
    2. Presto Misterioso (third movement)
Elegy, Op. 8b
    3. No. 1

Chapter 2
Fourteen Bagatelles, Op. 6
    4. No. 1
    5. No. 7
    6. No. 12
    7. No. 14
Ten Easy Pieces
    8. Dedication

Chapter 3
    9. *Etude*, Op. 18, No. 2
    10. *Allegro Barbaro*

Chapter 4
Improvisations
    11. No. 1
    12. No. 3
    13. No. 6
    14. No. 7

    15.　No. 8
From *Mikrokosmos*, Book 6
    16.　*Six Dances in Bulgarian Rhythm* (No. 1)

Chapter 5
Sonata (1926)
    17.　Allegro moderato
    18.　Sostenuto e pesante

Chapter 6
Out of Doors
    19.　"With Drums and Pipes" (1)
    20.　"Musiques Nocturnes" (4)
    21.　"The Chase" (5)

Chapter 7
Suite, Op. 14
    22.　Sostenuto (fourth movement)
Dance Suite
    23.　No. 4
    24.　No. 5

Chapter 8
    25.　*Rondo*, No. 1
Burlesques, Op. 8c
    26.　"Quarrel"
    27.　"A Bit Tipsy"
Dirge, Op. 9a
    28.　No. 1
Nine Little Piano Pieces
    29.　No. 4

Chapter 9
From *Mikrokosmos*, Book 6
    30.　Free Variations
    31.　Diary of a Fly
    32.　Ostinato

General Index

accents, 27, 51, 61, 63, 203, 217, 246
ad libitum, 29, 157, 233, 290
"allegro-barbaroso" stereotype, 288
Antichi Maestri Italiani, 221
Arabic music, 91, 108, 178, 185, 189, 190, 194, 195
Arányi, Jelly, 283–84
Ardeleana, 104
arpeggios, reverse, 30, 204, 265
Asheville, North Carolina, 280, 286n15
atonality, 37–39, 92

Babits-Makal Collection, 294
Bach, Johann Sebastian, 1, 51, 87, 187, 199, 200, 215, 222, 223, 225, 231, 233, 242, 244, 246, 266, 275, 288, 294
Works: *Anna Magdalena Bach's Notebook*, 226, 228; *The Well-Tempered Clavier*, 225
Backhaus, Willem, 14
bagpipe, 92, 100, 104, 106, 156, 193, 196, 235, 237–38
Baker, Henry, 292
Barber, Samuel, 79, 219
Bartók Archives, 289
Bartók, Béla: discography of recordings, 290–96; humor in music, 42, 117, 238,

254, 260, 261, 276, 295; metronome and timing markings, 41, 42, 78, 103; on atonality, 37–39, 92; on bitonality, 37–39, 52; on collecting folk music, 83, 84, 85, 86, 88, 89, 91, 92, 108; on criticism directed at folk music, 90; on editing music, xii, 293; on finding his path, 55; on form, 111; on general characteristics of folk music, 90–95; on "gypsy" music, 84, 87; on "new piano style," 35; on performance of folk tunes by peasants, 85, 89; on piano as an instrument, 254; on polytonality, 37–39; on teaching composition, 9; on teaching piano students, 10, 228, 244; on value of folk music and folk art, 83, 84, 85, 86, 87, 89, 109, 223; piano playing, 288, 289; "thematic extension of range," 239–40, 258
Bartók, Béla Jr., 160, 225
Bartók, Peter, xii, 82, 100, 113, 147, 187, 212, 226, 227, 246, 258, 274, 291
Basilides, Mária, 291
Beethoven, Ludwig van, 40, 103, 133, 142, 147, 178, 197, 199, 200, 223, 275, 279, 288, 292, 294, 295

Index of Bartók's Works

About the Author

Barbara Nissman is a pianist who has performed with many of the world's leading orchestras (including the Philadelphia Orchestra, New York Philharmonic, Chicago Symphony, London Philharmonic, BBC Symphony, Royal Philharmonic, Pittsburgh Symphony, St. Louis Symphony, and Cleveland Orchestra) and has worked with such distinguished conductors as Eugene Ormandy, Riccardo Muti, and Leonard Slatkin.

In 1989 she made history by becoming the first pianist to perform the complete piano sonatas of Sergei Prokofiev in a series of three recitals both in New York and in London. Her recordings of the complete Prokofiev Piano Sonatas (the first set made available on compact disc) were recently reissued on the historical label, Pierian Records.

Also well known for her writings and interpretations of the music of Alberto Ginastera, Barbara Nissman is the dedicatee of Ginastera's final work, the *Third Piano Sonata*. Her recordings of his complete solo piano and piano/chamber works have been reissued by Pierian Records. Scheduled for future release are recordings of music by Bartók, Liszt, and the five piano concertos of Prokofiev.

Performer, writer, lecturer, and frequent guest artist/teacher, Barbara Nissman has toured and given master classes throughout the United States, Europe, the Far East, New Zealand, and South America. Recently at the invitation of both the Moscow and St. Petersburg Conservatories, she presented recitals and master classes on Prokofiev.

A student of György Sándor, who was himself a student of Béla Bartók, Barbara Nissman received her bachelor's, master's, and doctoral degrees from the University of Michigan. She now lives on a farm in the Allegheny Mountains of West Virginia.